Pluralism and Oppression

Pluralism and Oppression

THEOLOGY IN WORLD PERSPECTIVE

R. Panikkar, T. Berry, J. Sobrino,
E. Dussel, and Others

EDITED BY

Paul F. Knitter

THE ANNUAL PUBLICATION OF THE
COLLEGE THEOLOGY SOCIETY
1988
VOLUME 34

UNIVERSITY
PRESS OF
AMERICA

Lanham • New York

Annual Publication • 34

Copyright © 1991 by

The College Theology Society

University Press of America®, Inc.
4720 Boston Way
Lanham, Maryland 20706

Co-published by arrangement with
the College Theology Society

"The Cosmology of Religions" © 1990
by Thomas Berry

"Christology from a Contemporary African Perspective"
© 1990 by Caritas McCarthy

"Theology in a Suffering World" © 1990 by Jon Sobrino

Library of Congress Cataloging-in-Publication Data

Pluralism and oppression :theology in world perspective /
R. Panikkar ... [et al.] : edited by Paul F. Knitter.
p.   cm. — (The Annual publication of the College
Theology Society : v. 34)
Essays in this volume were given at the 1988 meeting of the
College Theology Society at Loyola-Marymount University in Los Angeles.
1. Theology–Congresses.
2. Christianity and culture–Congresses.
3. Religions–Congresses.   4. Suffering–Religious aspects–
Christianity–Congresses.   I. Panikkar, Raimundo, 1918-
II. Knitter, Paul F.   III. College Theology Society.   IV. Series.
BR118.P58   1990   230—dc20   90–12709 CIP

ISBN 0–8191–7904–3 (cloth)
ISBN 0–8191–7905–1 (paper)

CONTENTS

INTRODUCTION
THE TOTALLY OTHER—THE UTTERLY NECESSARY

Paul F. Knitter

The essays assembled in this volume, all of which were given at the 1988 meeting of the College Theology Society at Loyola-Marymount University in Los Angeles, reflect and verify a growing conviction within contemporary Christian theology: if theologians are going to do their job properly, they have to somehow get out of their own backyards. For too long, theology has been an intramural affair, done within the churches, for the churches. Indeed, theology was meant to be "applied" or "proclaimed" to the world. But it was a one way street. During the Second Vatican Council, however, there flickered on the horizon a realization that has since become, for many, a brilliant noonday sun: not only do the "others" need us, but just as much—perhaps even more so—we need them. We cannot be church and we cannot carry on the task of drawing ever new treasures out of the old "deposit of faith" unless we do so *together with others*—"others" meaning people who are genuinely different from us. We must be confronted by, frightened by, embraced by those who see and feel the world differently than we do if we are to understand afresh and live anew the Gospel of Jesus Christ. In fact, the more the others are different, the more we can be nourished and enriched by them. The *totaliter aliter* (totally other) is the *totaliter necessarium* (utterly necessary) for the job of being Christian and doing theology.

A variety of factors and insights have coalesced to bring us to this realization of the utter necessity of embracing the totally other. Proponents of hermeneutical theory and method (e.g., H. G. Gadamer, J. Habermas, D. Tracy), advocates of anti-foundationalism in its philosophical statement (e.g., R. Rorty and R. Bernstein) or in its theological application (e.g., F. Schlüsser-Fiorenza, G. Lindbeck), prophetesses of feminist theory (e.g., C. Keller and R. Ruether) have clarified and confirmed what ordinary folk are realizing as they confront a world that is ever changing and increasingly plural: "truth" takes shape not within the neat mold of clear and distinct ideas but within the give and take of relationships; we encounter the real not via an *adequatio rei et intellectus* (an agreement between thing and intellect) but through a *conversatio cum aliis* (a conversation with others).

Two historical factors confirm the need we feel for such truth-revealing conversations. We are aware of the weight and pain of a past in which, in our sense of splendid self-sufficiency and superiority, we have effectively isolated ourselves from other cultures and other religions. Certainly, throughout the history of Christianity there have been encounters with other worlds, but rarely have we taken those other worlds seriously as conversation partners. Rarely did we expect to find anything of cultural or religious value that could add to or perhaps correct the truth we already possessed. Though dealing with other worlds, we have really been existentially isolated from them. This meant that our "dealings" with others usually led to making use of them for our own advantage. If they had anything to offer us, it was for the most part only in the raw materials, commodities, and novelties that could supply new and profitable grist for our economic mills. This history of Western, Christian exploitation and domination of other ways of being human and religious has often been told; and though it has sometimes been painted in overly lurid colors, the basic picture remains true. So today, these two ingredients in our historical memory—our isolation from and our exploitation of others—lend further weight and urgency to our growing awareness that as theologians we can carry out our task of revisioning Christian consciousness and praxis only if we are in a dialogue with others.

But who are the "we theologians" talked about in the preceding paragraph? Primarily, though not exclusively, they are those who— for better *and* for worse, for enrichment *and* for impoverishment— have assumed and then jealously stood watch over the theological enterprise: Western, First-World, middle-class (sometimes upper-class), white, males. To state the matter in commonplace imagery, Christian theology has, for the most part, been a business carried on by an international "old-boys club." It is we old boys who bear the main responsibility for the isolation from and domination of others that have characterized so much of Christian theology. So though all theologians, including Asians and Africans and females, are in profound need of the totally other in order to carry on the conversation toward truth, it is especially we old boys who feel (or should feel) this need and who are also in need of help and guidance in carrying on the conversation.

The conversations that make up the essays collected in this volume either articulate this need for the other or they try to speak the voice of the others in offering incentive and guidance that will enable those representing the "dominant theology" to let go of their dominance and embrace the other. The general topic for the 1988 annual meeting of the College Theology Society—"Theology in World Perspective"—was meant to be a call to the members to respond to the urgency of moving beyond our familiar words into the broader world of otherness. The planners of this meeting and this volume felt that the reality of otherness was to be found especially in the three faces of pluralism so evident in our contemporary world: the many other *cultures*, the many other *religions*, and the many *victims*. Thus, our discussions revolved around these three foci of "manyness" and "otherness."

But in our conversations at the 88 annual meeting, thanks especially to the presentation and presence of Thomas Berry, we became aware of another face of otherness that we had not explicitly "programmed" into our discussions. Berry's reminders of this "other" other was confirmed for us in the words and example of the Lakota shaman Mr. Buck Ghosthorse who spoke to us of Native American spirituality (but who felt uncomfortable in submitting a paper). Both Berry and Ghosthorse faced us with the otherness of *planet Earth*. Daily tortured and immolated on the altar of consumerism and technology, the Earth is certainly among the victims whose voice we must hear and whose life we must save.

In differing ways, each of the following essays deals with the otherness of culture, or religion, or victimhood. Raimon Panikkar's study, sustained by Robert Schreiter's response, warns that all this talk of embracing cultural otherness isn't as easy as it sounds. Indeed, to talk of a "transcultural theology" is to pose an impossible possibility or a dangerous necessity; Christian theology must abandon its notions of either being "above culture" or of expressing a "superior culture" and must take up the messy, dangerous, sometimes impossible task of living *crossculturally*. Caritas McCarthy and John McCarthy (no relation!) provide concrete examples of how such crosscultural exchange can be enriching (in Africa) and disrupting (in Japan). Robert Kress reminds us that in our openness to others, we must recognize those areas where we have something to offer and not just receive; he contends that American Catholicism has much to offer the universal church.

Proving that he is indeed both a "geologian" and a "theologian," Thomas Berry proposes that if the religions of the world today are to engage in an effective and relevant dialogue, they must do so on the basis of a universal cosmology or common creation-story and out of a shared commitment to saving the Earth and making sure the creation-story continues. As already noted, Berry's prophetic message—that among all the "others" that we seek to embrace, the Earth must occupy a parental priority—rang through most of the ensuing discussions. His call is critically sustained and made "more practical" through Rita Gross' Buddhist and feminist critique. Maura O'Neill adds another feminist voice in her challenging claim that the contemporary interreligious dialogue will not yield its needed fruits unless it is depatriarchized in both membership and method. A different, though no less complex, concern is expressed in Gerald Finnegan's warning that although the encounter with other religious paths requires Christians to revise their Christocentric particularity, if that particularity is lost, so is the value and fruitfulness of the dialogue.

Jon Sobrino's plenary address was another prophetic moment in our annual meeting's deliberations. Recognizing that cultural and religious plurality are essential ingredients in the theological mix of today, he urged that concerns for pluralism or for ecology should not obstruct the priority that the sufferings of the oppressed must play in Christian theological consciousness. Such an option for the suffering poor, obligation as it is, can become an occasion for the renewal of theology and church in that our "knowing through faith" (intellectus fidei) will be complemented through a "knowing through active love" (intellectus amoris). Confirming Sobrino, Susan Brooks Thistlethwaite urges him and other male Latin American theologians not to forget the other faces of suffering, for although there are many "los probres," there are many more "las pobras." Another spokesperson from Latin America, Enrique Dussel presents a scholarly challenge to North Americans and suggests that an openness to Marxism may facilitate a greater openness to the voice and plight of the oppressed. What it is like to read the stories of the Jewish bible from the perspective of the oppressed is made uncomfortably clear in Alice Laffey's different kind of analysis of Deuteronomistic history. Mary Hembrow Snyder uses that same liberationist perspective to envision new theological models for divinity and suffering. Recognizing the divisions that the voices of the oppressed and the concern for liberation have introduced among theologians and church leaders, William Portier attempts to reconcile some of those divisions, especially as exemplified in the theologies of Edward Schillebeeckx and Joseph Ratzinger.

In illustrating the need to do theology in world perspective—that is, in conversation with those who are our others—the fifteen essays in this book, taken together, give voice to the conviction, long-announced by Raimon Panikkar, that "I cannot ask, much less answer, the question 'Who am I?' unless I also ask and attempt to answer the question 'Who are you?' " We need the other to know ourselves. Only someone who is "totally other" than we can listen to us, live with us, and then respond and reveal to us the hidden presuppositions or assumed myths which ground our values and hopes but which are fully evident only to those who differ from us.

These essays also make clear that neither can we ask and answer the question "Who is our God?" unless we also ask and try to answer the question "Who or What is your God/Ultimate?" The embrace of otherness makes real and alive the traditional Roman Catholic affirmation of a universal revelation and the claim of Paul Tillich that there is a God beyond our God. Even when we want to insist that our Christ-centered revelation of God is "definitive" and "indispensable," we have to admit that it is not "entire" or "complete" unto itself. Finally, these essays show that the encounter with others will reveal to us not just the greater reality of God but also the greater reality of the Satan that lurks within us. This especially will result from listening—really listening—and acting with and for the victims of this world, for they will show us how our demons have often been their exploiters. We need these victim-others (human, animal, material) to recognize and cast out our demons.

But the final—or the pervasive—discovery made possible by the encounter with the other is that the other is not, in the final or fundamental analysis, really other. In genuine dialogue, we realize that in some sense, bordering on the mystical, the other is part of, one with, immanent to, our very selves. The extended experience of "doing theology in world perspective"—of conversing with, suffering with, working for the liberation of the other—brings us to the existential or mystical realization (enlightenment) that, again in the words of Panikkar, reality is theanthropocosmic: the material cosmos, humanity, and the divine make up a oneness-in-difference. In and through our differences we humans *are* our fellow human beings; we *are* the earth and animals; we *are* the divine. Only if we respect and nurture our differences and *at the same time* maintain our oneness through relatedness—only so can we have life and have it more abundantly.

If this volume can contribute in some small way to making such statements about oneness in diversity sound less "hokey" and more liveable, then all those who poured their energies into these pages— the essayists, the blind readers of the 38 originally submitted manuscripts, the translators, the typists, and the editor—could ask for no greater reward.

Part One

THEOLOGY IN A CULTURALLY DIVERSE WORLD

CAN THEOLOGY BE TRANSCULTURAL?

Raimon Panikkar

Our question is *new, biased, Christian,* and *legitimate.*

It is *new* because it entails a degree of historical reflection, critical self-introspection, academic scholarship, and secondary literature not available in other periods of Christian history. Manichaeism, for instance, had a crosscultural expansion for centuries and reached Taoism, Amidism, and other religions, but the question was never raised whether Manichaeism had a transcultural value.[1]

Our question is *biased,* because it assumes a particular understanding of theology and of religion which gives rise to our question about a transcultural theology. Seen from the outside, the primordial African religions, for instance, present a sort of common "religious negritude" which may lead one to ask about their transcultural values; but in fact, Africans did not ask this question—until timidly, in modern times, under Christian influence.

Our question is *Christian,* because of a kind of unformulated

Raimon Panikkar, Professor Emeritus (Religious Studies) of the University of California, Santa Barbara, studied chemistry, philosophy and theology in Spain, Germany, Italy, and India. Ordained a Catholic priest since 1946, he was a member of the first liturgical commission for Vatican II (under Cardinal Lercaro) and of the first Roman Synod during the Pontificate of John XXIII. He is General Editor of the Indic Theological Monographs of the Indian Theological Association and author of a Manifesto for a "Hindu-Christian Theology"(Jevadhara, 1979). He is also President of INODEP International (Institut Oecuménique pour le Développement des Peuples), Paris. He has published 29 books and around 300 major articles dealing with philosophy of science, metaphysics, comparative religions, theology of religion(s), and indology. Among his recent books are Myth, Faith, and Hermeneutics (Paulist, 1979), The Unknown Christ of Hinduism (Orbis, 1981), Blessed Simplicity (Seabury, 1982; Harper & Row, distributors), The Silence of God (Orbis, 1989).

expectation that there is a unique and "providential" proof that Christianity is, in some sense, above cultures.

Finally, our question is *legitimate*, for although it suggests a positive answer and evinces intellectual and vested interests, nothing prevents us from coming up with a qualified answer or even a plain no.

The Second Person of the Trinity, to use traditional language, "became" incarnated in Jesus of Nazareth, but Jesus himself never questioned whether he should or could have been born elsewhere and "elsewhen." He was the "son of Mary" and the "Son of Man". Only later did the early Christians introduce the idea of the "fullness of times" and the centrality of space (Israel, Jerusalem, Rome . . .). Likewise, Christian experience became incarnated in the surrounding cultural milieu, and so theology was born. But theology did not question whether its *theologumena* also made sense to peoples of other cultures. Later Christians reflected on their formulations and came to consider them the last word in space and time. When confronted with other cultural patterns, Christians used to speak about scandal and folly, rather than admit that Christian theology is the fruit of this tacit cultural dialogue. The dialogue was called, of course, refutation or apologetics.

I am oversimplifying the picture, for there were some thinkers well aware of the implicit dialogue. Nevertheless the situation of dialogue was hardly reflected upon in an explicit manner. In other words, the classical way in which Christian theology has moved through the centuries has been, by and large, as if theology were non-temporal and non-spatial, as if time and space were not theological categories. The troubling idea of a possible development of dogma emerged only in the last century. Still today, hardly any theologian dares speak of the *mutation of dogma*; most of them talk only of development. *Aggiornamiento* is all right, *retractatio* is abbhorrent, and *mutation*, unthinkable. *Quod semper et ubique* has been a Christian slogan.[2] *Eppur si muove!* Only recently, and quite timidly, has the sociology of knowledge begun to enter the awareness of Christian theologians.

Throughout history, official documents of the churches hardly acknowledged the spatio-temporal boundaries of their statements. Truth was considered to be atemporal. What was valid for Constantinople was considered valid for the entire world; pontifical documents inciting witch-hunting and justifying the torture of heretics have never been withdrawn. It all looked as if the theological enterprise were truly for a world without end. Implicit was the assumption that theological activity was somehow above the cultural mutability of purely human affairs.[3] Theology was considered to be above culture.

Let me make this point clear. Nobody would deny that sound theological activity requires a critical mind, a sensitive heart, and an acute power of reflection. The question under discussion is whether such theological activity is tied to a particular type of culture, whether to receive, understand, reflect upon the Christian fact—and even to believe in it—we need to belong to a particular culture or set of cultures. Is theology a transcultural value? Ultimately we have to ask whether the "christic fact" is not already a cultural fact.

Nor will anyone deny that every human statement is clad in temporal fashions and spatial features. Our question asks whether Christ "in a fashion which transcends the wisdom of all his interpreters"[4] has a universal message independent of all cultures. Yet our problem goes even deeper, for it must ask who or what is this Christ beyond and above interpretations. Or, from a less Protestant and more Catholic perspective, the question concerns the so-called substantial and thus, immutable and perennial, core of a divinely revealed *depositum fidei*.

Let me put it in an Asian way: What is the peculiar core which transmigrates from culture to culture and is born again and again in different forms? Is Swahili theology a reincarnation of Greek theology? Is the *karma of* John Sobrino a reincarnation of Cyril of Alexandria or, perhaps, Joachim of Fiore? In other words, how does the law of *karma* function in theology?

We shall distinguish three types of answers. I am fully conscious that there is no neutral viewpoint in matters religious and cultural. My perspective is based on the simple observation that there have been Christians throughout the ages who have interpreted themselves or their context in a threefold manner.

I. The Supracultural Claim

A certain type of Christian reflection claims to be above any culture, even though at times it shuns the very word theology. Karl Barth and Pius XII can serve as examples. The Christian message is supernatural; Christian revelation is the judgement on all religions; Christianity rightly understood stands above all cultural constructions of humanity. The church is the eschatological and supernatural human family: *signum levatum inter nationes* (Vatican I), *sacramentum mundi* (Vatican II). While religion and culture are human constructs, Christian faith is godly; it is not the human effort to ascend to the divine, but the fruit of the descent of the divine itself, as it has pleased God to manifest God's self to the world.

Contemporary questions about inculturation, adaptation, indigenization and the like often assume that the Christian fact stands above all cultural diversities and thus has a right of citizenship among all the cultures of the world. Christianity stands above all cultures and can be incarnated in any of them. When in such incarnation something is left behind or rejected, this very fact is taken to prove that the discarded doctrine or custom was not fully human. "The Church rejects nothing of all that is valuable and good in any culture and religion." This is a Christian attitude, at least fifteen centuries old, and repeated in unequivocal terms in the Second Vatican Council and in statements of the World Council of Churches.

To be sure, the evangelist, missionary, or theologian is advised to reach that naked *kenosis*, that mystical core, that supernatural faith which can be incarnated in any human culture. The Christian event is seen as a supracultural fact; and if until now it has adopted and adapted a certain garb, this is due to historical contingencies and/or the predominance of a particular culture over others; but, in itself, *per se*, nothing stands in the way of its taking flesh in the most remote and, for the western taste, most exotic cultures.

For over thirty years I have been personally grappling with this problem after having been taught, for a previous thirty years, that the church, as a supernatural entity, could be at home everywhere. I do not doubt the intention—and even good intention—of such an attitude. I only detect a contradiction in the intent *itself*. I used to ask the question whether in order to be a Christian, one ought to be spiritually a Semite and, intellectually, a Westerner. My partners in dialogue would readily admit that we should not confuse the Mediterranean garb of Christianity with its transcendent, mystical and supracultural core. I agree.[5] Indeed, my sympathies are for authentic mysticism. But neither religion in general, nor Christianity in particular, can be reduced to a formless, silent mystical core. The moment that the *muein* becomes conscious, and much more when it is translated into *legein*, it has to take names and forms (*nama* and *rupa*, the Indic traditions would say) that are no longer supracultural, but expressions of particular cultures. The standard response is to say that we have to do here with a transcendental relation that takes particular shapes and forms in different cultures. This has also been my own position in particular contexts. But this answer works well only under one *assumption* and presents an *intrinsic difficulty* or rather an inner contradiction if generalized crossculturally.

The *assumption* is what we can call the *theistic myth* proper to a limited set of cultures. It assumes in fact that it "has pleased God" to incarnate God's self in a particular culture and to make it the vehicle of a supracultural fact, imperfections of that culture notwithstanding. If there is a free and sovereign God, Creator of heaven and earth and Lord of history, nobody can prevent this God from doing or choosing whatever or whomever God wills. In other words, the christic event may be said to be supracultural, but the awareness of that event, let alone its interpretation, is far from being supracultural, for it assumes a set of beliefs that only make sense within a given cultural pattern. We can, therefore, speculate, as often has been done, that it is even providential that the Greeks came first, the Germanic tribes later, and the peoples of the East and of Africa will now "rejuvenate" and enliven Christianity. It is a legitimate thought and, at least since Tertullian, a factual one.[6]

But there is an *intrinsic difficulty*, which fast becomes a contradiction. Theology is said to be free to formulate, explain, and narrate the Christian event in the language of any culture. This works well as long as the picture of the new culture is somewhat homogeneous to and compatible with the picture of the older culture. But the conflict becomes *irresponsible* when this is not the case. The new interpretation, in fact, is rejected when it proves incompatible with the existing Christian tradition. But in this rejection, traditionally Christian criteria, of course, are used. This means that there seems to be a hidden agenda at work when the christic event is held up as sovereignly supracultural. The old pattern remains normative. Perhaps in an African milieu Christians might be allowed to celebrate the Eucharist and say "Pork of God" instead of "Lamb of God". There would be more resistance to permitting the Eucharist to be celebrated with tea and potatoes, or perhaps with "soma" alone. But can the christic event be culturally incarnated in a world in which there is no God as Supreme Being and no history as the scenario of revelation? Which supracultural criterion do we use to condemn all those "atheistic" and a-historical cultures, if not the criteria deduced from a particular interpretation of that allegedly supracultural mystery?

Where do we draw the line? I would argue that, until now, without a certain Semitic and Hellenic mind-set we are not even able to understand what Christianity is all about. The meaning of revelation, the notion of history, the idea of a personal God, and the like, are not even understandable without a particular *forma mentis;* such notions are not cultural invariants. Decades ago I called for the dekerygmatization of Christ in order to free him from any dogmatic proclamation.[7] Today I would ask whether we have to also de-historicize him.

The only coherent answer is one which renounces any claim of being above all culture and instead speaks of the scandal of concreteness and the challenge of the historical Christian revelation. We were all Gentiles and had to bow before the historical facts of a God incarnate. This leads already to the second option.

II. The Supercultural Claim

Let us then be humbly audacious and not be afraid to call things by their proper names. It is not true that theology is a *logos* on God, above and beyond culture. The clear fact is that Christianity bears the seal of a historically precise and superior culture. Christ may have been born poor, but he belonged to a refined and old culture. He was even of a royal family. He was a *kshatriya.* Christian revelation makes no sense in an uncultured climate, or in a "primitive" civilization. It requires a certain type of culture, a particular understanding of human history, a refinement of civilization. Within a certain human development there are, indeed, many possibilities, and there is no difficulty in accepting different cultural garbs to express the core of the christic fact; but this requires a certain degree of evolution—a superior culture that has transcended the inferior stages of human civilization. The old so-called "indirect methods" of evangelizing, which the French often baptized with the euphemism of "évangélisation de base," were based on this idea of preparing the ground by first civilizing the natives so that they could at least grasp what the missionaries were going to preach.[8]

Even though Christianity did not descend from heaven, chemically-pure and supranatural, it does belong to a superior culture and can become inculturated only among people with a certain amount of cultural sophistication. It presupposes a particular understanding of humanity. The first Christian missionaries in Korea had first to convince the natives that the human being is a sinner in order to preach redemption to them. We may not (yet?) ask whether we can understand the Bible without computer-language; but without a written culture, what we call Christianity today would make little sense. The human race is evolving, and Christianity belongs to the superior strata of that evolution. According to Scripture, the christic event took place at the end of times. We can understand, therefore, why the West today dominates the world and why western culture has spread all over the planet.[9] We may discuss how important a Plato or a Shankara are for theology; but with a Siberian shaman, there is not much we can do. In fact, we don't have to be romantics to recognize that today all the peoples of the world are trying to imitate the West and are thereby accepting more or less uncritically Christian infrastructures.

As much as we may abhor apartheid, we practice it theologically under other names and more subtle attitudes. The option for the poor and the Sermon on the Mount give ample food for thought and material for preaching, but their demands are taken only so far. The lilies of the fields are fine, but we don't know what to do with the weeds and tares. What place can they have in the Kingdom? Bismark was more sincere than many a theologian when he said that with the Sermon on the Mount one cannot run an Empire. After all, the Christian crusaders, conquerors, kings, and merchants also brought a higher form of civilization. The cross was accompanied by the menace of the sword, but was then followed by the "blessings" of the machine. It is all very intertwined.

Where do we draw the line? We all have a particular idea of humanness and humanization. Christian theology belongs to the higher echelons. *De catechizandis rudibus!* wrote St. Augustine in the year 400. Can everybody belong to the "World Church"? Can the culturally poor, "savages," prostitutes, primitives? Where are our *loci theologici?* Only among the "developed" countries? Or, perhaps, also among peoples on the "way to development"—but not among those who resist being "civilized"? Can one "christianize" without civilizing?

To be sure, theology as a conscious activity and critical reflection entails a certain degree of intellectual power. But does this require us also to assume a hierarchical view of cultures, or to speak about theology in an elitist manner which screens the raw materials suited for theology to make sure they are not too raw?

De facto, Christian theology, from the last millenium up to our times, has been linked with a certain complex of cultural superiority. This, however, was not always so—as we realize when we read Augustine between the lines and discover his nostalgia for the superior civilization of pagan Rome, or when we listen to the emperor Julian and feel his scorn at the lack of culture among Christians. We learn that Christians were by no means a cultural elite when we read Celsus, or study the centuries of "barbarian" theology, or listen to Nietzsche, or sit at the feet of some Vedantic master ridiculing the rough mentality of Christian missionaries. Wassilij Rozanov (1856–1919), that genial philosopher of religion, once said that western Christianity did pay heed to the words of Christ, but never took interest in looking at his face.[10] Besides his words (in Scripture), Christ has left us an *icon* of life.

Yet today, can we really defend a theology not linked with a certain degree of human sophistication?

Without going to extremes, we can say that the reaction against "academic" or "sitting theology" is healthy. Furthermore, we need not only contemplative theology, or a "kneeling theology:" (H. Urs Von Balthasar), but an active and practical theology. Even more, we need a theology in which both *logos* and *theos* once again mean "word" and "mystery." We have only to listen today to the cries of the so-called "tribals" in India, or the accounts of so many witnesses all over Africa, to realize the burdens of our doctrinal superstructures and the limits of our historical interpretations of the christic event—as if history were synonymous with reality. And so we have forgotten that theology is not for theologians but for the people.[11] Are we going to disqualify the so-called "theology of liberation"— better called "theology of life and death"[12]—because it does not fit into our academic theological language or does not use "scientific" methodology?

I submit that doing theology in culturally diverse worlds today demands a *kenosis* and a mystical insight which does not require belief in a superior culture.

Yet each period in time and each community in space draws the line on cultural requirements at different levels. Paul drew his bottom line by maintaining that at least one should be able first to understand, and then to believe, that there is one remunerator God. Others have been more strict, and others are prepared to be more generous.

To offer some extreme but telling examples: for some centuries the "native" peoples from Asia and Africa were not considered fit to become priests, let alone bishops in the Catholic Church. A native church was therefore simply not possible. Today the same church considers African polygamy incompatible with Christian ethics—but it has no major problems with atomic weaponry. In Roman Catholic theological circles in India, the stiff prohibition of *communicatio in sacris* is breaking down, and a Hindu-Christian theology is developing that would have been viewed as utterly impossible some half a century ago.[13] The line is movable, although each particular community in time and space draws it differently.[14] There may be a minimum of cultural sophistication, but this minimum is fluid. We cannot prove a priori that theology requires an objectively superior culture.

So let us examine the third possible option.

III. The Crosscultural Claim

We have seen that theology, because of its *logos* component, cannot logically claim to be above all cultures—that is, supracultural. Each culture has its proper *logos*, and every *logos* is housed in a culture. Each language is culturally bound. A possible *meta-logos* can only be a *dia-logos*, which creates a new language, a new culture, but it is not supracultural.

Because of its *theos* component, theology cannot consistently claim that it needs to belong to a superior culture—that is, supercultural. The divine is divine for all. "God is no respecter of persons" (Acts 10:34). The notion of a private Godhead makes no sense. God, in many traditions, is a proper name. But the very notion of God has a certain universal claim. God is, ultimately, a common name. To speak meaningfully about Dante or entropy requires a superior culture. To speak about God cannot have the same cultural restrictions.

Yet, *de facto*, and I shall argue also *de jure*, the theological activity has crossed cultural boundaries in the past, and is doing so presently, without necessarily having to indulge in cultural imperialism—difficult as that may sometimes be.[15] The crosscultural claim is justified. Culture is the house, not the prison of the human being.

I am purposefully using variations of one single word—supra-, super-, and crosscultural—in order to stress distinctions but not separation. So I am proposing the following assertions: First, anything human qua human belongs to the order of nature, and, as such, is somehow *beyond* culture. (I say "somehow" to guard against overstressing the polarity between nature-culture, for *logos* is also

rooted in nature). So there is a supracultral element in theology—
something belonging to the human being.

Second, anything which is not given by nature, and is tied to an
historical and datable event, is somehow *different* from other forms
of human existence, and, as such, is somewhat *above* certain cultural
forms, since it requires a certain degree of perfection. (The very
reflexive notion of the divine implies a cultural achievement.) In
this sense, there is a supercultural element in theology—as a human
perfection.

Third, anything which legitimately has not tied itself to a particular way of life and has claimed to be a message for the *anawin*, for
the poor representing the non-specialized and not particularly cul-
tured human beings, transcends the boundaries of one particular
culture and can be called crosscultural. In that sense there is a
crosscultural element in theology as a human activity not tied to a
particular human group.

May I ask the indulgence of "scientific" exegetes and interpret in
a nonfinancial way a sentence of Brother Jesus defending a woman?[16]
"You have the poor among you always." (Mark 14:7) This interest for
the poor, paradoxically enough, justifies the crosscultural value of
Christian theology. The poor are precisely those who have not "made
it" in any culture; they remain at the bottom-line. They are undiffer-
entiated, not culturally specialized. They are crosscultural, for they
are found in all cultures. Concern for brahmins or rabbis, scientists
or saints, white people or only free citizens requires certain cultural
options, but concern for the poor demands a crosscultural attitude.
The poor are always with us, in every culture. The *amha-arez*, "the
people of the land," are part of agriculture more than of human
culture.

In short, what is the meaning of crosscultural theology?

We have discarded the *universalistic claims* of a Christian theology (to have a value *above* and therefore *for* every other culture). In
spite of past theological explanations, this attitude today smacks of
philosophical immaturity and theological colonialism.

We have also discarded the *superiority claim* on paradoxically the
same grounds that Christian tradition refuted Pelagianism and Sem-
ipelagianism: it would make the understanding and acceptance of
the christic event dependent on "nature" (which we could translate
"culture")—that is, on something which conditions the Christian
experience *ab extra* and renders it dependent on something outside
of itself.

And yet we have also acknowledged that both attitudes cannot be totally excluded from Christian self-understanding.

I am aware that the theological task consists not in exposing private opinions, but in presenting the inherent polarity of Christian theology. Theology must be public, critical, and concerned with orthopraxis as much as with orthodoxy. In other words, Christian theologians want to be loyal both to the understanding of the christic event as disclosed to their own experience (which is always inserted in contemporary awareness) and to be unfolding of traditional, collective self-identity. The first condition entails, besides an obvious personal honesty, an openness to and recognition of the *novum* of our times. The second condition demands a reflective consciousness that attempts to articulate a plausible understanding of tradition which transcends private opinions, though it would not claim any extrinsic authority besides the convincing force of its own arguments. The authentic theologian does not need an *imprimatur* from the powers that be, but does look for a sacramental blessing from the community. This sacrament is also the voice of the cosmos. There is no theology without cosmology.

If we want to keep the biblical image, the theologian is rather like a shephard's dog which runs back and forth, sometimes getting ahead of the sheep and sometimes behind, barking, taking risks, making mistakes, the recipient of shouts and stones and a meager pittance—all this is part of its job of keeping the flock of the past in communion with that of the future. But a dog is loyal and asks no more.

This image mirrors our present-day situation. On the one hand, Christian theologians cannot ignore the traditional claim to universal validity—the famous or infamous "Totalitäts-" and "Absolutheitsanspruch". In one form or another, this claim is ingrained in Christian consciousness since the time of Jesus. Any authentic theology, while being a local theology limited by time and space, formulates at the same time something of the human condition that transcends local boundaries. The Christ-symbol has been constitutively linked—at least historically—with the alpha and omega of reality.

On the other hand, both the lessons of history and our present-day awareness make it impossible to overlook not only the dark side of such a totalitarian pretense, but also its sheer non-sense the moment it is formulated in whatever language.[17] How can one single phylum of human culture absorb or concentrate all the others?[18]

I am pleading for the *via media*, not for the muddled way. To explain the past does not mean to justify it or to explain it away. It means to understand the grounds on which the past was standing and which led to formulate convictions in the way they have been transmitted to us.[19] This hermeneutical rule, I suggest, applies not only to theology, but also to any interpretation of the past. If we take pains at interpreting the past, it is because we desire to understand a given situation, and, from there, to draw a deeper understanding of our situation.

In fact, Christians, children of their times as everybody else, did believe in the two positions which are for us no longer acceptable. I have elaborated *ad nauseam* that a new and deeper Christian self-identity may emerge if Christians give up those earlier claims and replace them with the crosscultural validity of the christic event. Neither exclusivism nor inclusivism is any longer convincing. Pluralism is the name of our third position.

This position is not the same kind of "strategic retreat" as is evident, still today, in the sad history of relations between modern science and Christian belief. It is, rather, an expression of healthy pluralism and the awareness of the relativity inherent in every human construct, act or position, including those activities allegedly performed in alliance with the divine.

In tune with such a healthy pluralism, and still within a genuinely historical and incarnational spirit, I propose the following crosscultural Christian principle: *The christic event has an inherent dynamism to take flesh wherever it can.* This "can" is *ambiguous, ambivalent,* and *not apodictic.*

It is *ambiguous* because it may lead in various directions, good and bad. It may led to impositions, conquests, and exploitations as well as to fulfillment, enhancement of life, and true conversion. It is *ambivalent,* because it may have opposite results—it may pacify, purify, and perfect a culture on the one hand, or harden, blind, and even fanaticize that culture on the other. It is *not apodictic* because the incarnational impulse cannot have any justification *a priori.*[20] We become aware of this impulse insofar as we experience the christic event to be connected with the destiny of the human race and with the very dynamism of Being. We are both actors in and spectators of the selfsame display of Reality. Not only the fate of the earth, but also the very life of the universe, is something about which we share the glory, the burden, and the responsibility.

We could play further with the metaphor of the incarnation and point out that the incarnation can take place only in a virgin's womb, in a poor milieu, and in a marginal culture, accompanied by astrological events. But there is no need to be allegorical. Theological incarnation is *de facto* not possible everywhere because Christian self-understanding in different time and space requires in each instance different conditions of possibility. Sometimes these conditions may not be present.

The same principle can be stated in a more positive light. It is the incarnational dynamism of the christic event itself, reenacted by its believers, that carries out such acts of inculturation. This is a delicate activity and Christians should be extremely careful not to repeat the cultural genocides of the past that resulted from their alliance with one particular culture.[21] There is always the danger that the Christian dynamism can degenerate into a trick to gain power or increase numbers, or make "followers"!

It is evident, therefore, that the incarnational enterprise evinces the previously mentioned ambiguity and ambivalence and can become unethical and, I would add, unchristian. The internal dynamism I am speaking about, which incidentally is not exclusive to the christic event, can be related to the principle that goodness spreads by itself (*bonum diffusivum sui*), so that any strategy or device to "make it work," or even to "give testimony," makes it spurious and harmful. This was, incidentally, the advice of Mahatma Gandhi to Christians: to attract by the perfume of their virtues.[22]

What I am saying is that there is a spontaneous fecundation among cultures, a positive osmosis among beliefs, a crosscultural enrichment that does not need to be an invasion of foreign goods, ideas, or people for the sake of profits, material or spiritual.

There is no blueprint for such a dynamism. It cannot be realized as an act of the conscious and external will (in order to gain some form of good). It has to emerge as a natural and spontaneous movement from an internal urge of the people concerned. An example of what I am talking about is the emerging Indic theology.[23] This theology is sprouting out of a double fidelity: to the religious traditions of the country and to Christian beliefs. Theologians are trying to harmonize the two traditions in which they live and believe. We are here at the antipodes of the "apologetics' " attitude and even of the "mission" mentality—though I recognize that these terms are undergoing deep changes in meaning.

This implies another reading of the classical text with which "missions" traditionally have been justified: "Go and teach all nations . . ." (Matt. 28:19) There have been abusive interpretations of this text which conclude from the injunction to teach the right to teach anything and to open schools. There are also the more subtle hermeneutical interpretations of modern exegetes. My reading is more radical. It uncovers an untheological *intrapolation* and an unconscious *extrapolation* of the meaning of the text.

The *extrapolation* is clear. Christians have read into those texts a Roman Empire mentality: *urbi et orbi, pax romana*, one civilization, and all the modern dreams of the same order, often with nice-sounding words, such as "one democracy," "world government," or "world church." The "all nations" of our text could not have meant modern Australia, just as the "darkness over the earth" at the death of Christ did not refer to that same continent, nor did the "idols" of Saint Paul refer to the *murti-s* of Hindu worship. I wonder if the "little flock" and the "one flock, one shepherd" could ever have meant an organization of one billion people with a monarch on the top. Such an interpretation has extrapolated into Jesus the mentality of a Roman lawyer or a statesman constituting an assembly (church) or founding a dynasty. It was the destiny of Christian history to have interpreted this text in this way. It is a legitimate interpretation. But unless we identify the christic event with history, it is not the only possible Christian reading.

The *intrapolation* is still more interesting. Even assuming Jesus Christ had the intention of establishing a world church as some dream of, the text would not have more authority than when he said that he should not go beyond the borders of Israel or when he commanded that we should live without money. He might have dreamt of a world without money as some dream of a world church. Both are dreams, although with the basic difference that one is a powerful utopia and the other, a dreadful nightmare.

In other words, neither interpretations envisioning Christendom nor those extolling Christianity are today any longer convincing. We need a vision of *christianness*.[24]

Summing up, the crosscultural value of the Christian event cannot be defended *a priori* as belonging to its very nature. Yet, there is an existential *nisus*, a dynamism, which urges Christians to formulate their truths in universal terms—whether they call such truth revelation or simply Christ. This urge belongs to the very movement of history. But this urge is neither unique nor can it claim special privileges; it is subject to all the contraints of history that we have described. The future of Christian history will show whether this effort at incarnation follows the pattern of the Grand Inquisitor or the spirit of Bethlehem, under the witness of the skies, the hospitality of animals, the astonishment of shepherds, and the bewilderment of the Magi. Without this mystic core, the entire christic event degenerates into a masochistic complacency in being humble or a sadistic drive to show the power of the Cross.

*   *   *

From all of these considerations, we can draw a threefold conclusion:

a) Christian theology is translatable only in as much as Christian theologians succeed in making those translations. It is not universally translatable in principle. The drive to translate belongs to the dynamism of history. Translation is not a neutral or easy human activity. If in times past translations were made in order to convert others, the irony of history shows now that good translations demand just the opposite: the conversion of the translator. You cannot immerse yourself in the universe of discourse of the other if you do not sincerely live in the universe of life of the other culture—i.e., if you do no make the foreign culture your own. I do not need to stress that I speak of real translations and not of transliterations.

b) Christian translations work both ways. They are introduced as foreign bodies into other cultures, and then, slowly, they are assimilated and transformed from within those cultures. This transformation is not necessarily only of the guest cultures; it can also provide a stimulation of the host culture to develop its own ways. An Indic theology of the Gospels, for example, may not result in attracting Hindus to Christianity; but it may contribute to strengthening, enhancing, and transforming Hindu beliefs—which is what the adjective "Christian" should mean.

On the other hand, Christian translations also modify the original tradition in an often unforeseeable way. For example, if we were to translate *agape* with *karuna*, *psyche* with *atman*, *Christos* with *abhisheka*, *logos* with *tao*, *theos* with *allah*, Christain theology would itself undergo a transformation. Each new term or image not only connotes a different universe of discourse; it also opens up the sluices for the living waters of the other culture. Once you introduce the notion of *dharma* into the West, for instance, you can no longer separate ethics from religion, nor can you reduce religion to doctrines. One might reply that Christians do not need Hindus and Buddhists to be aware of such dangers; still, without such eastern input, Christians would not have the reminder that the fragmentation of knowledge leads to the fragmentation of the knower.

In a word, the translation of a text demands the introduction of an entire context. The mingling of contexts is what brings forth strife and fecundation.

c) The double effect of the translation is not reduced to Christian theology, but has homeomorphic equivalents in other cultures. In this regard, Christian theology has no privileged posiion. A similar dynamism is detectable in many other cultures. Zen, for instance, is linked and yet not limited to the Buddhist religion.

The fact that the Christian tradition shares the same transcultural limits and promises with other religions in no way diminishes Christian life and self-understanding. Each culture and religion, like each individual being, is unique.

NOTES

1. For both facts and cultural differences, see the collected papers by H. Ch. Puech, *Sur le manichéisme et autres essais* (Paris: Flammarion, 1979); and Samuel N. C. Lieu, *Manichaeism in the Later Roman Empire and Medieval China* (Manchester: University Press, 1985).

2. "In ipsa item catholica ecclesia magnopere curandum est ut id teneamus, quod ubique, quod semper, quod ab omnibus creditum est. Hoc est etenim vere proprieque catholicum, . . . " S. Vincentius Lirinensis wrote in his famous *Commonitorium* in 434 (P. L. 50, 639).

3. The Pontificate of Pius XII in the Roman Catholic Church might be considered the acme of this mentality. "The Catholic Church does not identify herself with any culture: her essence forbids it." Pius XII, "Discourse to the International Congress of Historical Sciences," September 7, 1955 (AAS, 1955), p. 681. (My translation from the original French.)

4. R. H. Niebuhr, *Christ and Culture* (New York: Harper & Row, 1951), p. 2. It is clear that our perspective here does not attempt a typology such as that implicit in Troeltsch (*Die Soziallehren der christlichen Kirchen und Gruppen*, Tübingen: Mohr, 1912), or the fivefold typology of Niebuhr or the fourfold of Rupp (*Christologies and Cultures*, The Hague: Mouton, 1974). As a matter of fact, my three-partite division could be considered merely formal and thus not an alternative to those mentioned typologies.

5. See my brief paper "Deporre il manto mediterraneo" in *Humanitas* (1962), pp. 876–879, which in the euphoria of the Second Vatican Council was too well received without realizing its far-reaching consequences.

6. See R. Panikkar, "Chosenness and Universality: Can Both Claims Be Simultaneously Maintained?" in *Sharing Worship: Communicatio in Sacris*, P. Puthanangady, ed. (Bangalore: NBCLC, 1988), pp. 229–250. The entire book is an eloquent example of an Indic theology respectful of but not subservient to tradition.

7. See R. Panikkar, *Die vielen Götter und der eine Herr (Beiträge zum ökumenischen Gespräch der Weltreligionen)* (Weilheim: O. W. Barth, 1963).

8. See R. Panikkar, "Indirect Methods in the Missionary Apostolate: Some Theological Reflections," *Indian Journal of Theology*, 19 (1970) 111–113.

9. In his *Christianity in World History* (London: Edinbourgh House Press, 1964), Arend Th. Van Leeuwen is a sort of Hegel redivivus trying to link the linear development of history with the unfolding of Christian revelation. His other books, *Prophecy in a Technocratic Era* (New York: Scribner's, 1968) and *Development through Revolution* (New York: Scribner's, 1970), follow the same line. See *The Ecumenical Review*, 24 (1972) 107–109, and Rupp, *op. cit.*, 232ff. for a review of his later and earlier books.

10. "Das abendlandische Christentum, welches kämpfte, erstarkte, die Menschheit zum 'Fortschritt' führte, das menschliche Leben auf Erden ausrichtete, ging an dem, was an Christus die Hauptsache ist, vollig vorüber. Es akzeptierte seine Worte, bemerkte aber sein *Antlitz* nicht. Nur dem Osten war es gegeben, das Antlitz Christi aufzunehmen. Und der Osten sah, dass dieses Antlitz von unendlicher Schönheit und von unendlicher Traurigkeit war." *Das dunkle Antlitz. Metaphysik des Christentums*, in *Russische Religionsphilosophen. Dokumente*, Nicolai von Bubnoff, ed. and trans. (Heidelberg: L. Schneider, 1956), p. 115.

11. "Johann Strauss did not write his waltzes for musicologists but for dancers and lovers," Frederick Franck, "The Cosmic Fish," *Cross Currents*, 36 (1986) 283.

12. The expression is of the Salvadorean Baptist pastor, Marta Benavides, as reported by R. F. Bulman in his article, "Buddha and Christ," in *Journal of Ecumenical Studies*, 24 (1987) 72. I would even call it *theology of life or death*, for it is a theology of human survival.

13. "The sad fact about Christianity is that it never really got into the ancient spirit of India," writes a Christian theologian belonging to the ancient Syrian Christian tradition. J. B. Chethimattam, "Giving the Reason of Our Faith," *Jeevadhara*, 49 (1979) 72.

14. "Theology to be authentically Asian must be immersed in our historico-cultural situation and grow out of it," declares the final statement of the Asian Theological Conference held at Sri Lanka, January 7—20, 1979, and sponsored by the Ecumenical Association of Third World Theologians. See *Jeevadhara*, 49 (1979) 81. This statement only repeats what has been said time and again over the last fifty years by the majority of theologians of Asia and Africa. See *Theologen der Dritten Welt*, H. Waldenfels, ed. (München: Beck, 1982).

15. The otherwise magnificent articles on "Theologie" in the *Encyclopaedia Universalis* are all inserted within the framework of western culture.

16. Here I can remind scrupulous biblicists of Saint Thomas' exegetical freedom. He says, in fact, that ". . . omnis veritas quae, salva litterae circumstantia, potest divinae scripturae aptari, est eius sensus." *Quaest. disp. De potentia Dei*, q. 4, a. 1. (". . . every truth that, with the content of the literal meaning preserved, can be adapted to the holy scripture is its meaning."

17. My own theologumena are efforts in this same direction: the *Supername* to deal with the "no other name;" the *pars pro toto effect* to deal with the *Catholica*; the *homeomorphic equivalents* to deal with the different religions; the *Unknown Christ of Hinduism* (which is not the Christ known to Christians); my defense of *pluralism* up to the very pluralism of truth against sheer plurality and rigid uniformity. The names of some kindred spirits come to mind: Heiler, Rahner, Küng, Klostermaier, Cobb, Amaladoss, Chettimattam, Amalorpavadass, Pieris, Schlette, Coward, Knitter, Rupp, D'Costa, W. C. Smith, D'Sa, Krieger.

18. The modern literature on this issue is immense. I offer only a selected bibliography of mainly collected works that indicate contemporary trends: Otto Karrer, *Das Religiöse in der Menschheit und das Christentum*, 3rd ed. (Freiburg im Breisgau: Herder, 1936) (a pioneer work). Owen C. Thomas, ed., *Attitudes toward Other Religions* (New York: Harper & Row, 1969. Reprint: Lanham: University Press of America, 1986). Donald G. Dawe and John B. Carman, eds., *Christian Faith in a Religiously Plural World* (Maryknoll: Orbis Books, 1978). Nihal Abeyasingha, *A Theological Evaluation of Non-Christian Rites* (Bangalore: Theological Publications in India, 1979). Thomas Emprayil, *The Emerging Theology of Religions* (Vicentian Ashram Rewa: Vicentian Publications, 1980). Paul F. Knitter, *No Other Name? A Critical Survey of Christian Attitudes toward World Religions* (Maryknoll: Orbis Books, 1985). Harold Coward, *Pluralism* (Maryknoll: Orbis Books, 1985). John Hick and Paul F. Knitter, eds., *The Myth of Christian Uniqueness: Toward a Pluralistic Theology of Religions* (Maryknoll: Orbis Books, 1987). Leonard Swidler, ed., *Toward a Universal Theology of Religion* (Maryknoll: Orbis Books, 1987). M. M. Thomas, *Risking Christ for Christ's Sake* (Geneva: World Council of Churches Publications, 1987).

19. One may be ready to accept the monarchic principle and the ecclesiastical "theocracy" of Dante's *Monarchia* and Soloviev's *La Russie et l'Eglise universelle* provided one situates those two genial essays within their respective contexts and recognizes that the situation today has radically changed. This mutation is what makes Teilhard de Chardin susceptible of a reductionistic interpretation as if the future of humankind had to follow one single line of development.

20. See the doctoral dissertation by Donald Alexander, *Incarnation: A Model for Crosscultural Communication. A Study in Religious Methodology*, University of California, Santa Barbara, Interdisciplinary Doctoral Committee in Humanities, 1974.

21. Any student of sociology and ethnology will recall the controversies regarding "acculturation," "inculturation," "cultural change," "transculturation" and the like. For a summary introduction we may refer to the corresponding articles in the *International Encyclopedia of the Social Sciences*, 1968, and *Encyclopaedia Universalis*, 1985. Theological journals today are replete with articles dealing with this problem. See also the following publications: Donald J. Elwood, ed., *What Asian Christians Are Thinking* (Quezon City: New Day, 1976). Gerald H. Anderson and Thomas F. Stransky, eds., *Third World Theologies (Mission Trends, Nr. 3)* 1976 and *Faith Meets Faith (Mission Trends, Nr. 5)* (New York: Paulist Press, 1981). Hans Waldenfels, ed. *Theologen der Dritten Welt* (München: Beck, 1982).

22. "If I want to hand a rose to you, there is a definite movement. But if I want to transmit its scent, I do so without any movement. The rose transmits its own scent without a movement. . . .If we have spiritual truth, it will transmit itself. You talk of the joy of a spiritual experience and say you cannot but share it. Well, if it is a real joy, boundless joy, it will spread itself without the vehicle of speech. In spiritual matters, we have merely to step out of the way. Let God work His way. If we interfere we may do harm. Good is a self-acting force." *Young India*, January 19, 1928.

This topic was recurrent in Gandhi: "I have a definite feeling that if you want us to feel the aroma of Christianity, you must copy the rose. The rose irresistibly draws people to itself and the scent remains with them." *Young India*, October 15, 1931.

"A rose does not need to preach. It simply spreads its fragrance. The fragrance is its own sermon." *Harijan*, March 19, 1935.

"I take the simile of the rose I used years ago. The rose does not need to write a book or deliver a sermon on the scent it sheds all around, or on the beauty which everyone who has eyes can see." *Harijan*, December 12, 1936.

". . . let your life speak to us, even as the rose needs no speech but simply spreads its perfume." *Harijan*, April 17, 1937.

23. See Kaj Baago, *A Bibliography* (Library of Indian Christian Theology) (Madras: CLS, 1969), which contains literature since 1600 in European and vernacular languages; R. H. S. Boyd, *An Introduction to Indian Christian Theology* (Madras: CLS, 1969), which offers a primarily Protestant perspective. The following are mainly from a Roman Catholic perspective: J. Pathrapankal, ed., *Service and Salvation* (Bangalore: T. P. I., 1973). (This is a collection of papers from the Nagpur Theological Conference on Evangelization. The editing committee, not the editor, decided to modify some substantial points of the final conclusions of the Conference in order to take a more "prudent" position in regard to the Roman authorities.) I. Vempeny, *Inspiration in the Non-Biblical Scriptures* (Bangalore: T. P. I., 1983), in which the author argues "that the non-Biblical scriptures are analogically, yet truly, inspired by God." (p. xxi). D. S. Amalorpavadass, ed., *Research Seminar on Non-Biblical Scriptures* (Bangalore: NBCLC, no date). This is a collection of papers from the seminar on this topic in

1974, in which for the first time mainly Catholic theologians dared to pose the long burning questions concerning the relationship of the Bible and other Sacred Scriptures; at that time it seemed daring to call other scriptures "sacred". Michel Amaladoss et al., eds., *Theologizing in India* (Bangalore: T. P. I., 1981)—papers of a seminar held in Poona in 1978. P. Puthanangady, ed., *Towards an Indian Theology of Liberation* (Bangalore: Indian Theological Association, 1981), which collects papers of the annual meeting of the Association in which Latin America liberation theology is affirmed but recognized as inadequate for the Indian situation. Aloysius Pieris, *An Asian Theology of Liberation* (Maryknoll: Orbis Books, 1988)—an impassioned plea for the "religiousness of the poor" across religious frontiers.

24. See R. Panikkar, "The Jordan, the Tiber, and the Ganges," in *The Myth of Christian Uniqueness*, John Hick and Paul F. Knitter, eds. (Maryknoll: Orbis Books, 1987), pp. 89–116.

SOME CONDITIONS FOR A TRANSCULTURAL THEOLOGY RESPONSE TO RAIMON PANIKKAR

Robert J. Schreiter

I. The Need for a Transcultural Theology

Professor Panikkar has rightly made a case for developing a genuinely transcultural theology, that is, one that does not understand itself as supracultural (above any and every culture) or as supercultural (the gift of a superior culture to another culture deemed inferior). His case is rooted in a variety of considerations concerning how theology is to be expressive of the incarnation of the Gospel in each cultural situation. I would like to point out four such considerations that undergird this call for a new kind of theology.

First of all, a genuinely transcultural theology will permit a contextually sensitive description of the religious experience of believers and allow their confession of faith to ring true to their deepest realities and to resonate with the totality of their being and doing as humans. The experience of the presence and the salvation of God will not appear then as a kind of *Fremdkörper* in their lives, but as rooted centrally and completely in their existence.

Robert Schreiter is Professor of theology at Catholic Theological Union in Chicago. He earned his doctorate at the University of Nijmegen in the Netherlands under the direction of Edward Schillebeeckx. He has taught at Catholic Theological Union since 1974 and served as its dean for nine years. His books include The Schillebeeckx Reader (Crossroad, 1984), Constructing Local Theologies (Orbis, 1985), In Water and in Blood (Crossroad, 1988), and (with Mary Catherine Hilkert) The Praxis of Christian Experience (Crossroad, 1989). He is editor of New Theology Review and was formerly associate editor of Missiology. He is a Roman Catholic priest in the Society of the Precious Blood.

Second, a transcultural theology, as Professor Panikkar has outlined it, is also the source of the communicability of theology across
cultural boundaries. We usually think that the only way to have a
theology that moves across cultural boundaries is to create a theology that is a kind of common denominator among cultures and least
laden with the specificities of any given culture. But closer examination shows that the opposite is really the case. Such so-called
common denominators must have a home in some specific culture,
and so we get a supercultural theology (as Professor Panikkar has
defined it) rather than a transcultural one. A recognition of where
and how our theological expressions are situated is key to effective
communicability.

Third, only a theology firmly rooted in a culture can be geniunely
prophetic in that same culture. Transcultural theologies are not
about utter accommodation of the Gospel message to the contours of
a culture. But genuine prophecy never happens totally from the
outside either.[1] Prophecy is effective when it reorganizes knowledge
already part of the culture. To stand completely outside is to be
ignored. Thus, the more contextually rooted a theology, the more
acute can be its prophetic voice and action.

Fourth, a transcultural theology makes possible a solidarity between cultures in the pursuit of justice. By being rooted in the weal
and woe of one's own culture, one can become engaged in the
struggle for justice in another culture in a profound way. Solidarity
is a word bandied about rather easily, and sometimes its use smacks
of a king of "me-too" mentality of people who do not want to be
considered out of fashion. But a commitment to a transcultural
theology would make it difficult to profess solidarity too glibly.

All in all, the pluralism that Professor Panikkar has described
makes both supracultural and supercultural theologies unaccept-
able. A transcultural theology as he has outlined it makes a contextual approach utterly necessary. This would entail, it seems, parting
company with positivist theologies that assume that language and
concepts can be used without reference to their cultural origins, and
also with schemes that create a theology and then try to stuff the
world into it. In the face of the almost dizzying pluralism a world
church now faces, both of these temptations are real and some
theologians are succumbing to them. What will lead us to the
mutation in our theology that Professor Panikkar envisions?

II. Four Conditions for a Transcultural Theology

The task of developing genuinely transcultural theologies is a daunting one, and we are certainly at no more than the beginning phases of the task. As a way of focusing his proposal, let me suggest four conditions for developing a transcultural theology. These conditions affect the procedure in the theological process, and could be considered necessary, but not sufficient, conditions for such a theology. Much more is obviously required. But without attention to these four conditions, our efforts at developing transcultural theologies are bound to fail.

The first condition is an emphasis on *receiver-oriented methodologies* in our theology. This notion, borrowed from linguistics, emphasizes that true communication of messages across cultural boundaries will require a special sensitivity to the world of the receiver if that message is to be heard and understood.[2] Without attention to these methodologies, the message (in this case, the Gospel) may well reach the receiver, but the sender will have no idea how that message gets situated in the receiver's own universe of meaning. To assume that it will be located in the same place for them as it has been for the sender will generally prove to be a foolhardy claim. Often, if the message is perceived as utterly foreign and unrelated to the universe of the receiver, it will be isolated entirely from the other religious meanings in the universe. One then witnesses the development of dual systems within a single culture or community. A receiver-oriented methodology will ask the question: where are comparable religious symbols located in the receiver's universe and how is religious meaning communicated in that universe? Without getting to know the territory of the receiver and how changes are incorporated in the receiver's universe, any theology is bound to remain supercultural or disregarded as irrelevant.

A second methodolocial condition is that *otherness and difference* will have to be accepted as central categories to the theological enterprise. Theology tends to dwell more on categories of identity and to use otherness only in terms of a kind of apophatic utterly-transcedent. But in a pluralistic world, senses of otherness and differences have to be faced. This is especially important because otherness in actual life tends to get reduced to something else. Basically, when encounter with otherness goes awry, one of five things happens: (1) otherness is *homogenized* away (i.e., the other really isn't different after all—it just appears to be so); (2) otherness is *colonized* (i.e., treated as an inferior form of being and doing that needs to be elevated to our level; (3) otherness is *demonized* (i.e., becomes the object of all our repressed fears and anxieties—what Freud called projection); (4) otherness gets *romanticized* (another form of colonization, wherein the other is seen as superior but harmless); (5) or otherness gets *trivialized* (what is different does not really matter; it's the "essential"—non-other—that counts).

As these five pathways indicate, to take otherness and difference as important and central categories means to admit the importance of the question of power in the shaping theology. This entails understanding power in all its ramifications—coercive, unconscious, charismatic and otherwise—and not too readily identifying divine power.

A third condition is a methodology of *dialogical intentionality*. Put simply, this means that the direction of the theological reflection process must be guided by a truly dialogical intention, a sincere and sustained effort to learn as much as to teach, to be willing to change as much as to challenge. This goes beyond admiring in a culture what the sender finds to be exotic and really becoming engaged with the culture. Such a methodology has to continue to provide opportunities for learning and listening.

A fourth condition is a *multivalent criteriology*; that is, overcoming the need to have one single criterion that can determine the adequacy of a theology. If we live in many worlds, as Professor Panikkar has reminded us, then we should not be surprised that such complexity demands more than the utilization of one sole criterion. We need rather an interconnecting battery of criteria if we are to be really faithful to the Gospel.[3] Experience shows that we can err in many ways here. On a more conservative side, it is possible to think that linguistic formulations of one age can rise above any culture and serve as eternal criteria. On a more progressive side, necessary and sufficient conditions get confused, as though there were one criterion that makes all others unneeded (as in the formula, "if it doesn't liberate, it is not Christian").

Most of these comments have been about methodology and conditions. Let me close with just a few words on a foundational point in Professor Panikkar's presentation, namely, the centrality of what he calls the "christic event." The event of the incarnation of Christ represents both the problem and the possibility of a transcultural theology. For in our confessing of Jesus of Nazareth as the Christ, we are saying that the fullness of divinity could somehow reside and become manifest within the limitations of a first-century eastern Mediterranean culture, without that culture's forms becoming normative for subsequent generations of believers. There is both a problem and a possibility there, about the limitations and the potential of a culture. In this nexus between problem and possibility, the incarnation becomes the paradigm for a transcultural theology.

An additional thought that could be added is inspired by some of Professor Panikkar's work on the trinity. Does the doctrine of the trinity—three persons yet one God—not offer some clue to what unity, diversity and difference in Christian faith might mean? The theology of the trinity is a much underdeveloped area in western Christianity, and exploring once again this mystery may give us some new insight into the challenge of developing a genuinely transcultural theology.

NOTES

1. On the dynamic of prophecy, see especially Kenelm Burridge, *New Heaven, New Earth: A Study of Millennarian Activities* (Oxford: Basil Blackwell, 1969); Bryan Wilson, *The Noble Savages: The Primitive Origins of Charisma and Its Contemporary Survival* (Berkeley: University of California Press, 1975).

2. Sender and receiver methodologies are treated in Robert Schreiter, *Constructing Local Theologies* (Maryknoll: Orbis Books, 1985), ch. 3. On receiver methodologies, see also Richard Holub, *Reception Theory: A Critical Introduction* (New York: Muthuen, 1984).

3. Examples of such multivalent criteriologies may be found in Schreiter, chapter 5; and Anton Wessels, *Jezus zien: Hoe Jezus is overgeleverd in andere culturen* (Baarn: Ten Have, 1986).

CHRISTOLOGY FROM A CONTEMPORARY AFRICAN PERSPECTIVE

Caritas McCarthy

For a genuine world perspective in theology, full account must be taken of the increasing number of African theologians who reflect and write out of their experience of their own rich and distinctive culture. African perspectives come not only from Islam, which prevails throughout North Africa and in pockets throughout the continent, but also from African Traditional Religions and from a fast-growing African Christianity. Presently many African Christian theologians—Catholic and Protestant, men and women, indigenous and expatriate—have played a significant role, not only in creative Christian theologizing but also in giving written expression to African Traditional Religions, and in re-affirming religious beliefs, values, symbols, and rites which have been at the heart of African culture for centuries before the coming of Christianity. Thus today one can acquire something of the perspective of African Religions from those who present the Christian perspective. Many Christian

Caritas McCarthy, SHCJ, received her PhD in history from Catholic University of America, and her STD from the Gregorian University, Rome, Italy. She is presently director of the Humanities Interdisciplinary Program at Rosemont College (Rosemont, PA) where she is Associate Professor of History and lectures in religious studies. In 1987–88 she taught Christology at St Augustine's Major Seminary, Jos, Nigeria. Her concern that Christology studies be integrated with spiritual and historical theology has broadened to include the insights of other cultures, especially those of African theologians. She is preparing for publication an anthology of African writings on Christ. Since the publication in 1960 of her The Rule for Nuns of St Caesarius of Arles (Washington, DC: Catholic University of America Press) she has researched, lectured, and published on women's history and spirituality. In 1987 she published The Spirituality of Cornelia Connelly in the Edwin Mellen Press series "Studies in Women and Religion."

theologians are passionate in their desire to recover the profound traditional integration of religion and life, and the meaningful ancient beliefs, symbols, and rites of their peoples which they feel were needlessly, sometimes ruthlessly, suppressed by the Christian missionaries of the last century and a quarter.[1]

This essay will survey the writings of African Christian theologians of the last two decades who have focused on the central mystery of Jesus Christ; it will trace their search for Christological resonances in traditional African themes, their proposals of models for expressing the mystery of Christ which arise out of African life and culture. Like all theological models used throughout Christian tradition, they only approximate the reality they are expressing, but they do so in a way that approximates African reality as it is lived, and they open up new images to the world church.[2] This paper relies heavily not only on specialized studies, but also on recent surveys of African Christology, especially that of Raymond Moloney,[3] and of the volume *Chemins de la christologie africaine*.[4] The contribution I bring to this study is my use of and reflection on current Christological studies during a recent experience in Nigeria of teaching Christology to African seminarians and young African sisters, and of sharing community life with the latter. These experiences, as well as the directing of retreats and workshops in which the mystery of Christ was central, enable me to affirm personally the richness of African traditional religious values which contemporary Africans bring to their experience of the mystery of Christ. These experiences also enable me to affirm the validity of models proposed by the authors used for this study.

The authors surveyed in this review come from sub-Saharan African, east to west and south to Madagascar and South Africa; they reflect the experience of more than thirty nations and hundreds of tribal cultures. One might ask, therefore, whether there is a simply "African" Christological perspective, whether indeed this is not a homogenized fiction belying a rich cultural diversity. Theologians themselves from various parts of the continent, often working independently of one another through the last two decades, have found a growing convergence on "African" models for Christ, a convergence existing amid diverse ways of theologizing with the help of their models. Thus it has been affirmed that there are some fundamentally African ways of approaching the mystery of Christ, just as there is a fundamental African worldview.

In his search for models by which the African can most fully enter into the mystery of God-become-human, John Mbiti asked: "Where is He?" and answered ". . . in the realities of our African life, in African settings, in community structures, in traditional religious insights, in struggles for liberation, . . . energizing through the power of His Spirit."[5] Out of this search through the last two decades have come the following models of Christ: Proto-Ancestor, with all the rich implications this has for Christ's headship of the Mystical Body; Christ as Elder Brother, a preferred model to that of Christ as Chief, although the spokesman of the Chief is seen as a possible model; Christ as Master of Initiation, i.e., leader of the meaningful rites of passage which African traditional life has long included; finally and most importantly, those models which are most directly soteriological: Christ as Savior/Healer, Savior/Victor, Savior/Liberator. None of the models are without soteriological import. Mercy Oduyoye tells us that "the Christ of the popular theology of Africa is above all the one who saves." She defines "the African theological task" as "soteriology," and includes the liberation theologies from South Africa within the deep yearning of the whole continent for a savior.[6] Raymond Moloney notes that the themes of Christ as Ancestor, Master of Initiation, Healer, also focus on the person of the God-man as he is in himself.[7]

African theologians have found that they agree not only on certain basic "Christological resonances" in African belief and praxis, but also that they agree on a basic African worldview out of which models for understanding Christ emerge. It will be helpful to look briefly through African eyes upon the world. The Ghanaian scholar, Appiah-Kubi sees the following:

> At one with culture, religion is inextricably linked to the whole of life whose personal and communal activities it animates. The feeling of wholeness is an important aspect of African life. The celebrations of ritual ceremonies take place in common and for the common good. The spirit of solidarity plays a cardinal part in this, and the existence of the individual cannot be conceived outside the framework of one's integration in society. Religion therefore acts as a unifying factor in African culture. It is like the soul which keeps the whole body healthy.[8]

Thus we see that the African worldview eschews the dualism of sacred/secular, body/spirit, individual/society. All Africans agree on the centrality of community and have made their own Mbiti's beautiful expression of the intensely relational character of their life: "I am because we are; and because we are, therefore I am." Citing this, Appiah-Kubi goes on to say that a person is only truly and fully human in the company of others. It is in this context that he notes the importance of the rites of passage that "one has to go through" in order "to be accepted as a perfect man or woman in several African societies." It is essential to understand that "Religion permeates . . . especially the crucial aspects of life, namely marriage, birth, naming ceremony, puberty, illness, healing and death."[9]

Community includes those yet to be born, and "the living dead"— the ancestors. In order to be venerated as an ancestor in the spirit world one had to have led an exemplary life in the earthly community. Other intermediary spirits, both good and evil, are part of the Africans' world.[10] So, too, is the one Supreme God worshipped under different names and with varying rites and varying degrees of familiarity throughout the continent. Current scholarship on the African Traditional Religions rejects the errors of scholars and missionaries in the past who called these religions polytheistic.[11]

The African worldview has affinities with the biblical worldview; it is closer certainly than that of Europe and North America from which Christianity came to Africa. In one important respect African Traditional Religion and, indeed, the whole cultural heritage, differs from that of biblical peoples: Africans have not been "a People of the Book." Pobee says: "We have as yet no Scriptures of African Traditional Religion. But the urgent task is the collection of myths, proverbs, invocations, prayers, incantations, ritual, songs, dreams and so on."[12] Appiah-Kubi writes of the Independent Christian Churches that

> we must . . . see their theology in what they do, in their prayers and their self-help programs and not what they write. Their oral theology, as contrasted with the western liberal theology, is not the definition, but description; not the statement, but the story; not the doctrine but the testimony; not the book but the people; not the *Summa Theologia* but the song.[13]

These features of the African worldview, to which the Traditional Religions are integral, have been the fertile soil from which African Christian theologians have developed their models for Christ. This they do with passion, asking if there can finally "be genuinely African ideas of Christ which can be labelled . . . *MADE IN AFRICA*"?[14] Zulu Sofola calls for more depth to the indigenization process, saying that there has been a misdirected desire of African Churches to dress Christ in African clothes, without giving thought to the European soul with which Christ came to Africa. Unless Christ is presented to Africans in a manner acceptable to the African mentality, Christianity will remain alien and irrelevant. Christ must have an African soul, a soul that understands the realities of the African cosmos before he can respond to our lyrics, dances, and customs. He must first be liberated from the grip of Europeanism before he can be embraced by Africans in their quest for self-realization and liberation.[15]

The authors who express these sentiments come from the mainline Christian Churches, but they are being prodded constantly by the large, steadily increasing number of Independent Christian Churches throughout the continent of Africa. These churches have never lost touch with the integration of religion with African traditional life.[16] The challenges they pose and some insights they offer are now accepted by many mainline Christian theologians; the Christological efforts of the latter are one manifestation. Catholics and Protestants alike rejoiced when Pope Paul VI proclaimed in Uganda in 1969: "You may, you must have an African Christianity." At the Roman Catholic Synod of Bishops in Rome in 1974 the African Bishops rejected a theology of mere adaptation and proclaimed a theology of incarnation or inculturation.[17] And in March of 1988, the Vatican Secretariat for Non-Christian Religions directed African Catholic bishops to provide for studies of African Traditional Religions in all seminaries and houses of formation. A stated objective of this provision was the identification of "elements which Christianity could adopt . . ."[18]

What follows will be a brief descriptive survey of several images and figures proper to African life and worship through which the African can approach the mystery of Christ more authentically. The scope of the study does not permit extended theological analysis of the models proposed, nor of the full exposition their authors give them, nor analysis of the present status of Christianity in Africa. It is hoped that what is presented here will evoke continuing research, analysis and synthesis towards a truly African Christology.

Christ as Proto-Ancestor

In his recent book *Christ as Our Ancestor*, Charles Nyamiti notes that the importance for Africans of their ancestors as source of life and as vital mediator between earthly life and the spirit world cannot be overestimated.[19] Partain has said that "insofar as African Traditional Religion can be defined by specific 'religious actions,' the cult of the ancestors is its most common and essential activity."[20] Most African theologians find that the mediator role of the African ancestor and the regular sacred communication his descendents have with him offer much for understanding Christ. Only Aylward Shorter judges that the disadvantages outweigh advantages.[21]

But for Nyamiti the Christological resonances are powerful. He sees the ancestral mediator role as an apt preparation for faith in Christ as Savior.

> The Savior . . . appears as the highest actualization of the African aspirations sought for in the traditional ancestors. For what does the African desire from his ancestors if not their supernatural power and mediation in his favor, together with material and spiritual benefits, contact with God and his dead relatives? . . . By becoming Christ's descendent the African achieves not any kind of power, but God's own infinite personified power assisting him, and even identifying him mystically with it so as to become the intrinsic supernatural principle of his own being and activity.[22]

Nyamiti also finds that the recounting of the deeds of the ancestor in "effective memory form," and his becoming the archetype, the exemplar of behavior, make him an appropriate model for introducing the mystery of Christ and his relationship with his people. Nyamiti admits that there are hazards as well as strengths in the Christ-as-Ancestor model—e.g., that the ancestor, from having been "one-of-us"—as Christ was—only *acquires* a kind of supernatural status, and only when he passes to the spirit world.[23] Moloney was particularly concerned with this problem, noting that "the ancestor's promotion to a state of nearness to God suggests . . . adoptionism" rather than the uniqueness of Christ who was eternally divine, while becoming fully human. Moloney was also concerned with the "shadowy nature of the existence sometimes attributed to the ancestors."[24] Because of these problems, Moloney prefers the approach of Benezet Bujo to the Christ-as-Ancestor model, an approach grounded on what was an important element also for Nyamiti—ancestor as source of life. Moloney sees Bujo, after emphasizing the African God as the God of life, as "cutting away from the African model . . . from the physical descent that goes with it, when he centers our relationship to Christ as ancestor on the divine sonship of Christ as source and basis of our being born of God. As Son of God, Christ is ancestor in a unique sense . . . becomes the unique source of life. . . ." As *Proto-Ancestor*, Christ "is the perfection and fulfullment of the ideals which the God-fearing ancestors have always sought and stood for."[25]

Whatever the limitations of the ancestor—the lineage-head model for Christ—it is obviously a powerful model for Christ as Head of the Mystical Body. From the ancestor, within the tribe—one's community—Africans have received life and true identity: "I am because we are." Theologians believe that one of Africa's major contributions to western Christianity will be a deeper understanding of the unity of the human community in the Mystical Body, and a more authentic praxis of Christian charity. Meanwhile *Christ's* headship of his body has enlarged the African sense of community with a vision of an interrelatedness and an identity that transcends tribe and extends to the whole human community.[26]

Christ as Chief? Or Spokesman for the Chief?

In view of the "good soil" that African traditional life provides for understanding Christ as head of his body, it has been asked: "Does the Chief provide a Christ model?" There is fairly general rejection of this model on the grounds that colonialism discredited the chiefs, that the chiefs are too remote, that they have to be approached through intermediaries, that their authority is linked to a council of elders (whereas Christ's authority is unique and divine), and, finally, that they are not universally exemplary as are the ancestors. It will be remembered that the ancestors are those who so lived on earth as to be revered in the spirit world. The Ghanaian New Testament scholar Pobee has proposed that the powerful spokesperson—linguist—of the chief, who has full power to speak and act for him, might be proposed as a Christ figure. He cites the *Okyeame* of the Yoruba chiefs (Nigeria); Sawyerr cites the *Lavale* of the Mende chiefs (Sierra Leone) as examples. However, in general, the chiefs have not been considered as apt models for Christ.[27]

Christ as Elder Brother

But if the chiefship is unsuited to the person of Christ for Africans,

to represent Jesus Christ as the first-born among many brethren who
with him, together form the Church, is in true keeping with African
notions. . . . Our Lord's affinity to man . . . is a basis for presenting the
Church as the Great Family of which Jesus Christ is the head.[28]

From long pastoral experience in Sierra Leone, Sawyerr sees a
special reason why "an effort must be made to bring home the
mystical relation between Christ and the Christian . . . (Eph 2:19ff):"

> By it we are adopted into sonship with God, because . . . Jesus Christ
> was ordained to become the first-born among many brethren. Christians
> are equally ordained to be conformed . . . to the likeness of Jesus Christ
> (see Rom. 8:29, 1 John 3:2). This is man's true destiny, the means of
> overcoming the deeply ingrained feeling of insecurity which creates
> acute social and psychological problems even among Christian Afri-
> cans. The non-Christian African . . . has a ready-made formula for
> dealing with his difficulties. . . . He presumes witchcraft or a spirit . . .
> and performs the appropriate religious rites which restore his self-
> confidence and all is well again. . . . To the Christian this . . . is
> idolatrous. . . . But an attitude of total surrender to God seems difficult
> to sustain. . . . In the African situation the Incarnation should be so
> presented as to emphasize that Jesus Christ was the manifestation of
> God's love for man, God's sharing in human sufferings, God's victory
> over death and all the disastrous influences which throng man's every-
> day experiences. In short, African Christians should be helped to
> realize that Jesus Christ was born as I was, grew up as I did, . . . is elder
> brother.[29]

From the other side of the continent, de Carvalho, Methodist
bishop of Angola, finds also that, in Jesus, the elder brother, the
Christian African finds the "defender, mediator" which he lost in
giving up recourse to his traditional spirits and their rites:

> The incarnation in the African situation lies on the foundation of that
> African experience that Jesus Christ was an African . . . the older
> brother of the Africans. . . . The Africans found in the Independent
> Churches the risen Christ who became their brother, one of them. . . .
> For the majority of the Christians of Africa, the incarnate Jesus is the
> first born among many brethren (Rom. 8:29). The Virgin Mary herself
> is also our sister. . . . Jesus as our elder brother is perfectly understand-
> able due to the role that the older brother has in our society and
> culture; of a defender, mediator and protector.[30]

My own recent experience in West Africa affirms the power of the
role of the elder brother delineated by African theologians. The well-

known Mbiti expressed his sense of the grace that flows to African Christians from their felt experience of their relationship with Christ as elder brother:

> In Him the fulness of the brotherhood and sisterhood of humankind, dwells. All who share in Him, and in this solidarity, have mutual respect and equality of relationships. All forms of discrimination, exploitation and improper relationship are a negation.[31]

Christ as Master of Initiation

Bishop Sanon of Burkina Faso links Christ as Elder Brother with the evocative model of Master of Initiation, that is, the one who leads the members of the tribe through meaningful processes associated with various stages and events of life—birth, marriage, illness, death, and especially puberty, when one passes from adolescence to adult membership in the tribe and appropriates the tribal traditions, becomes a full person.[32] Mbiti had noted in 1968 that since the introduction of the New Testament, Africans have been able to identify with Christ in his initiation rites—his naming, circumcision, presentation in the temple both in infancy and at puberty, and his baptism.[33]

Moloney sums up the depth that Sanon has found in Christ as Master of Initiation:

> Christ . . . was also initiated into the fullness of God's plan by being brought to the perfection spoken of in Heb. 2:10, 5:9 and 7:28, . . . especially in his death and resurrection, which can be understood as a kind of initiatic ordeal through which one is transformed into a higher mode of existence. . . . Without the redemptive acts of the paschal mystery, Christ's initiation process would have no more than exemplary significance; but, through their causality on our redemption, Christ's initiation is truly the cause of our being initiated into a whole new mode of existence, and he is the one who leads us to fullness of life. . . . Our Lord comes to be seen as the Master of Initiation, the elder brother, (Rom. 8:29), at home in his Father's house (Luke 2:49), as befits a son (John 8:35), making others become children of the same household (Matt. 23:8, 10; Mark. 3:34f.). As in the initiation process, symbols are used as vehicles of the highest values of the community, so Christ leads us through symbols, especially the sacraments.[34]

Sanon writes with great feeling describing how only Christ has been able to lead to term the project hidden at the heart of the whole of the initiation tradition—the conduct of the human person to the full and authentic dignity of sons-daughters and brothers-sisters in the community of humanity. Like an ancient seer, he envisions his African disciples following on the initiation course founded by the ancestors. The disciples are "full of constancy and perseverence," taking word for word what the master puts forward, desiring what he designs, hoping to arrive where he leads.[35]

Christ as Savior/Healer

Contemporary African writings on Christ as Healer are abundant, convincing, and provocative. Appiah-Kubi says: "Jesus Christ is . . . conceived by many African Christians as the great physician, healer and victor over worldly powers *par excellence*. To many, Jesus came that we may have life and have it more abundantly."[36]

Aylward Shorter goes further and identifies the figure in African traditional life, once outlawed by Euro-American Christianity, who can now be seen to serve as a model for Christ—the "diviner-healer or witch-doctor." He notes the perceptiveness of R. Buana Kibongi who, as early as 1969,

> argued that the traditional *nganga* (doctor-diviner) is a healer and revealer, that this is precisely the role of Christ in the maximum degree, and that the African Christian encounters Christ in the light of his experience of the Christian priest as both God's doctor and God's evangelist.

Shorter goes on to note that the "implicit Christology of some modern African literature . . . and of Folk Christianity, confirms Kibongi's insight." He continues:

> The Christ-figures in the early moral plays of Wole Soyinka, and—to some extent—of his later political activist plays, present us with a savior who is both healer and teacher. Mission-related Christianity has found it increasingly difficult to integrate its priest-healers (and even its bishop-healers), but independent churches have mostly centred on a leader who has been hailed as a prophet healer . . .[37]

It was the independent churches (indigenous African Christian Churches) that gave Appiah-Kubi and others a clear picture of a Redeemer/Healer whom the African could "contact in a manner suitable to his own mentality and feelings." In the Euro-American "missionary churches . . . Jesus Christ seems to be a spiritual, intellectual or philosophical entity, . . . instead of being a dynamic personal reality in all life situations. Thus he seems to be absent in several crisis situations of the African life—birth, puberty, marriage, illness and death." The indigenous churches invite their people to bring their worries of unemployment, poverty, witch troubles, ill luck, enemy, barrenness, sorrow, blindness, etc., to Jesus who saves all who come to him in faith. These churches believe that Jesus, who is more powerful than evil spirits, heals the whole person, spiritually, psychologically, physically, within the believing community. They aim to supplement, not supplant, medical treatment with rites using prayers, visions, dreams, oil, water and ashes. Appiah-Kubi finds that

> the commonest reply one gets to the question "Why did you join this or that Indigenous African Church?" is "I was ill for a long time. I tried all forms of treatment, but to no avail. I was advised by a friend to go to prophet so-and-so. I did and now I am better. "Praise the Lord!!"[38]

Shorter, like Appiah-Kubi, has found his model for Christ akin to the Christ of the New Testament:

> Jesus was a medicine man in his own culture and a worker of wonders. . . . [He] used the techniques of popular healers and exorcists of his time, and, to that extent, at least, he was like a traditional diviner-healer or witchdoctor.

Shorter continues with what he and his African colleagues agree is the great contribution which the African model for Christ as Healer can make to world Christianity:

> Jesus shared the integrated approach to healing which characterizes the so-called witchdoctor. . . . In antedating medical science Jesus escaped its limitations, notably its comparative lack of interest in the environmental, social and moral aspects of healing.[39]

Appiah-Kubi reminds us frequently that, for the African, illness involves the whole person, "the relationship of the patient with the spiritual or supernatural world, and with members of the society." There is no "clear distinction between religion and medicine." The healing ministry of the Euro-American mission churches has lost its sacred character, its social control functions, its subjective influence on society, its meaningful moral terms. . . . The conspicuous absence of Jesus Christ from almost all the life crises raised a lot of questions in the mind of the African Christian.[40]

Emefie Ikenga-Metuh has also spoken of the "big question mark" left by past "methods of Christianization," e.g., methods lacking a model for Christ as *Integral* Healer. He noted in 1985 that

Westernization in most cases was limited to the adoption of western life-styles, without the western christian or secularist convictions. Under these circumstances, the roles of diviners and medicine-men have been greatly enhanced. Many of them have emigrated to the urban areas where their customers include the new educated, and christianized westernized elite—politicians, students, judges, civil servants, business men who approach them with traditional as well as new problems arising from the tensions of modern life. Thus divination, fortune-telling and medicine-making services have continued to thrive and their roles have expanded far beyond the limit of their traditional religious roles. They now flourish in the urban areas where pressure of modern life created crisis situations of a different kind to which they have so far adequately responded.[41]

Obviously the role of Christ as Integral Healer is one most apt for African quest for "wholeness of life"; it is also one of the most challenging and perhaps most promising for Euro-American Christianity. Shorter, who advocates its use in pastoral ministry, is quick to point out its hazards: like any model, it is exposed to the dangers of literalism and misinterpretation. He notes, among other negative possibilities, the propensity of cults toward the marvellous, the too-direct linking of physical and moral healing, the insistence on immediate results which renders the holistic healing ministry "transient and ephemeral." He recommends that the mainline Christian churches return in faith to a renewed study of the New Testament Jesus as Revealer-Healer and to a new openness to what the Revealer-Healer of African Traditional Religions can teach us.[42]

Christ as Savior/Victor

Accounts of Christ as Healer link the concept, and sometimes the title, of Christ as Victor. In an early and provative Christological essay Mbiti suggested that the image of Christ Victor—bestower of resurrection, of future life—is particularly suitable for Africans, not because it emerges from present cultural models, but precisely because it responds to "the yearning and longing of our people," fills "an obvious gap," even "a vacuum."[43] Very recently N. Onwu has referred to somewhat the same potential for a Christ who fulfills and carries forward traditional concepts: "Africa has no concept of a future kingdom. Jesus' teaching about the kingdom offers meaning to human existence and thus satisfies Africa's spiritual yearnings.[44]

But Nyamiti is less absolute in his synthesis of the total African picture when he speaks about "traditional salvific myths." He believes that

> . . . to those tribes who hold that salvation has not yet been realized, . . . Christ's redemption, will be welcomed as good news. . . . To those whose teachings bear some traces of that doctrine [Redemption] the Christian messages will serve as the perfect accomplishment of that teaching.[45]

Christ as Savior/Liberator

It is obvious from the profoundly soteriological emphasis of African Christology that the figure of Christ as Liberator underlies many of the images that arise from the African concept of savior.

Thus a group report of a consultation of the World Council of Churches in 1977 read:

> To both Asian and African peoples Jesus Christ is the liberator from all that keeps them in bondage, in fear, in domination, in oppression, in religious distortion, whether in political, economic, psychological or social terms. He is the liberator from all that robs them of their dignity as full human beings and hampers them from full realisation of their true potentials. He is the liberator from Karma, transmigration, caste system, tribalism, racialism, etc. He has come to announce good news to the poor, to proclaim release for prisoners and recovery of sight for the blind, to let the broken victims go free and to proclaim the year of the Lord's favor (Luke 4:18 f.) It is not enough to list what Afro-Asians are being liberated from without stating what they are liberated for. They are liberated for love, for loving relationships with their fellow beings and God.[46]

This group had been dealing chiefly with Christologies of inculturation which have been the major concern of this essay. But, as

Moloney and Ukpong point out, contemporary African theologians, especially in the flagrantly oppressive racist regime of South Africa, have also been writing and preaching Christologies of liberation.[47] These arise not from the African Christian communities' reflection on Christ in the light of its centuries-old traditions, but on Christ and the kingdom in the light of present and severe oppressions under which the community lives. Christologies of liberation involve a more extensive and detailed exposition than is possible in this essay. Here only a few indications can be given of current developments including the emergence of women among the liberation Christologists.

Moloney agrees with Ukpong that there is an African liberation theology, related to that of Latin America but with its own distinctive characteristics. Within Africa itself one must distinguish between theology in South Africa and that on the rest of the continent. Among South Africans there is a strong emphasis on the black Christ, an emphasis that needs to be studied in relation to black Christology of North and South America. Moloney notes that Albert Nolan's *Jesus before Christianity* is "closer theologically to the work of the Latin Americans than to that of black theology," but that the "concern for justice is clearly a product of the same situation as that of black theology."[48]

Above South Africa, where the nations throughout the continent are ruled by Africans themselves, there is not the same emphasis on the black Christ. Shorter says rather sweepingly "the African Christian . . . stubbornly points out that in actual historical fact, Christ was not black. . . . In so far as, according to Black Theology, Christ's blackness stems from his solidarity with the black oppressed, even this claim is undermined by the existence of black oppressors. The Deity, as the Nigerian playwright Wole Soyinka has pointed out, "can no longer be identified along the simplistic color line."[49]

Recently N. Onwu of Nigeria has reiterated this position on the black Christ—"Christ's color is irrelevent"—while admitting that a "white Christ" is indeed often seen as "tied up with the colonialism and neo-colonialism that created realities of hunger, unemployment, repression, racism and Third World violence."[50]

Significantly Onwu has described a role for Christ as Liberator in the actual situation in which many independent nations of Africa presently find themselves, that is, plagued by tribalism, political and economic instability, and corruption. He calls for a critical biblical hermeneutic which allows Jesus' message to confront "neo-colonialism and individualism," and allows for the proclamation of a living Christ who liberates and unifies humanity, and creates a human community, a new social order. Indigenization must be profound enough to allow the "Person and word of Christ to confront Africa's worldview."

> Vulnerability and under-development are basic features of the African situation. Coincidentally, they were the problems which angered Jesus. They should form the core concerns of a biblical hermeneutic for Africans.[51]

African Women's Models for Christ

Increasingly in the last two decades African women have emerged as theologians and have taken up Christological concerns. They have joined male theologians in supporting Christologies of inculturation, recognizing the need of their people to approach Christ through the realities of their traditional life experience, and to be liberated from a Europeanized Christ.[52] They have turned to that woman's experience so central to African community life—that of the mother in labor and giving birth, and have found, as Christ himself did, a powerful image of his Paschal experience.[53] They have pondered deeply the New Testament image of Christ as Mother:

> . . . in Christ all that we know of perfect womanhood is revealed. He is the caring compassionate nurturer of all. Jesus nurtures not just by parables but by miracles of feeding. With his own hands he cooked that others might eat. . . . Jesus is Christ—truly woman (human) yet truly divine, for only God is the truly compassionate one.[54]

In Christ they have found the assumptions of their traditional society transcended: "The Christ of the woman of Africa upholds not only motherhood, but all, who like Jesus of Nazareth, perform 'mothering' roles in bringing out the best in all around them."[55]

African women theologians do not support all that has been proposed in Christologies of inculturation, showing that in some ways these perpetuate the male bias that has prevailed both in their traditional African societies and in the Christian missionary churches to which African women have belonged since the nineteenth century.[56] From the oppressions which women have suffered from both groups they turn to Christ for liberation. They ask now that their Christian churches present an authentic New Testament model of Christ who related to women with esteem, and who saw them as fully human, equal in dignity to men; they ask for an ecclesial praxis consonant with this model.[57]

Christologies of liberation have become a focus for several women theologians; they believe that the liberation of women will be a key to liberation from oppression of whole societies of men, women, and children. Louis Tappa of Cameroun expresses this forcefully:

> The African woman is at the bottom of the scale. . . . She incarnates the mass of the poor and oppressed. . . . When this woman has really come to understand the message of liberation that Jesus bears, she will be able to take her brothers by the hand and lead them to the way of liberation that is ours.
>
> . . . The principle that makes it possible for some to profess Christianity while being racist is the same principle that enables one to profess Christianity while keeping women in a lower position than men. . . . Christology is really at the center of this discussion, for Christ is the source of our faith, Christ is the norm of our faith, Christ is the content of our faith.[58]

It has been said that the emerging African Christologies have not yet sufficiently influenced the pastoral scene.[59] Several women theologians write with a pastoral emphasis. Mercy Oduyoye and Elizabeth Amoah closed their "The Christ for African Women" with a pastoral reflection which can serve as an appropriate conclusion for this essay:

> Finally the only way we can convince Africa that Jesus of Nazareth is uniquely the Christ of God is to live the life we are expected to live as Christ-believers. Do not call "Lord, Lord" while ignoring the demands of God.
>
> Christology down the ages, though derived from the experiences of the early companions of Jesus of Nazareth and those of their immediate associates, has been formulated in response to the actual historical realities of each age and place. Persons have contributed by the way each perceives and experiences Christ. "Christ" has been explained through imagery, cosmology, and historical events understood by both "speakers" and "listeners." This process continues in Africa. One thing is certain: whatever the age or place, the most articulate Christology is that silently performed in the drama of everyday living.[60]

NOTES

1. See, for example, the twenty-one essays in *African Theology en route*, Kofi Appiah-Kubi and Sergio Torres, eds. (Maryknoll: Orbis Books, 1983) passim. Jean Marc Ela in *African Cry* (Maryknoll: Orbis Books, 1983) often strikes this same note.

2. Avery Dulles, *Models of the Church* (New York: Doubleday, 1974), pp. 13, 27–28, gives a definition of models which seems to fit the work of contemporary African Christologists. Aylward Shorter treats of the need the universal church has for Africa's contribution in *African Christian Theology* (Maryknoll: Orbis Books, 1977), pp. 30ff.

3. "African Christology," *Theological Studies*, 48 (1987) 505–15.

4. F. Kabasélé, J. Doré, R. Luneau, eds. (Paris: Desclee, 1986).

5. John Mbiti, "Some Current Concerns of African Theology," in the volume he edited, *African and Asian Contributions to Contemporary Theology* (Bossey: World Council of Churches, 1977), p. 7. For the African worldview, see also Appiah-Kubi, "Jesus Christ—Some Christological Aspects from African Perspectives," pp. 51–52, in the same volume.

6. Mercy Amba Oduyoye, *Hearing and Knowing* (Maryknoll: Orbis Books, 1986), pp. 97–108 and "The Value of African Religious Beliefs and Practices," in *African Theology en route*, pp. 114–16. See also Moloney, pp. 506, 508, 515, and Charles Nyamiti, *Christ as Our Ancestor: Christology from an African Perspective* (Gweru, Zimbabwe: Mambo, 1984), p. 81.

7. Moloney, p. 506.

8. Appiah-Kubi, "Response" to "Roman Catholic Perspective," in *Christ's Lordship and Religious Pluralism*, Gerald Anderson and Thomas Stransky, eds. (Maryknoll: Orbis Books, 1981), p. 122; see also his "Jesus Christ," p. 53.

9. Appiah-Kubi, "Response," p. 122; "Jesus Christ," p. 56.

10. Nyamiti, pp. 15–16, 69–71.

11. See, for example, Emefie Ikenga-Metuh, *African Religions in Western Conceptual Schemes* (Ibadan: Pastoral Institute, 1985), p. vii–xiii, and passim; Geoffrey Parrinder, *West African Religion*, 2nd ed. (New York: Barnes & Noble, 1969), pp. 23–25.

12. John S. Pobee, *Toward an African Theology* (Nashville: Abingdon, 1979), pp. 21, 82; N. Onwu, "A Hermeneutical Model for Africa," *Theology Digest*, 34 (1987) 124–25.

13. Appiah-Kubi, "Jesus Christ," pp. 64–65.

14. Ibid., pp. 53–54.

15. *African Theology en route*, p. 136.

16. *African and Asian Contributions*, passim, especially pp. 53 ff.; also Lawrence Njoroge, "African Christianity: A Portrait," *Chicago Studies*, 26 (1987) 112–17.

17. Shorter, *African Christian Theology*, pp. 20–21.

18. *Catholic Standard and Times* (Philadelphia, PA), May 12, 1988, p. 26.

19. Nyamiti, pp. 7–9, 148–50; however, Pobee, p. 18, and Nyamiti, p. 15, both note that the Masai of East Africa are an exception to this generalization.

20. "Christians and Their Ancestors: A Dilemma of African Theology," *Christian Century*, 103 (Nov. 26, 1986) 1066.

21. Shorter, "Ancestor Veneration Revisited," *Afer*, 25 (1983) 197–203.

22. Nyamiti, pp. 69–70.

23. Nyamiti, pp. 7–8, 19–24, 146–48.

24. Moloney, p. 510.

25. Moloney, p. 511, citing Benezet Bujo, *Afrikanische Theologie in ihrem gesells-chaftlichen Kontext* (Dusseldorf: Patmos, 1986); "Nos ancêtres, ces saints inconnus," *Bulletin de théologie africaine*, 1 (1979) 165–78; "A Christocentric Ethic for Black Africa," *Theology Digest*, 30 (1982) 143–46.

26. Moloney, pp. 511–12; Bujo, "A Christocentric Ethic," pp. 143–46; Damian Lwasa, "Traditional and Christian Community in Africa," in *African Christian Spirituality*, A. Shorter, ed. (Maryknoll: Orbis Books, 1978), pp. 141–50.

27. For some support of the chief model and his linguist see Pobee, *Toward an African Theology*, pp. 94–98; for rejection of the model see Harry Sawyerr, "Jesus Christ—Universal Brother," in *African Christian Spirituality*, pp. 65–67.

28. Sawyerr, pp. 66–67.

29. Sawyerr, pp. 65–67.

30. Emilio de Carvalho, "What Do the Africans Say Jesus Christ Is?" *Africa Theological Journal*, 10 (1981) 17.

31. Mbiti, *African and Asian Contributions*, p. 102.

32. "Jésus, Maître d'initiation," in *Chemins de la christologie africaine*, F. Kaba-sélé, J. Doré, R. Luneau, eds. (Paris: Desclee, 1986), 143–66.

33. Mbiti, "Some African Concepts of Christology," in *Christ and the Younger Churches*, ed. G. Vicedom (London: SPCK, 1972) pp. 56–57.

34. Moloney, p. 507.

35. Sanon, pp. 156–57.

36. "Jesus Christ," p. 62.

37. A. Shorter, "Folk Christianity and Functional Christology," *Afer*, 24 (1982) 136; *Jesus and the Witch Doctor* (Maryknoll: Orbis Books, 1985). See also E. deRosny, *Healers in the Night*, (Maryknoll: Orbis books, 1985).

38. "Jesus Christ," pp. 53, 55, 63.

39. *Jesus and the Witch Doctor*, pp. 3, 12–13.

40. Appiah-Kubi, "Jesus Christ," pp. 61–62

41. Metuh, pp. 167–68.

42. Shorter, *Jesus and the Witch Doctor*, p. 25.

43. "Some African Concepts," pp. 53–54.

44. "A Hermeneutical Model for Africa," *Theology Digest*, 34 (1987) 125.

45. Nyamiti, pp. 34–35.

46. *African and Asian Contributions*, p. 101

47. Moloney, pp. 505–506, 513–15; J. Ukpong, "The Emergence of African Theologies," *Theological Studies*, 45 (1984) 521–29.

48. Moloney, pp. 513–15.

49. Shorter, "Folk Christianity," p. 135.

50. N. Onwu, "A Hermeneutical Model for Africa," p. 124.

51. Onwu, p. 126.

52. African women theologians have made significant contributions to two recent publications of Third World women theologians: V. Fabella and M. Oduyoye, eds. *With Passion and Compassion.* (Maryknoll: Orbis Books, 1988); J. Pobee and B. Von Wartenburg-Potter, eds. *New Eyes for Reading* (Geneva: World Council of Churches, 1986). Women theologians are included in *African Theology en route*. See also M. Oduyoye, *Hearing and Knowing* (Maryknoll: Orbis Books, 1986). P. Stadler, "Christological Approaches in Africa," *Theology Digest*, 31 (1984) 219–22, recognized the contributions of women.

53. Oduyoye, "Birth," in *New Eyes for Reading*, pp. 41–44; see John 16:21.

54. Oduyoye and E. Amoah, "The Christ for African Women," in *With Passion and Compassion*, p. 44.

55. Ibid., p. 45.

56. Ibid., pp. 43–45.

57. See, in *New Eyes for Reading*, E. Amoah, pp. 3–4; G. Eneme, pp. 28–32; B. Ekeya, pp. 59–67; M. Oduyoye, pp. 68–80. In *African Theology en route*, R. Zoe-Obianga, pp. 145–49.

58. "The Christ-Event from the Viewpoint of African Women: A Protestant Perspective," in *With Passion and Compassion*, pp. 33–34.

59. Moloney, p. 415.

60. *With Passion and Compassion*, p. 45.

WHO IS SEBASTIAN RODRIGUES?
CROSSCULTURAL PERSPECTIVES ON RELIGIOUS IRONY AND THE SELF

John McCarthy

So tightly wound around the topics of rationality, intelligibility, control, and continuity is the western understanding of the self that its unraveling has been an inevitable product of twentieth century thought. Psychoanalysis, sociology, historical study, critical theory, deconstruction, new narrative and poetic forms, new cosmologies, and more all intersect in their conviction that, however the self might be understood, its discussion can no longer be confined to individuality, conscious self-presence or, personal will. The encounter with non-western traditions in which the self is measured by radically dissimilar scales of time, person, and cosmos has only hastened this process of unraveling. This paper takes up the topic of the "unraveled self" in the light of such contemporary and crosscultural contexts. In what follows I will maintain that the Japanese writer, Shusaku Endo, in the novel *Silence*, presents a theological hermeneutic of the self forged in a situation where categories of individuality, accepted traditions, cultural definitions, and social customs are not available. This failure of categories occurs precisely because of the encounter of a western, Christian individual—a character by the name of Sebastian Rodrigues—with a Japanese culture radically different from his own. If this analysis proves to be adequate and helpful, then it suggest one set of topics for a theological hermeneutics of the self at home in a world religious context.

John McCarthy (Ph.D., University of Chicago, 1986) is an Assistant Professor of Theology at Loyola University of Chicago and Chairperson for Publications and Research for the College Theology Society.

The analysis properly begins with the obvious question, "Who is Sebastian Rodrigues?" But to ask "Who is Sebastian Rodrigues?" is to pose a question which immediately splinters. First, it is a question of sheer information; the name "Sebastian Rodrigues" is not a household term. Second, it is a question of literary composition: namely, what are the processes of characterization used to establish "Sebastian Rodrigues" as both *homo fictus* and *homo sapiens?* Third, it is a question of narrative interpretation: given the inscribed textual structures, how might the name "Sebastian Rodrigues" be read as an element within the larger narrative? Fourth, it is a question of fundamental, and in this case, theological, hermeneutics: namely, given the narrative centrality of "Sebastian Rodrigues," what is the scale which the narrative suggest as appropriate for identifying what it is to be a "self" as Christian? The questions of information, characterization, narrative interpretation, and theological hermeneutics are, at minimum, all pieces of the larger, controlling question, "Who is Sebastian Rodrigues?" The central claim of the paper is as follows: "Sebastian Rodrigues" names a deeply, if not infinitely, unstable character. This unstable character may be appropriately described as ironic. The irony invites the reader's attempt to restabilize the character and yet the instability of the character blocks its reconstruction. In as much as the characterization of Sebastian Rodrigues suggests the narrative measure of a "self," specifically as Christian, it discloses an understanding of the "self" as deeply, if not infinitely ironic. The "self"—both Sebastian Rodrigues and the reader—are victims of the expectations of a stable and independent self, an expectation measured as inappropriate by the narrative ironies. The narrative renames this disruption in character, "a different love."

The First Splinter: Information

To set about developing this thesis it is necessary to return to the splinter questions, and here narrative information is indispensable. "Sebastian Rodrigues" is the name of a seventeenth century Portuguese Jesuit missionary in Shusaku Endo's novel, *Silence*. *Silence* is the fictionalized account of this character's journey from Portugal to Japan and his subsequent life at a time when the persecution of Christianity became state policy. Rodrigues begins his journey with both appropriate missionary zeal and the news that his former teacher, now missionary, Fr. Ferreira, has apostatized. The journey to Japan becomes a double mission: to spread the Christian faith and to find out what has truly happened to the teacher whom Rodrigues held in such esteem. The voyage halfway around the world is difficult, but the difficulty is not its primary characteristic. The journey's highlight—or lowlight—is the introduction of the sniveling, stinking character, Kichijiro. A Christian, he has himself apostatized. As the narrative progresses his desire for prestige combined with his former beliefs compel him to alternate between a safe allegiance to, and a frightened denial of, his Christian faith.

Entering Japan at night, Rodrigues is immediately stashed away for protection in a hillside hut. Initial fears of capture soon recede, and, with guarded courage, Rodrigues and his companion priest, Francis Garrpe, cautiously engage in their sacramental efforts. This delicate peace changes abruptly with the visit of the magistrate, Inoue's, soldiers. The suspicion of Christian activities is announced and threats are made, all based on the ominous suggestion that someone from the village has informed the official. Hostage taking and the offer of large sums of blood money become the twin pressures used to identify fellow Christians and the hidden priests. As the measure of non-involvement with Christianity each villager is ordered to step or spit on an image of Christ or Mary—the fumie. The test of one's adherence to Christianity becomes the test of desecration. Several Christian villagers refuse to apostatize, but Kichijiro does. Rodrigues and Garrpe watch these scenes from the hillside and are informed about them through messangers. The priests come to recognize that their presence and protection is purchased with the suffering and death of the villagers. Separating, the two priests leave the immediate area of the village. But Inoue is dogged in his pursuit and torture of Christians with the ultimate intent of capturing the foreign missionaries. In time, Rodrigues and Garrpe are captured. Both refuse to apostatize, but the pressure to do so escalates quickly. Garrpe is brought to the seashore where two villagers are wrapped in straw mats. Unless he denies his beliefs, he is told, the villagers will be taken off shore and pushed into the water. Garrpe's refusal initiates a sequence in which both villagers and he meet their death. Rodrigues, meanwhile, is forced to view the entire scene from a hilltop. His former expectations of a victorious martyr's death as the crown of missionary activity all but receive their final blow. Yet Rodrigues still does not apostatize.

Not long after, Rodrigues meets his former teacher, Ferreira, who he discovers has indeed apostatized. A mixture of respect, understanding, loathing, disbelief, and fear separate and join teacher to student. With a feeble interchange, Ferreira attempts to convince Rodrigues to step on the fumie, yet Rodrigues remains steadfast. Ultimately put in a cell with the expectation that he may still meet the martyr's death by hanging upside down in a pit of excrement, Rodrigues awaits his fate. The silence of the cell is broken by what he takes to be the snoring of the guard outside his door. A visit from Ferreira reveals that the sound is not snoring but Christians, who have already apostatized, hanging in the pit until Rodrigues denies his faith. It is at this point that he agrees to step on the fumie. Endo writes:

> "It is only a formality. What do formalities matter?" The interpreter urges him on excitedly. "Only go through with the exterior form of trampling."
> The priest raises his foot. In it he feels a dull heavy pain. This is no mere formality. He will now trample on what he has considered to be the most beautiful thing in his life, on what he has believed most pure, on what is filled with the ideals and the dreams of man. How his foot aches! And then the Christ in the bronze speaks to the priest: "Trample! Trample! I more than anyone know the pain in your foot. Trample! It was to be trampled on by men that I was born into this world. It was to share men's pain that I carried my cross."
> The priest placed his foot on the *fumie*. Dawn broke. And in the distance the cock crew.[1]

After this scene Rodrigues is held under house arrest, forced to take the name, wife and home of a dead Japanese man, Okada San'emon, and compelled to take part in state measures insuring that Christianity is cut off at the roots in Japan. Sebastian Rodrigues is Okada San'emon, a character who dies in isolation in Japan about thirty years after the apostasy. Thus the novel ends.

The Second Splinter: Characterization

This plot outline provides an initial response to the question "Who is Sebastian Rodrigues?" But, as Wolfgang Iser notes, summarizing the plot of a novel does more to alienate than involve the reader. It furnishes a necessary but incomplete grasp on the whole of the text. This marginal grasp is, however, a prerequisite for the second splinter question: what are the techniques of narrative characterization used to establish Sebastian Rodrigues? It is with this investigation that the claim made regarding character instability can be developed. The central instability of the character is the absence of an intelligible and coherent pattern of values and reasons from which directed action might be initiated. This is not to say that Rodrigues is incapable of performing action, nor that his actions become random, nor that there is not a rationale for each of his actions; it is to say that by the narrative climax, what Rodrigues had thought to be a intelligent and coherent pattern of values and reasons has dissipated leaving him and the reader faced with a future devoid of any stable pattern by which to interpret and initiate inevitable future actions.

A variety of narrative techniques establish the instability. Four are of particular importance—namely, the narrative of a journey, structured misdirection, disperate points of view, and identity mergers. First, the journey narrative: the geographical journey becomes the mirror of the character's journey. At the journey's origin, Portugal, everything seems stable: Rodrigues' identity as a missionary, his education, his plans, his picture of Jesus. It is truly home, the locale from which his bearings are taken. The journey from this home is the journey from these stable bearings. Japan becomes "the swamp" in which missionary ideals are subverted, his education reversed, his plans frustrated, his picture of Jesus trampled. In Japan Rodrigues has no place to live. He exists in hiding, sometimes under a floor; he lives on the road or in a prison; he finally dies in the house of a dead man. Like the journey, Rodrigues is characterized by the distance from Portugal and not by the return to it. Both he and his journey end in homelessness.

Second, the novel trades on a structural misdirection of both the character and the reader. Initially Rodrigues' understanding of the missionary/martyr is a seemingly commendable matrix of strong belief, noble individuality, and heroic virtue. Like his memory of the seminary image of the risen Jesus emerging triumphant from the tomb, he is determined to be religiously victorious, to "suffer steadfastly even unto death." There is no textual indication suggesting that this character matrix should be understood as idiosyncratic or fanatical. Indeed, the opposite is the case: if the reader does not confirm this matrix as plausible, even appropriate, the latter events of the text lack tension. The stable character calls for a stable reading of this character. But as the narrative progresses the stability of character and reading is dismantled. Places, beliefs, expectations, and allegiances are reversed; the matrix which explains action from the side of the self as agent shatters, and likewise the perspective for

reading the character as a unified self vanishes. The initial direction
becomes a misdirection.

Third, the text is written from at least four points of view. Not
only are they different but these viewpoints are ordered to create an
increasing sense of distance from the stability of the initial characterization. The text begins as a series of letters composed by Rodrigues in diary-like fashion. The first forty percent of the novel is
first person. All action and description up to the point of Rodrigues'
capture are thus portrayed. The next fifty percent of the text is an
omniscient, third person narrative, but one which is clearly more
concerned with the thoughts and actions of Rodrigues than of any
other character. The last ten percent of the text contains a mixture
of viewpoints: a short section repeating the omniscient narrative; an
account from the diary of a Dutch trading clerk; an account from the
diary of a Japanese officer overseeing Rodrigues, and a translation of
official reports. The ordered change of viewpoints reiterates the
distance from the stable characterization at the beginning of the
novel: the narrative moves from the first person diary/letter to the
diary accounts written by minor officials, to the distant and offical
report of times, dates, and burial costs. In the end, Rodrigues is
literally the money it takes to dispose of the body. The distant third
person wholly replaces the seemingly stable first.

Fourth, there is a series of merged identities which further frag-
ments the initial stability. The technique used is the embedded
parallel story. The narrative of a seventeenth century missionary is
told in tandem with the gospel story of the capture, suffering, and
death of Jesus. The tandem telling is strengthened not only because
the narratives are both stories of capture, but because Rodrigues
identifies his actions and fate so closely with that of Jesus. Like Jesus
he preaches God; he is stalked, betrayed by a follower, and captured.
The series of merged identities which the tandem tales generate—
Rodrigues and Jesus, Kichijiro and Judas, Inoue and Pilate, the
villagers and the disciples—likewise seem stable. But this is again
dismantled when the tandem tales suddenly go off at odd angles.
The possibility of martyrdom is denied Rodrigues; he must live
when others die. It is as if the gospel narrative were to be rewritten
to deny Jesus the possibility of death, and instead to narrate the
death of the disciples, one by one, until Jesus denied the preaching
of the Kingdom of God. The hope for a stable key to read the
narrative of Rodrigues' character fails. Rodrigues becomes simultaneously Jesus, Judas, Peter, the Pharisees, Kichijiro, Ferreria, the

Japanese official, and the dead man, Okada San'emon. Once defined identities merge as multiple instabilities.

These four examples by no means exhaust the characterization of Rodrigues but in concert they are sufficient to show the instability of Sebastian Rodrigues as narrative character, as one who by the end of the text lacks an intelligible and coherent pattern of values and reasons from which directed action might originate.

The Third Splinter: Textual Interpretation

If the reader of Silence follows the techniques of characterization, he or she has taken a journey similar to Rodrigues. Stability, identity, individuality, hope for victory, security of religious convictions— all these have been initially granted only to be taken away by reversals, frustrations, mergers, and distances. In a significant sense the narrative development of character in Silence can be termed disjunctive; whatever Rodrigues was in the beginning he is not at the end, right down to his name. For the reader the issue at the end of the text is the possibility of creating a whole character for the name "Sebastian Rodrigues," or, alternatively, of making sense of the radical disruptions based on an anticipated unity of character. The issue of a constructed whole at the completion of the reading is a different issue from following the local strategies. While it may not be difficult to create or observe a coherence between a limited set of episodes within the narrative, it is difficult to see the coherence of the character in the narrative as a whole precisely because the narrative strategizes to destabilize a unified reading. Since neither the character nor the point of view provide a convenient resolution for the instability of the central character, the reader seems left with four major options: a) to dismiss the text itself as flawed, either aesthetically, religiously, morally, or philosophically; b) to read it as a narrative of either the failure or the attainment of character; c) to read it as a critical deflation of a series of cultural or religious conventions; d) to read it as a text which challenges the reader to join wholeness with instability in such a fashion that the disjunction does not become contradiction but dialectical self-limitation. Because of the instability of the central character all four of these readings are possible. I will focus on the latter two readings as more appropriate for reasons to be stated below.

The first reading, the text as significantly flawed, presumes the presence and defensibility of some measure of character external to the narrative by which the instability could be rendered as flaw. Such a reading will likely (but not necessarily) suggest some norm of stability which includes elements of the initial character matrix: individuality, heroic virtue, faithfulness, etc. These elements function not only to establish character and an initial point of view, but also to establish a consistently reiterated norm by which the character may be evaluated in the end. "This is the way human beings, especially faithful believers, should be; Sebastian Rodrigues claims to be both; this is the way Sebastian Rodrigues should be; he is not, and thus should not be held up as a Christian hero." But it may likewise suggest a much less conservative critique: that the novel is not one of character at all but of place, so that the incorporation of issues around the name "Sebastian Rodrigues" rather than around "Japan," or "the sea," or "the mountaintop" is a flaw in composition. It is not a novel of character at all, but rather a clash of locales and customs in which Sebastian Rodrigues is but a pawn. Both of these readings tend to value an extrinsic measure of character, favoring, on the one hand, religious or metaphysical individualism, and, on the other, a potential deconstruction of the category of character. Neither of these readings is incoherent. Indeed the mildly deconstructive reading could capitalize on the destabilizing techniques as well as the geographical associations of the text to form a potentially comprehensive interpretation. Yet to carry out either of these readings the burden on the interpreter is to present the largely extrinsic measure by which the character of Sebastian Rodrigues is judged unworthy of composition or reception, either as unfit example or an ontic Chesire Cat.

The second reading accepts what seems to be a narrative certainty: that this is a story about the character, Sebastian Rodrigues, and is thus a narrative of character. As such it can then be read as a narrative of character failure or achievement. To read it as a story of character failure is a significant variation of the conservative reading suggested above. To carry out such a reading, the initial stability of the character must be accepted as normative. The narrative is then that of a fall. But rather than being judged as unfit or even weak, the character is understood as overwhelmed, as one to be both admired and pitied, to be read empathetically rather than judicially. Salvation is not "earned the old-fashioned way-by works;" it is a gift in an almost tragic situation. Such a reading need not be weak. It does tend to be normative, and thus demands from the interpreter a convincing statement of what it means to "stand" before the "fall."

Such a statement may reassert the initial matrix as the norm, or it could emphasize, in the fashion of Dostoevsky's "Grand Inquisitor" or Camus' *Fall*, the impossibility of standing up to either the demands of Christ or those of human existence which place freedom or autonomy at the heart of the self.

If the narrative is read as one of character then it may be read not only as failure but also as attainment with surprisingly little adjustment. In such a reading Rodrigues moves from a first naive and narcissistic understanding of the Gospel narrative to one fixed by the unforeseen experiences of discipleship. Serenity and confidence are not the marks of this attainment; loneliness, ridicule, and exile are. And yet even in this unenviable state Rodrigues—and the reader—know something more about the Gospel narrative and discipleship. First naiveté has moved to a second, troubled, realité. Again this reading need not be weak. Rodrigues is not a comic book martyr. The initial matrix of character traits with which the story begins is significantly altered by the end so that character attainment is not victory but a mixture of wisdom, compassion, perseverance, and awe; and it is Sebastian Rodrigues who undergoes this journey.

While these readings may take their respective places within the plurality of responsible interpretations, I want to focus on two additional candidates—the critical and, especially, the dialetical reading.

The Fourth Splinter: Fundamental/Theological Hermeneutics

With these two readings the fourth splinter of the initial question, "Who is Sebastian Rodrigues?" is finally encountered—namely the splinter of fundamental/theological heremeneutics. By a fundamental hermeneutics I mean an interpretation which discloses a meaning or meanings of the text derived not only from the surface strategies of the text but also from the fundamental topics which generate these strategies. Here the question which suggests the fundamental hermeneutic is this: what does the text proffer as the measure of the *self* as *Christian*. The reflection of "Christianity" in this text is explicit and tense. Christianity is a foreign religion with universal claims in a Japanese culture deeply suspicious of both theism and the West. The exposition of the topic of the "self" is much less explicit, but, I would suggest, is fundamental. The self is transformed from the independent center of action capable of overcoming other, less able, centers of action, to an interdependent web of

intersecting lives, times, places, and values, called "another kind of
love." It is in both the critical and the dialectical hermeneutics that
these fundamental issues are brought to light.

The strength of both of these readings lies in their recognition of
the strategies for characterization. The third reading, what I have
termed the critical reading, takes full advantage of the disjunction
between Sebastian Rodrigues as western, male, ecclesial, missionary
in the beginning of the narrative, and Okada San'emon/Sebastian
Rodrigues as transplanted Japanese official, apostate, and married at
the end. It certainly is possible to view this reversal as a narrative of
critical disclosure. At the end of the text Sebastian Rodrigues—and
the reader—are aware that the initial expectations are not simply
unmet but flawed: martyrdom is not heroic death; westernized
Christianity is not universal and timeless; the self is not the individual who can be measured by the success of his or her own plans for
actions. The combination of Christian identity with ecclesial adherence, heroic virtue, unyielding individualism, and westernized images of Jesus builds the character of Rodrigues over a narrative fault
no less dangerous for this character than the San Andreas fault is for
the future of California. The quake must come, but unlike California,
Sebastian Rodrigues is initially unaware of the subterranean fissure.
At journey's end, however, the radical reversals have given the lie to
what was formely the case. More of the same—the reassembling of
the previous actions and traits which went to make Rodrigues who
he had been—is not the solution to the issues of measuring the self
in the Christian context. It is not only, or even primarily, character
attainment that is at issue. What is at issue is the critical reappraisal
of Christianity as systematically distorted in a colonizing culture.
After Rodrigues' apostasy, and within the rapid shifts of emotion,
point of view, and character identity, the text reads:

> As Ferreira spoke to me his tempting words, I thought that if I aposta-
> tized those miserable peasants would be saved. Yes, that was it. And
> yet, in the last analysis, I wonder if all this talk about love is not, after
> all, just an excuse to justify my own weakness.
>
> I acknowledge this. I am not concealing my weakness. I wonder if
> there is any difference between Kichijiro and my self. And yet, rather
> than this I know that my Lord is different from the God that is preached
> in the churches.[2]

The "different God" is an uncertain voice in a sea of silence, a
voice which neither judges allegiance nor intervenes to change the

course of human action, but a voice which murmurs, which is at the same time a person's projection of compassion and fear met with human need and unbending historical structures. Not only is this Christianity far from Portugal, it is far from victory, from hierarchy, from assertions and doctrines, from robes and rituals, from most attitudes and behaviors commonly associated with the term "Christian."

This reading of the narrative as a critical disclosure of the inherent instability of the initial matrix of values that establishes the character of Rodrigues differs substantially from reading the text as a narrative fall or achievement. Less focused on the character as an independent entity, it understands the destablization of the assumed Christian matrix as the indispensable condition for any possible reconstruction of the character on the part of the reader. But such a reading tends to exhaust itself in criticism, in the identification and dissolution of a deceptively stable set of rules used to apply the adjective "Christian."

I want to suggest, however, that there remains at least one more reading which understands the name "Sebastian Rodrigues" more constructively: as the task of the reader to combine the instability of the character and the whole of the narrative without the unwarranted imposition of either a false stability or an easy dismissal of character unity. What follows is an outline of a reading which draws on the critical negations and disclosures of the previous reading, and suggests that the trace of Sebastian Rodrigues remaining is the trace of the ironic character understood as a "different love." This outline is simply that, an outline of one critically responsible reading which suggests a textual measure of the self as Christian in the light of Endo's "Sebastian Rodrigues."

This reading begins with the last first-person passage of the story:

> Kichijiro wept softly; then he left the house. The priest had administered that sacrament that only the priest can administer. No doubt his fellow priests would condemn his act as sacrilege; but even if he was betraying them, he was not betraying his Lord. He loved him now in a different way than before. Everything that had taken place until now had been necessary to bring him to this love. "Even now I am the last priest in this land. But Our Lord was not silent. Even if he had been silent, my life until this day would have spoken of him."[3]

1) Rodrigues here is not wholly undone; the collapse of initial stability is neither a total annihilation of character, nor chaos, nor

the abrupt end of the story. The character as the independent source of action surely recedes as the subsequent third person accounts indicate. The trace that remains is that of transformation and the disclosure of something different, of an indistinct voice that breaks the deafening silence of the novel.

2) The emphasis, however, is not on an alternative stability; the disclosure is not a reconstruction of the character but a trace that marks both the critical dissolution of a colonizing Christianity and the hint of something else—a new love.

3) The trace of character—the fact that Rodrigues does not completely dissolve into apostate or victorious martyr, into Judas, Christ, Peter, Kichijiro, or Okada San'emon without remainder—is a disclosure of the true tensions within the character as a "self."

4) Because the text is less explicit in its discussion of the character as "self," our approach here must be one of indirection. Paradox is a first approximation of these tensions. By the end of the narrative Sebastian Rodrigues is, but is not, Sebastian Rodrigues; he is likewise Okada San'emon. By the end of the narrative Rodrigues is an individual, and he is not; he is Ferreira, Kichijiro, Judas, Christ, etc. By the end of the narrative Sebastian Rodrigues is the Christian, but he is not; he has denied Christ at the very word of Christ. By the end of the narrative the silence of God is unbroken but the silence is broken; Rodrigues' life speaks.

5) But the paradox is only a first statement of the narrative reversals, the logical scaffold upon which the literary irony opens. Irony is a notoriously slippery term. It most generally describes the situation in which one thing is said and another thing is meant. Incongruity and reversal are at the heart of irony. Whether it be verbal, situational, dramatic, or comedic, an implicitly simultaneous disjunction, often involving some ignorance on the part of an actor or audience, character or reader, propels the incongruity beyond simple contradiction or juxtaposition toward some possible reconstruction, often the reverse of what was said or expected.[4] For paradox the incongruity is the simultaneous assertion of true but contradictory propositions. Irony shares with paradox both simultaneity and incongruity but potentially drives to resolution through strategies of reversal.

The incongruity of Sebastian Rodrigues and Okada San'emon is not only paradoxical; it is ironic. Clearly the character has changed; clearly the changes are radical. To make a whole of the narrative around the character of Rodrigues is to bring into focus the beginning and the end of the text at the same time, to view Rodrigues as simultaneously missionary and apostate, priest and not priest, Jesus and Judas. The key to the incongruity is reversal: as missionary Rodrigues is an apostate, but as apostate he is missionary; as not priest he can truly hear Kichijiro's confession in a fashion which as priest he could not. As Judas he saves those in the pit and as Jesus he acts to deny Jesus.

6) If the reversals were so clean then a clear code for interpretation of these character ironies could be derived from the text: when this is said, then this, its reverse, is what is meant. But ironies may not be that easy to control. Wayne Booth provides a very helpful map of ironic literary strategies in his text, A Rhetoric of Iron.[5] Among his categories a fundamental distinction is made between stable and unstable irony. He writes:

> At last we cross that formidable chasm that I have so long anticipated—the fundamental distinction between stable ironies and ironies in which the truth asserted or implied is that no stable reconstruction can be made out of the ruins revealed through the irony. The author—insofar as we can discover him, and he is often very remote indeed—refuses to declare himself, however subtly, for any stable proposition, even the opposite of whatever proposition his irony vigorously denies. The only sure affirmation is that negation that begins all ironic play: 'this affirmation must be rejected,' leaving the possibility, and in infinite ironies the clear implication that since the universe (or at least the universe of discourse) is inherently absurd, all statements are subject to ironic undermining. No statement can really mean what it says.
>
> The consequences of the differences between these kinds are immense. What we do with a work, or what it does with us, will depend on our decision, conscious or unconscious, about whether we are asked to push through its confusions to some final point of clarity or to see through it to a possibly infinite series of further confusions. No other step in the never completed process of mastering the arts of interpretation is more important than discovering how and when to cross and recross this borderline with agility and confidence.[6]

The distinction between stable and unstable irony is quite helpful for the project of responding to the controlling question, "Who is Sebastian Rodrigues?" If the incongruities are ironic in a stable way then the pleasure of the text is achieved in the task of resolving the unstable character into a stable one beyond the text as the measure of the Christian self through the reversal of the final characterization: eg. the apostate is the believer; the self is the other and not the individual, etc. To a certain extent this seems appropriate; the trace of the character is read as the reversal of the final fortunes. But the danger here is the re-establishment of a stability for the measure of the self as Christian after the text has been at pains to destablize the character. Booth is again helpful by suggesting a distinction between local and infinite instability. Locally unstable ironies are those in which the scope of the irony is limited to a structure within the whole which is itself stable. Thus while one scene or one character may not admit to resolution by reversal, the narrative as a whole does. The infinitely unstable irony unhinges the narrative as a whole, so that even the seemingly stable events or characters may be understood as other than what they appear to be. If it is the case that the establishment of character in *Silence* is unstable, then the trace of ironic character at the end cannot move too quickly to the stabilization of a coded reversal, but must allow for the possibility of infinite irony as the measure of the self.

7. An appropriate set of critical categories for explaining the possibility of this infinite irony is provided by Wolfgang Iser in his analysis of textual blanks, negation, and negativity.[7] It is neither possible nor necessary for the purposes of this essay to explain in detail the wealth of Iser's analysis. Suffice it to say the following: Iser understands the fictional text to be an instance of communication, an event, in which the text uses a certain repertoire of techniques and a certain strategy of combinations to create a framework which both provides a guide for interpretation while at the same time requires from the reader creative reconstruction. The text does not tell the reader what to do but rather provides the structures—as well as blanks—which necessitate the active response by the reader to make sense not only of what is said but of what is not said. He writes of blanks:

> The blank, however, designates a vacancy in the overall system of the text, the filling of which brings about an interaction of textual patterns. In other words, the need for completion is replaced here by the need for combination. It is only when the schemata of the text are related to one another that the imaginary object can begin to be formed, and it is the blanks which get this connecting operation underway. They indicate that the different seqments of the text are to be connected, even

though the text itself does not say so. They are the unseen joints of the text, and as they mark off schemata and textual perspectives from one another, they simultaneously trigger acts of ideation on the reader's part.[8]

The text is less the decipherable code than the coercive invitation. The blanks need not be the ciphers of authorial failure but may well be the textual voice of demand upon the reader. As such, it is appropriate, but not exhaustive, to say that the text is constructed in the construction of the reader and as the construction of the reader. This is not the open floodgate for any possible reading of the text, but at the same time, it is clearly a recognition that all fictional texts exceed the stability of the didactic text in the incorporation of spaces, gaps, or blanks as essential to the communication.

Negation functions at the local level to call into question standards and assumptions both from within and without the text. It is by the negation of expectations or conventions that the blank is most often produced. Iser again:

Negation produces blanks not only in the repertoire of norms but also in the reader's position, for the invalidation of his norms creates a new relationship between him and the familiar world. This relationship is determinate, in the sense that the past is negated, but indeterminate in that the present is not yet formulated. The formulation takes place—or the blanks are filled—when attitudes are adopted through which the text can actually be experienced by the reader.[9]

Iser's strongest claim, however, is regarding "negativity." He writes:

Unlike negations, negativity is not formulated by the text, but forms the unwritten base; it does not negate the formulations of the text, but—via blanks and negations—conditions them. It enables the written words to transcend their literal meaning, to assume a multiple referentiality, and so to undergo the expansion necessary to transplant them as a new experience into the mind of the reader. . . . But we must not forget that negativity is the basic force in literary communication, and, as such, it is to be experienced rather than to be explained. If we were able to explain its effect, we would have mastered it discursively and would have rendered obsolescent the experience it provides.[10]

In a text like Endo's where characterization *is* destabilization, negativity of the infinitely unstable irony cannot be discounted as a responsible reading.

8. Iser's material does no more but no less than provide a critical apparatus for explaining the possibility and shape of infinite irony at the narrative level. Infinite irony seems to court, if not directly become, the literary expression of absurdity, a situation of radical instability which issues in the negation of all meaning and the call for, at best, courage if not suicide. Such a reading cannot be wholly dismissed as one possibility in light of the instability and irony of Rodrigues. But, as Booth notes, infinitely unstable irony need not issue in absurdity.[11] For Rodrigues the remainder of the radically destabilized character is simply termed "a different love."[12] But what is the self which corresponds to this different love?

First, Rodrigues has become a *series of others*, a name not his own. He is the intersection of Portugal and Japan, of colonial Christianity with a Japan which refuses to be wooed, of the gospel story with human torture, of the desire for self-establishment by the martyr's death with the unbending refusal of history and culture to play accomplice to this end. Second, more than the convergence of forces, external and internal, Sebastian Rodrigues is the *point of compassion* which no longer accepts the logics of victory, allegiance, and heroism. Such traditional logics spell death—not for the hero, but for those who follow. Third, emptied of the possibility of being the rebel, the victor, the self-contained individual, the faithful ecclesiastic—all of the acceptable possibilities of his western culture— Sebastian Rodrigues is finally *a response* to a situation in which the silence of another's torture is broken by an ironic denial. In that denial Sebastian Rodrigues becomes a "new love," one who identifies with Kichijiro in mutual forgiveness, one who translates, teaches, and lives sure of nothing but that apostasy was life-giving. Sebastian Rodrigues is the self emptied of a rational and coherent plan of predictable action and reestablished as responsive, if yet troubled, love. "Sebastian Rodrigues" names this possibility of the self, one who dissolves over others with the failure of all previous measures to secure the self. Serenity, victory, return, recognition— all these vanish as possibilities for the self. But drawing this measure of the self is, at the same time, drawing the reader into the gaps set up by the negation of the original character. Not a program, not a plan of action defined by a new character description, the reader is left with the phrase, "a different love," and a story of forgiveness, the mutual confession of Kichijiro and Rodrigues. Endo's hermeneutic of the Christian self is that of one emptied, infinitely emptied, not to be rebuilt as the independent individual but as forgiving and compassinate lover.

With an infinite irony resulting from an encounter and clash of cultures, Endo's hermeneutic of the self challenges traditional, secure western notions of the Christian self. Theologically Endo's hermeneutic brings together a kenotic Christology[13] with a theology of love[14]. It is doubtless the case that the portrayal of Christ, presented initially through images of victory, beauty and power, is confronted and corrected by an image of the battered Jesus on the fumie. Likewise, the story of Sebastian Rodrigues is doubtless the mirror of this transformation in the central character. A kenotic anthropology becomes the narrative reflection of a kenotic Christology. The character of Rodrigues does not, however, end in dissolution even with the collapse of all the previously accepted categories for self-interpretation. The kenosis ends in an ironic and shattering echo of I Cor. 13, a situation in which speech, prophecy, knowledge of mysteries, feeding the poor, self-sacrifice, and all other possible criteria used to establish the worthy self fail. Faith and hope grow dim, but love remains. And not only does it remain but it remains as the only action left on the other side of the startling kenotic voice of Jesus uttering, "Trample, trample." Kenosis here is not placed on a trajectory which traditionally issues in return to exaltation, glory, and praise. Rather, it is placed on a trajectory of compassionate action in which the emptied self is disclosed as the fitting origin[15].

In a recent issue of *Concilium* devoted to Christian Identity, Pierre Bühler[16] suggests that modern Christian identity has lost the traditional indices by which it can be recognized. Attachment to a church, adherence to a body of doctrine, a certain type of moral behavior—all of these seem to prove increasingly less appropriate as scales of Christian identity. Bühler argues that this means neither the absence of Christian identity nor the dissolution of Christianity in subjectivity. At the same time the plea for a new Christian positivism in doctrine or action will not meet the need for a new Christian identity. He suggests rather that Christian identity relies on the correlation of three factors: a) the interplay of relations of those who call themselves Christian, in order to avoid an easy subjectivity; b) the examination and clarification of the language which is used to articulate faith; and c) a trial of practical relevance in order to draw Christian action beyond private desire or ethical formality. On this latter he remarks:

Thus committing himself (sic) to the round of practical tasks, the subjective Christian exposes his (sic) convictions to the decisive test: do they allow me to place myself convincingly in the world and to open myself to the demands which are made on me? Do my convictions enslave me, or do they give me the freedom to love my neighbor as myself? In this ethical examination the behavior will be on the look-out—in all restraint and humility—not for reassurring confirmation, but rather for discrepancies and faults which will be for him (sic) the crisis within which his (sic) identity can grow and mature.[17]

Bühler's analysis suggests that the decisive test of Christian identity is ultimately the convergence of conviction, community, and reflection in the action of love of neighbor. It is this sense of Christian identity which is iterated and deepened in Endo's narrative reflection. The kenosis of the divine form and the central character in this extreme situation of cultural clash issue in a kenosis of language, cultural pattern, and traditional formulations. These usual indices of the Christian self give way to an unexpected orthodoxy—loving compassionate action, reflectively appropriated.

Ultimately the narrative does not return to a formulaic understanding of what is Christian, nor does it suggest alternative formulations. A distant, third-person narrative takes over. For those who are what Frank Kermode calls pleromatists,[18] there is something, dissatisfying about this lack of a return to a formula. And yet this formulaic desire may be but another way to wrench a kenotic Christology, and the consequent anthropological and dogmatic kenosis, from its tensive relation to a theology of love back to a victorious theology. The encounter with traditions and thought patterns aware of the problems of understanding the self as independent, conscious and controlled individuality reminds us that these may not be the most fitting resources for understanding the Christian self in a contemporary world. At this intersection of kenosis and love in a world religious context, the Christian may ultimately need to read Shin'ichi Hisamtsu's Vow of Mankind alongside of 1 Cor 13.

Keeping calm and composed, let us awaken to our true self, becoming fully compassionate human beings, make full use of our gifts according to our respective vocations in life; discern the agony both individual and social and its sources, recognize the right direction in which history should proceed, and join hands without distinction of race, nation or class. Let us with compassion vow to bring to realisation mankind's deepest desire for self-emancipation and construct a world in which everyone can truly and fully live.[19]

"Who is Sebastian Rodrigues?" has been the controlling question of this investigation. But if the question is one which exceeds simple textual clarification and moves toward a fundamental hermeneutic of the self as Christian, then the name "Sebastian Rodrigues" provides little help if conventions are what is sought. If Rodrigues is as deeply ironic as I have suggested, then the standard conventions of what establishes a self are called into question. Heroism, victory, allegiance, individuality, witness, all have become inappropriate scales. The infinitely ironic scale is an unsure, troubled, outreaching love which at once seeks and gives forgiveness, and in so doing reveals the self as at best a trace, a voice, a remainder, engaged in compassionate love with other voices and traces on similar journeys.

NOTES

1. Shusaku Endo, *Silence,* William Johnston, tr. (New York: Taplinger Publishing Company, 1980), p. 259.

2. Endo, pp. 263–264.

3. Endo, p. 286.

4. The analysis relied on here is that of Wayne Booth in *A Rhetoric of Irony* (Chicago: University of Chicago Press, 1974), esp. pp. 33–44.

5. Booth, p. 235.

6. Booth, pp. 240–242.

7. Wolfgang Iser, *The Act of Reading: A Theory of Aesthetic Response* (Baltimore: The Johns Hopkins University Press, 1978), esp. pp. 180–231.

8. Iser, pp. 182–183.

9. Iser, p. 217.

10. Iser, p. 226.

11. Booth, p. 269.

12. Endo, p. 286.

13. Typically the *locus classicus* of the 19th and 20th understanding of "kenotic Christology" is the hymn found in Philippians 2:6–11. It has been noted frequently that a "kenotic Christology" is a misnomer for in fact what is described in the hymn in not simply "an emptying out," but rather a prior "form," an "emptying"— understood as taking the form of a slave, the likeness of humankind and death—as well as exaltation. For the moment I am focusing specifically on *kenosis* as emptying.

14. It is precisely this that Paul does in Philippians. Theologically this is regularly overlooked by an exclusive focus on either humility or glory. Within Philippians, this uncharacteristically Pauline hymn is located in an exhortation to love and compassion.

15. The analysis of *Silence* by Douglas Hall, "Rethinking Christ: Theological Reflection on Shusaku Endo's *Silence*," *Interpretation,* 33 (1979) 254–267, and Jean Higgins, "East-West Encounters in Shusaku Endo," *Dialog and Alliance,* 1 (1987) 12–22, place primary emphasis on Endo's narrative dislodging of western, victorious theologies. Both end their analyses with an appeal for a more adequate theology broadly understood as kenotic. Higgins briefly touches on the topic of compassionate action but seems to understand this as suffering with one's fellows (p. 18). For both, the theological interpretation relies on a theological kenosis. The suggestion in this essay is that the interpretation of the text is better served by recognizing both the kenotic God/Christ/humanity as well as a theology of love. To loose the tension between these two is ultimately to dissolve the character of Rodrigues and a theological hermeneutic of the self.

16. Pierre Bühler, "Christian Identity: Between Objectivity and Subjectivity," in *Christian Identity,* Christian Duquoc and Casiano Florista, eds., *Concilium,* 196 (1988) 17–27.

17. Bühler, 25.

18. Frank Kermode, *The Genesis of Secrecy: On The Interpretation of Narrative* (Cambridge: Harvard University Press, 1979), p. 72.

19. Quoted in Masao Abe, "Transformation in Buddhism in Comparison with Platonic and Christian Notions," in Duquoc and Florista, *Christian Identity,* p. 54.

THE AMERICAN CATHOLIC CHURCH—A NEW WAY OF BEING CATHOLIC

Robert Kress

Insofar as this year's theme is "how the Christian religion/church can be challenged and enriched by listening and responding to the voices that speak for other cultures, or for other religions/spiritualities,"[1] one might suspect, from the title of this essay, that it has clearly missed the mark.

However, it is precisely to dispel such suspicion that I have chosen this topic. The unique development and character of American Catholicism is not really understood in America itself and certainly not in Europe. As a leading German theologian noted several years ago, "Here in Germany we know very little about the Church in the USA, indeed, in all honesty, nothing." Whether this leads to or proceeds from the understanding that the American Catholic Church is nothing more than a tail, cropped at that, of customary European Catholicism is a variation on the chicken and the egg conundrum. I do recall that a professor of modern church history at Innsbruck responded thus to an American complaint that he included nothing about American Catholicism in his course: "When anything worth including happens there, I shall include it." This was in 1954. The

Robert Kress is professor and chair of the department of theological and religious studies at the University of San Diego. He has published widely on various theological topics, especially ecclesiology. He has degrees in philosophy, theology, and education from the University of Notre Dame, the University of Innsbruck, the University of St. Thomas (Angelicum), Rome, and St. Meinrad College. His most recent book is Holy Church, Sinful Church (Michael Glazier). In 1990 his book The People's Church: The American Transformation of Roman Catholicism will be published by Harper & Row.

same ignorance of the American Catholic experience is responsible
for the refusal of Latin American liberation theologians to pay any
attention whatsoever to what should be a very fertile source of
theological and ecclesiological insight for them.[2] The fascination of
Latin American liberation theology for European theologians and
intellectuals surely exposes the Middle European roots of that theology, no matter how intense the protests that it has been conceived,
born, and nurtured in Latin America.

Be that as it may, what is new about American Catholicism and
what can be learned from it for the future of the universal church?
We must preface our answer with a brief survey of the development
of Christianity in its European mode. Then we shall look at the
precisely American Catholic experience and development. Finally,
we shall point out the differences and the significance of these for
the future.

I. The Establishment of Christianity

European Christianity results from the encounter of Hebrew religion, Greek culture, and Roman law and politics. This is a truism,
but one which cannot be repeated too often. One need only imagine
how Christianity would have developed and how it would look today
if the apostolic missionary journeys had gone principally south into
Africa or east into Asia. This statement is in no wise invidious. I
intend no comparisons of value, only of empirical and historical
reality. To say that the western movement and development of
Christianity was practically and historically inevitable is probably
also correct. But this inevitability confers eternal value on neither
the development itself nor any individual elements therein.

How is this "inevitability" to be understood? Certainly not as
some sort of metaphysical determinism. I use the term only to
emphasize that as a religion in the world, it is most likely that
Christianity will have received and adapted certain understandings
and practices from the *saeculum*, the secular world, in which it
found itself. Here "inevitable" is equivalent to the German "*selbst-
verständlich.*" It is possible to argue, as some do, that Christianity
not only adapted, it also capitulated. This is the argument of the
Free Churches which have found in the Constantinian and Theodo-
sian establishment of Christianity as the official religion and church
of the Roman Empire a Fall equal to that of Adam and Eve. Although
we shall emphasize some of the baneful influences of this develop-

ment in western Christianity, we do not share that or other overly pessimistic evaluations of the Constantinianization of Christianity.[3] This would be ultimately negative only if it were absolutized and judged to be the only acceptable form of the church in the world.

In this essay we shall focus on the influence of the Roman Empire, especially its law and its polity on the Christian church. Until the persecutions ceased, the relatively small number of Christians would have had little opportunity, desire or need to adapt Roman political institutions to their own social organization. However, after the persecutions and after the great influx of the "masses" into the church, the question of social organization became critical. If the orderly life of the church was already a theme and problem in the earliest Pauline churches, as all the epistles clearly indicate, how much more so would it be in the great CATHOLICA!

That the church was always structured in some way is clear, however great the variety of the organization may have been.[4] Even the rapid development into some sort of monarchical episcopate does not have to be attributed solely to human and clericalist ambition and lust for power. In accord with the great theological and political insight of Harry Truman, "The buck stops here" finds a practical organizational and structural form in every society. Even the Marxists found that a troika does not work. Although both generally Jewish and specifically Essenian or Qumranian organizational principles influenced the social organization of the early Christians, the decisive influences on the western church clearly came from Roman praxis.

What this meant for the church became clear early on, as Joseph Ratzinger has so well pointed out. Originally the church was to be an *adelphotes,* a brotherhood or sisterhood. Again, it is clear in the New Testament that this fellowship was neither anarchical nor egalitarian. The church was an articulated society in which various members enjoyed various roles, all of which were necessary for the good of the whole body. But, whatever these gifts and roles, all, even governance *(kubernesis)* were to be exercised in a brotherly and sisterly manner. However, as Ratzinger reports, already by the time of Cyprian, the brotherliness had diminished. Cyprian still referred to his church corporately as "Beloved Brother." Otherwise he limited the use of the singular brother to only bishops and clerics, not individual Christians, and he himself was addressed as "beatissime et gloriosissime papa." The use of brother as the "title" of all Christians continued to decline, and was eventually restricted to clerics and monks among themselves. Eventually the very term "brother" was replaced by "collega," a term from Roman law. The original brotherhood had become the "collegium," a development which continued in the increasing use and final domination of Roman legal terms—and concepts!—such as "ordo" and "corpus" to describe social elements of Christianity.[5]

It is important to emphasize this early "Romanization" of Christianity so that we do not attribute all subsequent developments to the Constantinianization of Christianity. However, it is also clear that the Constantinian event and heritage have been decisive in the actual formation of western Christianity and its transformation into Christendom. Two elements from the Constantinianization of Christianity have been decisive for Catholicism—the understanding of the church as a society and the understanding of office in the church. We shall begin with the latter.

What Constantine did most of all was transform the Christian population from a persecuted illicit religion to a licit, then to a favored religion and, finally, to the official state religion and church. The consequence of this was the genesis of what Joseph Cardinal Ratzinger has called "an imperial universal Church as against a really theological conception in which it is not the emperor but Rome (=papacy) which plays the decisive role." Later on he also explains: "The mixed theological and political model of the pentarchy, which was not in any way seen as the fruit of mere historical accidents or political expediency, was then admittedly increasingly overlaid by the imperial model of the state Church, in which the functions of the Petrine ministry devolve upon the emperor: the emperor becomes the actual executive organ of the universal Church."[6] This second statement makes clear that Constantinianization affects not only the western understanding and practice of the church, but the eastern as well.

Here we are clearly in the realm of Caesaropapism. The now distinguished, although not to be separated, sacred and secular were then not even distinguished. They were united, indeed, homogenized. As such, they constituted the much vaunted societas perfecta, the perfect society, sufficient in every way unto itself. But we know that in fact this society was far from perfect, and that the imperfection probably afflicted the church more than the state.

Whether originally imperial or later monarchical/princely, the Constantinian and Caesaropapist mood permeated Christianity and its socio-political form, Christendom. The various reformations in the sixteenth century altered this situation only marginally in Europe. The dissenting Anabaptist and Free Church believers were too few in number and too weak in power to effect a change in the established European churches. Their choice was to flee the corrupt old world and migrate to the new world. After the ecclesial divisions which accompanied these various reformations, the Anglican, Lutheran, Roman Catholic, and the Calvinist Churches continued the imperial and monarchical model on a smaller scale. This was given legal status in the *Pax Augustana* of 1555: "*Cuius regio, eius religio.*" As the saying (not merely a popular folklore insight, but a *Rechtssprichwort*) has it, "Dux Cliviae papa est in terris suis" (The Prince of Cleves is the pope in his own territories). The assertion that the Lutheran Reformation was a lay movement is patently false. It was a movement of clericalists, both ordained and academic, and of the princes, who thereafter functioned as the traditional hierarchs had in the pre-reformation church. In the *evangelische Landeskirchen* (Lutheran Provincial Churches) the prince functioned as the *Summus Episcopus*, supported by a consistory of pastors. This situation lasted until the fall of the monarchy in 1918!

The Constantinian spirit also flourished in Roman Catholicism. Whether the pope or the emperor happened to have the upper hand at any given moment is important, but not most important. Most important is that whether pope or emperor, the mode of leadership in the church was imperial and monarchical.

At some moments the "Church" belonged to the emperor or the prince. Thus arose the *Eigenkirchen* as well as the *jus patronatus*, in which the civil authority played the decisive role in determining the administration of the church by controlling the naming of bishops and pastors. At other times the "state" belonged to the pope, without whose blessing the civil authority could not take office and become official. In either case, the two swords distinguished by Gelasius were all too often smelted into one.

This background enables us to understand the theological evolution of official leadership and membership in the church. As the civil ruler was the monarch by divine right, so was the ecclesial ruler, when and insofar as the two were not the same person, a monarch by divine right. The monarchical papacy, and the monarchical episcopacy, insofar as local bishops could get away with it, were not considered particular contingent, factual, historical, developments, which could have been otherwise. No, they were, as the phrase had it, *jure divino*—by divine right. They were the direct and immediate consequences of God's will. This understanding of the papacy—and, it must never be forgotten, of the church itself—is nowhere better illustrated than by Dominic Palmieri's book, revealingly entitled: "Treatise on the Roman Pontiff, with a Prolegomenon on the Church." His understanding is straightforward: "The form of Church government (its *regimen*) is therefore monarchical by divine law. . . . Therefore, through the power conferred on Peter, Christ established the form of a monarchical regime in the Church. . . . Christ himself immediately conferred supreme power on Peter alone; others share in this power only through Peter and in dependence on him."[8] Yves Congar has correctly called this the "courant hiérocratique" of church history.[9]

All this is significant for the understanding of administrative leadership and hierarchical office, as well as for the understanding of the church itself. Against a background like this, one can readily understand the pretensions of a Pope Pius IX who is reputed to have proclaimed, "La tradizione sono Io" (I am tradition!). The church is subsumed (*aufgehoben*) into a privileged class or caste. Thus, we have been treated to such proclamations as: "The Supreme Pontiff occupies the summit of the Church and can be called The Church." "Papa ipse Ecclesia" (The Pope—himself the Church!). Of course, the ecclesiastically ambitious will not allow themselves to be totally deprived of participating in this privileged position: "The Pope and the Lord Cardinals [Note—no longer brothers, not even colleagues, but Lords!] are in the Roman [Catholic] Church in such a way (so intensely) that they themselves are this very Church itself."[10]

In such a view, the people, or simple faithful as they were preferentially called, are either eliminated or reduced to a lower class membership. They could not be simply eliminated, for then the pope and cardinals would have had no one over whom they could rule. Hence, only the second option was preferential. From Gratian's "two kinds (*genera*) of Christians . . . the clerics . . . the laity" there is a direct path to Pius X's declaration that "The Church is essentially a society of unequals comprising two categories of persons, pastors and flock. . . . As for the multitude, it has no other right than to let itself be led, and, a docile flock, to follow its pastors."[11] It is no wonder, then, that a French theologian thought it possible, indeed necessary, to call for an ecumenical movement within the Catholic Church.[12]

The imperial, monarchical mentality has consequences not only for internal church affairs. It also affects the church's relationship with the world. Either the world is subjected entirely to the church, as in the old Caesaropapism during periods when the papacy was in the ascendancy, or else the world is divided from the church and declared to be profane, and hence of secondary value. In this division, care for the superior sacred and saving values is assigned to the clergy and monks, for the inferior secular and transient and even tempting values to the laity.[13] Unfortunately, this divisive mentality is clearly evident in the addresses of Pope John Paul II.

A final consequence of the monarchical mentality should be noted. It flows fittingly from the very word itself, for etymologically monarchy comes from the Greek *mone* for single, sole, alone, and *arche* for principle, beginning, source. Clearly, the monarch is the sole source, whence proceeds all else. This understanding is clearly evident in the theories of papal power within and without the church. It is also evident in the colonialism which the central Roman Church has practiced in regard to the local churches throughout the world. A singular example of this was the Chinese Rites controversy, which amounted to canonization of western and Roman cultural Catholicism and the excommunication of all other cultures. Today we are familiar with the complaints of so-called Third World Catholic Churches about excessive Roman centralism and its twin offspring, imperialism and colonialism. We should recall, however, that only in 1908 was the American Church released from the tutelage of the Congregation for the Propagation of the Faith and no longer regarded as a mission country. And we should also equally not forget that since the condemnation of Americanism, a heresy which never existed in America, Roman policy toward the American Catholic Church has hardly been that of a sister church, but that of a matriarchal church in regard to a daughter whose definitely deviant proclivities require close supervision and constant correction.

Against this background we can now proceed to examine the unique history and development of American Catholicism, and precisely how it differs from the European.

II. A Free and Voluntary People's Church

A major incentive for European Christians migrating to America was flight from the established churches of Europe. This was true for continental Anabaptists as well as English Puritans. It was probably these dissenting Christians who gave the American colonies and nation its most distinctive traits. Among them must be counted the

Catholics who fled the established state Church of England. Before we elaborate on the Roman Catholic settlers of Maryland as Catholic Dissenters, we must set the stage by briefly describing the general American religious situation in which they found themselves.[14]

America was an explicitly religious nation. The founders who migrated from Europe migrated for explicitly religious reasons, especially freedom of religion. Associated with this was a sense of national vocation inspired by their Puritan millenarianism. This was the hour when God was giving the world a last chance to become the holy and just city God had always intended it to be. Hence, the migration from the old world to the new was not merely a migration, it was a mission. For the Puritans it was an "Errand in the Wilderness" to which God had called them. Through virtuous living they were to establish "the holy city built on a hill" which was then to serve as a "beacon to all nations."[15] The Isaian metaphor used by Vatican I to describe the church is obvious here.

As soon as the Puritans found themselves in the majority and in political power, they established themselves as the official church, a blatant contradiction of their fundamental tenet.[16] The Quakers in Pennsylvania and the Catholics in Maryland resisted this temptation. Established official churches in the colonies persisted into nationhood, the last state to disestablish being, as one might expect then and now, Massachusetts. However, even in the colonies, establishment was always precarious. This was the case not only because of the fundamental emphasis on freedom, but also practically because of another fundamental element in the American religious experience, pluralism.

From the very beginning the European exploration and experience of the new world were religiously pluralist. There were not only the French and Spanish Catholics, who are not quite as important for our considerations here as the English Protestants, but also the other Europeans who settled the eastern seaboard. Even among the Protestant settlers there was a pluralism which ensured that the established colonial churches could never rest easy. Not infrequent missionary incursions from the other colonies and churches saw to that. It also ensured that there would be no national official, established state church once the colonies became the American nation.

This pluralism also ensured a third essential element in the general American religious experience, competition. Just as there was a free market in commerce, so was there a free market in religion. All the churches were (more or less, some mostly less!)

welcome in the new world, but they would have to compete on their own for membership and public status and influence. They could not rely on the support and patronage of the civil government for their religious mission. Obviously this free market was extremely restricted where a church had been established. Nonetheless, even in established colonies there were missionary incursions from the outside.

The unique nature of the American religious experience is also visible in the American Revolution or, better, the War of Independence. In contrast to the classical revolutions of Europe (Enlightenment, France, Russia) which were all anti-religious, anti-clerical, anti-church, anti-God, the American Declaration of Independence invoked precisely the Deity in support of itself and of the freedoms it sought for its citizens. Furthermore, again in contrast to Europe where revolution and independence from the king and state meant revolution and independence from the pope/bishop and the church, American churches were generally on the side of freedom and the freedom fighters. This is true of the churches as such, not only of individual Christians. The Latin American situation has been much like the European. The revolutions of Brazil in 1819 and of Mexico in 1917 were extremely hostile to the Roman Catholic Church, although nearly all citizens of both countries were at least nominal members of that church.

Although even Protestant America was religiously pluralist, it was predominantly Free Church Protestant. Seymour Lipset has gone so far as to claim that "The United States is the only Protestant country. By 'Protestant' I am referring to Protestant sects as opposed to State Churches. . . . The majority of Americans . . . from practically the beginning of the Republic down to the present have been members of churches that are not supported by the state and, in turn, do not support the state."[17] Free Church is not an easy concept. One can accent either the tendency to sectarianism, self-righteous elitism, exclusivism, biblicism, anti-sacramentalism, anti-hierarchicalism (although one must note immediately that leaders within Free Churches often display the same imperial and monarchical attitudes and tendencies as those in explicitly hierarchical churches) or one can accent the overwhelming emphasis on free and voluntary membership in a given church.[18] In actual Free Churches, of course, all these and other elements are present in varying degrees. It is important to be aware that both opponents and proponents can be tendentious in selecting the elements to be emphasized.

As a nation America has never had an official state religion or church. Nonetheless, there was a sort of unofficial official religion and church—a non-denominational Protestantism of the Free Church tradition. This unofficial official religion lasted until about the middle of this century when it began to erode for various reasons. There were two principle factors for this development. The increase of the non-Protestant population reduced the domination of the old Protestant majority. A series of court decisions more or less eliminated the customary Protestant symbols from the public life of the nation. Examples are the elimination of Bible reading in public schools and of the Bible as that upon which the oath was taken in courts and for installation in public office. Unfortunately, this development can be the object of only extremely moderate rejoicing on the part of Catholics and other traditional religions. The public square has hardly been left empty. Secular Humanism has clearly replaced the old non-denominational Protestantism as the nation's unofficial official religion. And, in keeping with the biblical admonition, the last state is, in all likelihood, worse than the first.[19]

A final element of the general American religious experience must be mentioned, an unfortunate one. It is the anti-Catholicism so endemic and virulent in American history that Arthur Schlesinger once felt compelled to remark to John Tracy Ellis: "I regard the prejudice against your Church as the deepest bias in the history of the American people."[20] Some are wont to date this anti-Catholicism from the nineteenth century immigrations and call it Nativism. This is entirely wrong. Anti-Catholicism was imported from Europe by the earliest immigrants, especially from England in the form of the anti-Irish, anti-Catholic penal laws. It has since waned at times and changed its form many times, but it has never died, and shows no sign of doing so today.

American Catholics as Dissenters

Into this religious landscape Catholic pilgrims from England, under the leadership of Lord George Calvert, Baron of Baltimore, sailed in 1634 aboard the Ark and the Dove, to begin a unique event and achievement in the history of Christianity in general and Roman Catholicism in particular.

There is a superficial resemblance between the beginning of the Catholic Church in America and of Catholic Christendom in Europe. In both cases there was a general context of persecution, in which a noble played a decisive role. However, there the similarity ends and a decisive change occurs. Constantine freely and deliberately chose to establish the church, Lord Calvert freely and deliberately chose not to establish the church. Constantine's Edict of Toleration eliminated religious toleration and freedom. In spite of the anti-Christian persecutions, the Roman Empire had had a strangely inconsistent history of religious toleration toward its subject peoples. Calvert's (and Maryland's) Edict of Toleration established religious toleration and freedom. The critical question was, could the Roman Catholic Church, so long and so prototypically the established religion, the state church, survive in this new condition in the new world.

The striking answer is that it not only survived, it thrived. And in so doing, it has provided another "Model of the Church," another mode of being Catholic.

First of all, and something that is nearly always overlooked, the American Catholic Church was founded by a layman. He was accompanied by priests, but the founding and the guiding force was a layman. His lay leadership was not the royal patronage and lay investiture of Europe, which subjected the church to the civil lord. It was, rather, an investiture of the church with freedom from civil governmental patronage (jus patronatus) so that the church's pastoral administration and activity would not be subservient to secular authorities.

It is also important to note that Lord Baltimore refused to establish Catholicism as the official church, even when he had the power to do so. Here too is an achievement much ignored and unappreciated. Calvert was able to make this decision even though he was a loyal and devout Catholic. Neither contemporary theory nor practice provided justification or paradigm for such a decision. A decision that would be commonplace for us today was extraordinary for Calvert, requiring unusual creativity and audacity.

Not only did Calvert refuse to establish Catholicism as the official state religion of the colony. He also refused to provide official state support for normal pastoral care. He remained steadfast in this resolve even under threats of excommunication when the Jesuits, who provided the pastoral care, complained that the Maryland assembly, failed "to provide or shew any favor to Ecclesiasticall persons, or to preserve for the church the Immunitye and priveledges which she enjoyeth every where else."[21]

This may well have been the most important single decision and act, both practical and symbolic, in the history of American Catholicism. Practical, for only a few years later Puritan Dissidents from neighboring Virginia invaded Maryland, unseated the Catholic government, and established their church. Catholics had fortunately already been forewarned, by one of their own, that they would have to survive on their own freely and voluntarily raised resources—they could expect none from the state. Symbolic, for it was a decision of the American Catholic Church, at the very beginning, freely, by a layman, and constitutive for all subsequent American Catholic history.

Calvert laid the foundation for that later Catholic development which some sarcastically call the "edifice complex." A contemporary Catholic conceit complains condescendingly about the American Catholic fascination and preoccupation with organization and institutions. However, there was no other way for Catholics to survive, much less thrive. Furthermore, it was but the Catholic articulation of that general phenomenon in free and democratic societies already emphasized by Alexis de Tocqueville: "Free association of the citizens could then take the place of the individual authority of the nobles, and the state would then be protected from both tyranny and license."[22] What the nobles had provided for both church and state in aristocratic societies the free and voluntary associations of citizens would have to provide in democratic societies.

Calvert also provided another foundation for the development of American Catholicism. He clearly understood that his settlement in the new world would not separate, but would positively correlate religion, politics, and economics. Neither would they be subsumed into one another in the old European monarchical and Caesaropapist fashion. Free, mutual cooperation of all citizens with one another in these three crucial areas of human life would result in the enhancement of all citizens in all three areas. Just as Catholics were the first to practice the precisely American virtue of religious toleration and freedom,[23] so would they also be exemplary practitioners of that trait also observed by de Tocqueville:

> Another observation can be made which applies to the clergy of every communion. American priests do not try to divert and concentrate all of people's attention on the future life; they freely allow them to give some of their hearts' care to the needs of the present, apparently considering the good things of this world as objects of some, albeit secondary, importance. . . . while they are ever pointing to the other world as the great object of the hopes and fears of the faithful, they do

not forbid the honest pursuit of prosperity in this. Far from trying to show that these two worlds are distinct and opposed to each other, they seek to discover the points of connection and alliance.[24]

Of course, such concourse of religion and prosperity is not without dangers. But could it be worse than the dangers inherent in establishment? On the other hand, religion could become an excuse or rationalization for prosperity—the complaint of some economically secure clericalists, whether religious or tenured academics. But who would want to say that this danger is greater than, or even as great as, the customary schizophrenic spirituality which simply divides this world from the next and reduces this world to the status of either temptation or test. A prosperous citizenry is, of course, a problem for elitists whose guidance is more likely to be questioned and even rejected by those whose prosperity has enabled them to be more independent. Manifestations of this problem cover the ideological spectrum today. From the left and the right, clericalists of all persuasions clearly find the prosperity of the people problematic.

The American Catholic Church has also made a clear commitment to the republican, democratic form of limited government. Although Catholics have customarily been accused of being unreliable democrats, and although official Catholic doctrine has only reluctantly accepted the republican idea, American Catholics really never hesitated. Observers as diverse as Alexis de Tocqueville, Harriet Martineau, and Henry Steele Commager have commented upon the preferential option of American Catholics, both corporately and individually, for democracy.[25] The Roman Catholic Church would not catch up with the American Roman Catholic Church officially until the Second Vatican Council.

Originally the American Catholic Church even evinced a democratic preference in inner-churchly matters, as Harriet Martineau's prophetic observation clearly implies: "The Catholic body is democratic in its politics, and made up from the more independent kind of occupations. The Catholic religion is modified by the spirit of the time in America; and its professors are not a set of men who can be priest-ridden to any fatal extent."[26] Note that she says "modified" and not corrupted or completely changed. Note also that she says Catholics are not priest-ridden. To this point we shall return in our conclusion.

This same democratic spirit was obvious in John Carroll's plans for an "ordinary national Church" in communion, certainly, with the papacy.[27] His choice of words is unusually significant, for "ordinary" is the proper title, in Latin technical theological and canonical terminology, for a residential bishop with full status and jurisdiction. The "Ordinary" is the eccesial administrator who is so by full right, in contrast to various kinds of ad hoc administrators who serve for particular purposes and particular periods, totally beholden to a superior administrator. Carroll's "ordinary" American Church would have had a certain independence, not separation, from European models and Roman praxis. It would have, in the much later words of Vatican II, "respected and fostered the spiritual adornments and gifts of the various races and peoples . . . admitted the fashions from every period according to the natural talents and circumstances of peoples and the needs of the various rites."[28] It is not fanciful to speak of an American rite, for as is clear by now, in the American nation and culture the Catholic Church found a way of being the Catholic Church which is not merely an extension or imitation of the European way. Carroll's "ordinary" American Church would have incorporated American understandings and practices into its life, its piety, its polity, its theology. He himself was elected to the episcopacy by his fellow priests and proposed this as the proper way for all bishops to be selected.

For many reasons, both internal and external, Carroll's plans for a truly American Catholic Church failed. Externally, economic depression was accompanied by a revival not only of revivalist Protestantism but also of the crassest anti-Catholicism. Internally, the pastoral care of increasingly numerous and pluralist immigrant Catholics and the general shortage of priests for this task overwhelmed all other considerations. Little time and energy remained for the planning and implementation of a truly new way of being the Catholic Church. Furthermore, Roman centralism began to reassert and even intensify itself in the aftermath of its mauling by the French Revolution and Napoleon. Unfortunately, John Carroll himself contributed to the failure by some of his own personnel and policy decisions. The magnitude of the failure of Carroll's plans for a truly American Catholic Church is indicated by the fact that only thirty years after John Carroll had insisted that the national clergy had the right to choose its own bishops, his second successor was informed by Rome that he had no right even to be consulted in the naming of bishops.

However, all was not lost. At least in theory Carroll had clearly established that even in the West local churches did not have to look like the customary established churches of Europe. American Catholics had also established, in practice, that the Catholic Church could not only survive, but also thrive without establishment and state support. They would continue to do this throughout their history and still do, to the dismay of critics both liberal and conservative. Eventually John Courtney Murray would explain to the Romans, and to us too, that the state's role in the "care of religion," as the established phrase had it, was adequately performed by providing for and protecting religious freedom for its citizens.[29] In so doing, Murray would "only" be providing a theological elaboration of John Carroll's claim at the beginning of the hierarchical American Church: "if we have the wisdom and temper to preserve [religious and civil liberty], America may yet come to exhibit a proof to the world that general and equal toleration, by giving free circulation to fair argument, is the most effectual method to bring all denominations of Christians to a unity of faith."[30] And, we might add, all citizens to a unity of nationhood.

Some American Catholics continued to carry the torch of John Carroll for a truly American Church. Among them were a few Bishops like John England, but bishops, as one might expect, found the European aristocratic and monarchic model of the episcopacy more fulfilling personally and professionally. Also among the advocates of an American Church were those lay people who have come to be lumped under the negative sobriquet of "Trusteeism." For example, Irish Catholics in South Carolina and Polish Catholics in Milwaukee argued that the jus patronatus of the Catholic nobles of Europe would henceforth by exercised by the Catholic people of America.[31] However, as James Hennesey remarks: "Neither Rome nor most American bishops accepted the argument. They understood the age-old European model of intermediate lay involvement through princes. Immediate lay involvement as a consequence of newfangled democratic forms was beyond their comprehension. It was a demand for extension to the United States of the jus patronatus, with the sovereign people as a 'patron,' and it was rejected."[32] And, we may surely add, it still is beyond both comprehension and acceptance.

But even this rejection can serve as a sort of negative cipher for the point we are making. On the basis of their American experience, American Catholics refused to accept the old established and aristocratic church of Europe as the only acceptable form. Although they were rejected, they were not defeated. They did not leave the church, thereby also leaving it in the sole possession of the Europeanizers. They stayed, to continue their quest, however they could, for a truly American Church.

Other significant advocates of "an ordinary American Church" include Isaac Hecker, founder of the Paulist Fathers. He is significant in a special way. His call for greater participation of the laity in the life of the church was rejected, as was the original call of John Carroll for a greater role of the priests in the administration of the church. The imperial spirit had begun to pervade the American Church. In a sort of chain reaction, bishops imitated the papal refusal to share responsibility with them by refusing to share responsibility with priests and people, and priests imitated their bishops by refusing to share with the people. Serendipitously, at this time the bishops were not yet so out of touch with the people.[33] Since the clergy's concerns generally coincided with the people's, partly an unintended beneficence of Protestant persecution, the people were able to cooperate with both priests and bishops in the enhancement of the life, both sacred and secular, of the Catholic population at large. Bishops, of course, and priests too, tended to misunderstand this cooperation of the people. They interpreted it as obedience, in keeping with the kerygma of Pope Leo X: "The nerve of all ecclesiastical discipline (order) [is] obedience, which is also the font and source of all virtues."[34] As Peter Blau has pointed out, however, the totalitarian leader can command "obedience" only as long as he delivers the goods to the people.[35] Certainly the circumstances of the times, especially the virulent anti-Catholicism which accompanied the increasing Catholic immigration, helped to preserve the communion of people, priest, and bishop and to provide all three with common goals and goods to be achieved. But neither the legendary affection and courtesy of the American Catholic people for their priests nor their mutual cooperation in mutually beneficial enterprises should lead one to the conclusion that the people were ever overwhelmed by episcopal and priestly pretensions of superior insight and holiness. The reality was quite different from the interpretation that certain clergy were pleased to give it.

Nonetheless, American Catholicism has been able to avoid that anti-clericalism which has been so harmful to the churches of Europe and Latin America. And there seems to be a basic reason for this. In America the Catholic Church has never been established; it has always been free and voluntary. People were Catholic because they wanted to be, freely and voluntarily. Hence, they could also better tolerate inadequate church administrators and "leaders." The people did not depend on the leaders, the leaders depended on the people. This was the American way, civil as well as ecclesial. The initiative of the people as well as the cooperation of priest and people are well illustrated by the mutual benefit societies. These organizations of the people often had as their first priority the securing of a priest to be their pastor. Even in the context of lay initiative, then, there was still a fundamental cooperation with the clergy.

Increasing Roman emphasis on hierarchial prerogative echoed through the American episcopate. Without noble blood and lineage, the American bishop could nonetheless find the "Prince Bishop" of Europe an appealing model. Once again the Protestant persecution of American Catholics had an unintended benefit. Even the most autocratic of bishops were forced by this external condition to remain in communion with the people of their diocese. The role played by non-establishment in this matter is so clear that it need be only mentioned.

Another fortunate consequence of the persistent anti-Catholicism in the nation was the existence of a common enemy for all Catholics, clergy and laity alike. The low social, economic, and political status of the immigrant Catholics, the anti-Catholicism, and the mutual benefit societies ensured that the American Catholic Church was always a public church.[36] It has always been active in the public sphere, in social matters such as education, health care, labor, etc. Clergy and religious played important roles in this public participation of the church. Nonetheless, as impressive as their contribution has been, it has hardly surpassed that of the people. The American Catholic Church is justly famous for its Labor Priests. On the other hand, one must recall that priestly participation by and large followed that of the people, who, after all, were the workers. Symbolic of this reality, and not restricted solely to the realm of labor, is Cardinal Gibbons' defence of Catholic participation in the Knights of Labor. It was not he who organized the workers or led them into the movement. It was they who took the initiative. He "merely" defended them against Roman, and American, hierarchical interference.

Here I want to emphasize that I have no intention of denigrating the enormous contribution of priests and religious to the development of American Catholicism. That would be as petty as it would be false. However, I do want to emphasize that in a free and voluntary democratic society, there are various kinds of leadership.[37] Hierar-

chical administrative leadership may not be the most effective kind
and, in any case, it depends entirely on the "leadership" of the
people. Without establishment of the church, there is no state
enforcement agency to compel people either to enter the Church to
begin with or to participate once they have entered. One of the
entirely noteworthy achievements and characteristics of the American Catholic Church has been the close communion and cooperation
of priest and people. And this should be recalled, especially in an
age when many are tempted to dwell on the excesses of some clerics,
past and present.

Furthermore, although immigration has lessened, it has not
stopped. This is true of both legal and illegal immigration, and the
latter must by no means be restricted to only the Mexican migrants
in the Southwest. In a sense there is a double Hispanic migration
taking place in the United States today. There is the continuing
entrance of Hispanic immigrants into the American nation from the
outside. There is also the entrance of American Hispanic Catholics
into the mainstream of the American Catholic Church from the
margins where they had geneally resided until now.

There is another sort of "immigration" in Catholicism today. By
this I mean the significant presence of "particular" (not particular-
istic) groups such as charismatics, more intensely ideological liberal
and conservative Catholics, all sorts of "spiritualities," and perhaps,
most significantly of all, the migration of women into the public
sphere of the church. All of these had always been present in the
church to some degree or other. But the changed condition of
American culture and society in general and the changed condition
of the American Catholic population in particular make the voluntary cultural pluralism of Catholics different. There is a great tendency to underestimate the past influence of women in the church
because their public status was generally quite restricted. However,
public status and serious influence are hardly to be equated. On the
other hand, it is also important to be aware of the importance a
change in the public status of various constitutencies has for a
society, ecclesial and civil alike. Consequently, just about the time
the American Church might have thought that it could relax and rest
because its extreme pluralism had come to some sort of completion,
it is faced with migrations, both internal and external, which may
be as intensely pluralist as anything that is has known in the past.

One final element in the American Catholic experience must be
noted. Except for the core of the original Maryland Catholics, Amer-

ican Catholics have by and large started out at the bottom of the social ladder. Only slaves and former slaves were lower than Catholics in all matters: social status, education, professions, economics, etc. Catholics have written a remarkable success story in American history. As various studies have indicated, of discernible religious groups, contemporary Catholics rank high, indeed, second only in comparison with Jews, in regard to levels of success and achievement in the various categories used to measure this.[38] Of course, not all Catholics have made it to the top, and perhaps many are still near the bottom. However, as an empirically discernible subpopulation in the larger American society, the Catholic achievement has been extraordinary.

Even more extraordinary is the fact that this social achievement has been made in and through the church, yes, let us be so bold and say it, even the institutional church. The papal complaint that the greatest scandal in the nineteenth century was the loss of the working classes to the church was not and is not true in the American Catholic Church. It is probably the greatest indication of the general ignorance of the true history and nature of the American Catholic Church that this statement was taught and taken as true in American Catholic schools which had been built precisely by workers who had not been lost to the church. Here is to be emphasized once again what was only mentioned above: If the American Catholic Church had not been a public church from the very beginning, it would not have been at all. The American Catholic Church is living proof and witness that the church need not be and has not always and everywhere been either restricted to the sanctuary or subservient to the state which has established it. It is possible to be Catholic and prosperous simultaneously. This needs to be emphasized constantly today, lest we be drowned in the romance of poverty and pauperism which pervades the entire ideological spectrum, including Pope John Paul II and Cardinal Ratzinger, the American Bishops and their socially concerned clericalist advisors, the political theologians of Europe, the liberation theologians of Latin America and other less developed nations, and their secular counterparts.[39]

Just as people are not poor because they have sinned, so also are people not prosperous because they have sinned. In all this, sin plays an insignificant role. What is significant is economic and commercial ability and enterprise. Clearly, the free American society has been extremely fertile in enabling people in general, not just the aristocratic few, to prosper and enjoy the good things of this world.

That it is not perfect need not be belabored here, since that is both obvious and the belaboring has obviously been chosen by some as their life's vocation. As Alexis de Tocqueville noted above, American Catholics have found it possible to emphasize this world and achievement therein without rejecting the world to come. This may well be the most outstanding achievement of the American Catholic Church, namely the ability to be both religious and prosperous.

After all, the classical critique of religion (Nietzsche, Feuerbach, Marx, Freud) has maintained that religion can flourish only in the soil of oppression and suppression, exploitation and alienation, unfreedom and slavery. Once these negative social conditions have been removed, religion will automatically perish. However, in the United States of America this has not been the case. It has not been the case especially in the American Catholic Church. Perhaps the classical critique does apply to the established European Christianity which the above-named critics knew and disdained. In that case human emancipation also meant religious and precisely Christian emancipation—to be free from the emperor/king and his riches was to be free from the church and its riches, which had also been his riches. However, in America the "riches" of the church are the accomplishment achieved by the people, not the booty wrested from the people.

And, as Andrew Greeley has shown, the prosperity of the Catholic people has not resulted in the oft-feared and prematurely deplored embourgeoisement of the American Catholic population.[40] It has resulted in the enhancement of the fundamental American Catholic dream of an ordinary American Catholic Church. And what is the nature of the American Catholic Church?

It is a free and voluntary people's Church, able to survive and thrive in a free, pluralist, secular, democratic, and prosperous society. It is able to be and do this precisely because it is its own church, not the European church, not an appendage of the European church.

It is not hostile to the European church, whence it came. It is grateful. It is not hostile to the central Church of Rome, the symbolic and administrative center of the whole worldwide Catholic Church. It is grateful.

But it also knows that it is its own church. As such it has the right to its own independence, not separation, but independence, as an "ordinary Catholic Church" in communion with the worldwide church and with Rome. It has the right not only to listen to the rest of the church, it also has the right to be heard.

III. The American Catholic Church for the Whole Church

And what will the rest of the church hear when (perhaps better, if) it listens to the American Catholic Church?

First of all, it will hear that local churches can dissent, not from Catholicism, but from particular cultural forms of Catholicism. As I write this, there is much talk about dissent in the American Catholic Church, especially in regard to certain areas of sexual morality. However, as important as the current discussion may be, it is clearly dwarfed by the initial American Catholic dissent described above, namely from the established state church ecclesiology which had dominated Christianity for over a millenium. Local churches will also learn that one can dissent and still be loyal to the universal and papal church. Dissent is not treason. Of course, not every dissent need be true and holy, but then neither does every consent.

Local churches will also learn that their dissent need not be appreciated, or even, for that matter, understood—not right away and not for a long time. As late as 1895, when Catholicism was flourishing in America and languishing in Europe, Pope Leo XIII could not refrain from the following caution in his otherwise laudatory if condescendingly hierocratic letter to the American Catholic Church:

> But moreover . . . thanks are due to the equity of the laws which obtain in America and to the customs of the well-ordered Republic. For the Church amongst you, unopposed by the Constitution and government of your nation, fettered by no hostile legislation, protected against violence by the common laws and impartiality of the tribunals, is free to live and act without hindrance. Yet, though all of this is true, it would be erroneous to draw the conclusion that in America is to be sought the type of the most desirable status of the Church, or that it would be universally lawful or expedient for State and Church to be, as in America, dissevered and divorced. The fact that Catholicity with you is in good condition, nay, is even enjoying a prosperous growth, is by all means to be attributed to the fecundity with which God has endowed his Church, in virtue of which unless men or circumstances interfere, she spontaneously expands and propagates herself; but she would bring forth more abundant fruits if, in addition to liberty, she enjoyed the favor of the laws and the patronage of public authority.

As the "yet" and the "but" clearly indicate, Pope Leo XIII had obviously learned and understood nothing from and about the

American Catholic experience. If the church is to be "free to live and act without hindrance," it cannot enjoy the "patronage of the public authority." If anything was clear from the Constantinianizion of the church, that surely was. One cannot emphasize too often that freedom is a problem for the clericalist hierocratic spirit, whether this be the ordained religious or the academic intellectual kind.

Several years ago I remarked to a very moderate(!) German theologian that I did not think that Pope John Paul II understood the United States of America and the American Catholic Church, and that this was why his comments on America so often missed the mark. The theologian replied lapidarily, "He does not understand the West." This need not be surprising, since papal Polish experience would have been intensely influenced by aristocratic Catholicism, Polish messianism, and Nazi and Marxist invasions and occupations. Whatever may the case with the West, that Pope John Paul II does not understand America, especially insofar as it is a free, voluntary democratic society has been strikingly certified by George Huntson Williams in his generally laudatory biography:

> From his only examples of communities of acting it is evident that the author has no idea of the scope, vigor, resourcefulness, and abiding role of "voluntary associations" in what he calls the society of "individualism," associations which are by no means "limited to self-interest," for they often go far beyond self-interest in sometimes self-sacrificial, sometimes prophetic, criticism for its good as well as their own. . . . With an incredible want of objective observation with respect to the voluntary associations . . . of the land he had twice visited at the time of the completion of *The Acting Person* in translation . . . the author regards every voluntary association in the Anglo-American tradition as individualistically selfish.[42]

And thus he must also regard the entire American nation as individualistically selfish. Of course, this criticism is not peculiar to John Paul II alone. It pervades the recent writings of Joseph Cardinal Ratzinger in whose *The Ratzinger Report*,[43] for example, I have counted excoriations of selfishness and materialism on at least 34 pages. They are generally directed at the West, but especially at the United States. It seems clear that we may be the great Satan not only in the eyes of Muslim ayatollahs. Of course, anyone who has labored through Robert Bellah's *Habits of the Heart*,[44] that classic of liberal academic-intellectual clericalism, knows that some Americans themselves delight in propagating the same criticism. What is common to all these critics, of course, is their fear, that the freedom and prosperity of the "common man," of the people, makes them less pliable and more resistant to the manipulations of those who know better what is good for the people than the people themselves. Marie Augusta Neale's criticism of Bellah's civil religion thesis is equally applicable to his *Habits of the Heart*—Bellah speaks not as scholar but as a priest.[45]

I have included the above for a definite reason. The future, shy of apocalyptic cataclysm, will feature a world that is free, voluntary, prosperous, educated, professional. It will not be perfect, its citizens will not be perfect. But neither will they be the serfs ecclesiastical and academic clericalists have been accustomed to direct, and, indeed, lord it over. Given these circumstances, other local churches will do well to study the American Catholic experience, for thus far at least it has demonstrated that in such a society religion in general and Catholicism in particular can flourish. The American Catholic Church is as different from the customary European model as any of the Third World churches which we are assured by many are aborning as the churches of the future. It is this reality to which I call attention here, not for the sake of proclaiming a model which can be carbon copies, but which can be studied with profit.[46]

The churches of this new world will have to reckon with a church membership for whom Pius X's exhortation that the flock has but to be docile, submissive, and tractable (the German word "gefügig" is most appropriate here) is as ridiculous now in practice as it was then in theory. Rather, the local churches elsewhere will have to reckon with a membership like the one prophetically—and gleefully—described by Andrew Greeley in America:

> As humiliating as it may be to Church leadership [here he means hierarchical officials], it would seem that they have influence on their people only when their people decide to permit them to have such influence. The authority of government apparently rests on the consent of the governed, not only in civil matters of the United States but also in Catholic ecclesiastical matters.
>
> Those Church leaders who might in some of their darker moments wish that they could be rid of the contentious, opionated, independent professional-class Catholics who are now becoming typical are wasting their time. The well educated Catholic professional is here, he/she is here to stay and not about to leave the Church. But not about to participate in the Church on any other terms but his or her own.[47]

The "Christian religion/church [not only] can be challenged and enriched by . . . other cultures." It has been—in the American Catholic Culture and Church, a free, voluntary, people's Church.[48]

NOTES

1. From the letter (April 4, 1988) of Paul Knitter, editor of this volume, seeking contributions.

2. The German author of the letter will remain anonymous. In the same letter he also notes the German fascination with the liberation theology of Latin America. This strange affinity is strikingly illustrated in a collection of essays edited by Norbert Greinacher, *Konflikt um die Theologie der Befreiung* (Einsiedeln: Benziger, 1985). The book is all the more striking since it limits liberation theology to the Latin American kind, and ignores the many others with which we are so familiar in America. The ignorance about and disdain of the United States of America is indicated right in Greinacher's foreword, where he refers to the "United States of North America," a non-existent nation. He there complains about American intervention in Latin America, conveniently forgetting, as his kind is wont to do, that America has also had to intervene in Europe, not infrequently.

3. Obviously excessive is the exuberance of M. D. Chenu, "La fin de l'ère constantinienne," in *Un concile pour notre temps*, Yves Congar, ed. (Paris: Cerf, 1961), pp. 59–83.

4. Robert Kress, *The Church: Communion, Sacrament, Communication* (New York: Paulist, 1985), pp. 161–213.

5. Joseph Ratzinger, *Das neue Volk Gottes* (Düsseldorf: Patmos, 1969), pp. 207–212.

6. Joseph Ratzinger, *Church, Ecumenism, Politics* (New York: Crossroad, 1988), pp. 76, 94.

7. Georg Schwaiger, "Reformation," in *Handbuch der theologischen Grundbegriffe*, vol. 2, Heinrich Fries, ed. (Munich: Kösel, 1963), p. 398.

8. Domenico Palmieri, *Tractatus de Romano Pontifice Cum Prolegomeno De Ecclesia* (Rome: S. C. de Propaganda Fide, 1877), pp. 427–443.

9. Yves Congar, *L'église de saint Augustin à l'époque moderne* (Paris: Cerf, 1970), 271. In the same volume Congar shows how the theology of the church moved from emphasis on ministry to power, the power being both royal and sacerdotal: passim, especially pp. 15, 259.

10. Harding Meyer, *Das Wort Pius IX: "Die Tradition bin ich."* (Munich: Kaiser, 1965), pp. 35–40. Yves Dongar, *Jalons pour une théologie du Laicat* (Paris: Cerf, 1954), pp. 71–73 for the other quotations and many more like them.

11. Gratian, *Concordia discordantium canonum*, C. 7, C XII, q. 1, ed. Friedberg, I (Leipzig: 1879: Graz, 1959), p. 678. H. M. Legrand, "L' avenir des ministères: bilan, défis, tâches," *Maison Dieu*, 124 (1978) 29, has assembled the quotation from Pius X along with many others of the same ilk. Of all this, the observation of Yves Congar is most apropos. This is a ':'juridical definition of the Church as a perfect society, hierarchical and unequal . . . of which the primary article was the distinction by divine right and divine law between clergy and laity." Congar, "Regard sur le Concile Vatican II," in *Unterwegs zur Einheit: Festschrift H. Stirnimann* (Frieburg: Herder, 1980), p. 773.

12. J. P. Audet, with Alfons Deissler and Heinrich Schlier, "Priester und Laie in der christlichen Gemeinde: Der Weg in die gegenseitige Entfremdung," in *Der priesterliche Dienst* (Frieburg: Herder, 1970), p. 151.

13. Robert Kress, "The Theological and Ecclesiological Foundation of the Social Mission of the Church," *Charities USA* 15, 5 (1988) 1–7.

14. For the general background of this section of the paper, see Jay Dolan, *The American Catholic Experience* (Garden City: Doubleday, 1985) and James Hennesey, *American Catholics* (New York: Oxford, 1981).

15. Paul Johnson, *The Almost Chosen People* (Rockford, IL: The Rockford Institute, 1985).

16. Martin Marty, *Righteous Empire* (New York: Dial, 1970).

17. Seymour Lipset, "Religion in American Politics," in *Capitalism and Socialism*, Michael Novak, ed. (Washington: NEI, 1979), p. 61.

18. On the Free Church, see Franklin H. Littell, *The Anabaptist View of the Church* (Boston: Starr King, 1958) and Donald Durnbaugh, *The Believers' Church* (New York: Macmillan, 1968).

19. John Courtney Murray had already detected this and observed that the "new Nativism" was not so much classical Protestantism as it was the new naturalist secularist humanism. See Donald Pelotte, *John Courtney Murray: Theologian in Conflict* (New York: Paulist, 1976), pp. 17–19.

20. John Tracy Ellis, *American Catholicism* (Chicago: University of Chicago Press, 1969), p. 151.

21. John D. Krugler, "Lord Baltimore, Roman Catholics, and Toleration: Religious Policy in Maryland during the Early Catholic Years," *Catholic Historical Review*, 65 (1979) 67. This article also contains valuable material on the positive correlation of politics, economics, and religion in the Maryland experiment.

22. Alexis de Tocqueville, *Democracy in America*, J. P. Mayer and Max Lerner, eds., George Lawrence, tr. (New York: Harper & Row, 1966), p. 8; see also pp. 560–565, 655–664, and passim.

23. A point usually overlooked or surpressed and properly recalled and emphasized by Theodore Maynard, *The Story of American Catholicism* (New York: Macmillan, 1960), p. x.

24. de Tocqueville, *Democracy*, p. 414.

25. de Tocqueville, *Democracy*, pp. 265–266, 415. Henry Steele Commager, *The American Mind: An Interpretation of the American Thought and Character Since the 1880's* (New Haven: Yale University Press, 1950), p. 193.

26. Harriet Martineau, *Society in America*, vol. 2 (London, 1837), p. 237.

27. James Henesey, "The Vision of John Carroll," *Thought*, 54 (1979) 322–333.

28. Vatican II, *Constitution on the Sacred Liturgy*, nn. 37, 123.

29. For example, John Courtney Murray, "The Declaration on Religious Freedom," in *Vatican II: An Interfaith Appraisal*, John Miller, ed. (Notre Dame: University of Notre Dame Press, 1966), pp. 565–576.

30. John Carroll, *An Address to the Roman Catholics of the United States of America by a Catholic Clergyman* (Annapolis, 1784), p. 115; reprinted in *The John Carroll papers*, 3 vols., Thomas O'Brien Hanley, ed. (Notre Dame University Press, 1976), I, pp. 82–144.

31. Dolan, *American*, pp. 181–186.

32. Hennesey, *American*, p. 95.

33. As they are today, as is correctly contended by Andrew Greeley, *American Catholics Since the Council: An Unauthorized Report* (Chicago: Thomas More, 1986).

34. Leo XII, "Exsurge, Domine," Mansi, 32, 1053; translation in *Readings in Church History*, Colman J. Barry, ed. (Westminster, Md.: 1985), pp. 634–640.

35. Peter Blau, *Exchange and Power in Social Life* (Wiley, 1964), pp. 115–167; *The*

Dynamics of Bureaucracy (Chicago: University of Chicago Press, 1963), pp. 207–230; *On the Nature of Organizations* (New York: Wiley, 1974), pp. 243–262, 323–348.

36. See Robert Kress, "On the Free-Churching of the Roman Catholic Church in the United States of America," *Proceedings of The Association for the Scientific Study of Religion* 1987, Jack Weir, ed. (Abilene: Texas Christian University, 1987), pp. 51–59.

37. And the same applies to the church. Robert Kress, *The Church*, pp. 161–212.

38. Andrew Greeley, *The American Catholic: A Social Protrait* (New York: Basic, 1977). A summary is in Greeley, *American Catholics*, p. 48.

39. On the romanticism of Karl Marx in general, see James Billington, *Fire in the Minds of Men: Origins of the Revolutionary Faith* (San Francisco: Harper/Colophon, 1983). On the manifestation of this Marxist romanticism in his epigones, especially Ernst Bloch, whose influence on Johannes Baptist Metz and other political and liberation theologians is well known, see Robert Vander Gucht, "Der Marxismus," in *Bilanz der Theologie im 20. Jahrhundert*, Herbert Vorgrmiler and Robert Vander Gucht, eds. (Freiburg: Herder, 1970), pp. 328–338, especially 335–337. On the romanticism in political and liberation theology, see Robert Kress, "Theological Method: Praxis and Liberation," *Communio*, 6 (1979) 118–121; Michael Zoeller, "Wer für die rechte Sache kaempft," *Frankfurter Allgemeine Zeitung*, July 5, 1988, p. 29.

40. "Those who suggest that the 'embourgeoisement' of American Catholics means less concern about the poor or the oppressed are, according to the evidence, simply wrong. . . . There is not the slightest bit of evidence that economic and occupational success and religious change in the last quarter century have diminished these concerns." A. Greeley, *American Catholics*, p. 48.

41. Leo XIII, "Longinqua Oceani," in John Tracy Ellis, *Documents of American Catholic History*, 3 volumes (Wilmington: Michael Glazier, 1987), II, p. 502.

42. George Huntson Williams, *The Mind of John Paul II* (New York: Seabury, 1981), p. 212; see also pp. 380–381.

43. Joseph Ratzinger and Vittorio Messori, *The Ratzinger Report* (San Francisco: Ignatius, 1985).

44. Robert Bellah et al., *Habits of the Heart* (New York: Harper & Row, 1985).

45. Marie Augusta Neal, "Civil Religion, Theology, and Politics in America," in *America in Theological Perspective*, Thomas McFadden, ed. (New York: Seabury, 1976), p. 102: "He speaks more as priest than sociologist. . . ."

46. There is a remarkable similarity between the experience of the Catholic Church in America and the current experience of the Catholic Church in southern India. See Thomas Gannon, "The Catholic Church in India," *America*, February 15, 1986, pp. 112–117.

47. Greeley, *American Catholics*, pp. 33–34, 98.

48. I hope to expand all of this into a book tentatively entitled *The People's Church* to be published in 1990 by Harper & Row.

Part Two

**THEOLOGY IN A RELIGIOUSLY
PLURAL WORLD**

THE COSMOLOGY OF RELIGIONS

Thomas Berry

The universe itself is the primary sacred community. All human religion should be considered as participation in the religious aspect of the universe itself. We are moving from the theology of religions and the anthropology of religions to the cosmology of religions. Especially in the past fifty years in America there has been intensive interest in the sociology of religions and the psychology of religions, but even more interest in the history of religions. All of these fall within the general designation of the anthropology of religions. Because none of these have been able to deal effectively with the evolutionary story of the universe or with the ecological crisis that is distrubing the earth in all its basic life systems, we are being led on to the cosmological dimension of the religious issue both from our efforts at academic understanding and from the practical issues of survival.

What is new about this sense of the religious mode of being of the universe is that the universe itself is now experienced as an *irreversible time developmental process* rather than as an abiding seasonal renewing universe. Not cosmos but cosmogenesis.

Thomas Berry is a historian of cultures and a writer with special concern for the foundation of cultures in their relations with the natural world. He was director of the graduate program in the History of Religions at Fordham University from 1966 until 1979. Founder of the Riverdale Center of Religious Research in Riverdale, New York, he has been its director since its beginning in 1970. He was president of the American Teilhard Association from 1975 until 1987. He has published a book on Buddhism and one entitled The Religions of India, *as well as a number of articles on the more significant human issues of the present. For the past ten years his writings have mainly been concerned with ecological issues. His book,* The Dream of the Earth, *was published in 1988 by Sierra Club Books.*

Also our knowledge of the universe is primarily through our *empirical observational sciences* rather than through intuitive processes. We are listening to the earth tell its story through the signals that it sends to us from outer space, through the light that comes to us from the stars, through the geological formations of the earth, and through a vast number of evidences of itself that the universe and its various components manifest to us.

In its every aspect the human is a participatory reality. We are members of the great universe community. We participate in its life. We are nourished by this community, we are instructed by this community, we are healed by this community. In and through this community we enter into communion with that numinous mystery whence all things depend for their existence and their activity. If this is true for the universe entire, it is also true in our relations with the earth.

From its own evidences we now know the story of the universe as emergent process in its fourfold sequence: the galactic story, the earth story, the life story, the human story. These constitute for us the primodial sacred story of the universe.

The original flaring forth of the universe carried the present within its fantastic energies as the present expresses those original energies in their articulated form. This includes all those spiritual developments that have occurred in the course of the centuries. The universe in its sequence of transformations carries within itself the comprehensive meaning of the phenomenal world. In recent secular times this meaning was perceived only in its physical expression. Now we perceive that the universe is a spiritual as well as a physical reality from the beginning.

This sacred dimension is especially evident in those stupendous moments of transformation through which the universe has passed in these fifteen billion years of its existence. These are moments of great spiritual as well as great physical significance; the privileged sacred moments in the Great Story. The numinous mystery of the universe now reveals itself in a developmental mode of expression, a mode never before available to human consciousness through observational processes.

Yet all this has seldom meant much to our modern western theologians. We remain concerned with scriptural interpretation, spiritual disciplines, our social justice programs, studies of liturgy, the history of Christianity, interreligious dialogue, psychology of religion, and religious pedagogy—all of them studies with little concern for the natural world as the primary bearer of religious consciousness. This is one of the basic reasons why both the physical and spiritual survival of the planet earth have become imperilled.

Presently we in the West think of ourselves as passing into another historical period or undergoing another cultural modification, a continuation of the long series of historical transformations that have taken place in the past and which are continuing on into the future. This is quite understandable. If we think, however, that the changes taking place in our times are simply another in the series of transformations that move from the classical-mediterranean period through the medieval to the industrial and the modern periods, we are missing the real order of magnitude of the changes taking place. We are at the end of an entire religious-civilizational period. In virtue of our new knowledge, we are changing our most basic relations to the world about us. These changes are of a unique order of magnitude.

Our new acquaintance with the universe as irreversible developmental process can be considered the most significant religious and spiritual, as well as the most significant scientific, event since the beginning of the more complex civilizations some five thousand years ago. At the same time we are bringing about the greatest devastation that the planet earth has ever experienced in the four and a half billion years of its formation. Such at least is the opinion of Norman Myers, a specialist in the biosystems of the planet. In his estimation we are bringing about an extinction spasm that is liable to result in ". . . the greatest single setback to life's abundance and diverstiy since the first flickerings of life almost four billion years ago."[1]

This is a remarkable statement. We are changing the chemistry of the planet, we are disturbing the biosystems, we are altering the geological structure and functioning of the planet, all of which took hundreds of millions and even billions of years to bring into being. In this process of closing down the life systems of the planet, we are in fact devastating a sacred world, making of the earth a wasteland, little realizing evidently, that as we lose the more gorgeous species of life on earth we thereby lose modes of divine presence, the very basis of our religious experience.

Because we are unable to enter effectively into the new mystique of the emergent universe that is available to us through our new modes of understanding, we are unable to prevent the disintegration of the life systems of the planet that is taking place through the misuse of that same scientific vision. Western religion and theology have not yet been able effectively to address these issues or to establish their own identity in this context. Nor have other religious traditions been any more successful. The main religious traditions have simply restated their belief and their spiritual disciplines in a kind of fundamentalist pattern. What I have indicated as our new experience of the religious being of the universe and of the planet earth is not perceived on any widespread scale within academic theological or religious circles.

We cannot, it seems to me, resolve the difficulties we face in this new situation by setting aside the entire scientific venture that has been in process over these past two centuries, especially during this twentieth century. It will not go away. Nor can we assume an attitude of indifference toward this new context of earthly existence. It is too powerful in its total effects. We must, it seems to me, find a way of interpreting the process itself. If interpreted properly, the scientific venture may even be one of the most significant spiritual disciplines of these times. This task is particularly urgent just now since this new mode of understanding is so powerful in its consequences on the very structure of the planet earth. We must learn to respond to its deepest spiritual content or else submit to the devastation that is before us.

I do not consider that fundamentalist assertions of our former traditions can themselves bring these forces under control. We are not engaged simply in academic inquiry. We are involved in the future of the planet in its geological and biological survival, as well as in the future of our human and spiritual well-being. We will bring about the physical and spiritual well-being of the planet entire or there will be neither physical nor spiritual well-being for any of our earthly forms of being.

The traditional religions have not dealt effectively with these issues or with our modern cosmological experience because they were not designed for such a universe. Traditional religions have been shaped within a dominant spatial mode of consciousness. The biblical religions, although they have a historical developmental perspective in dealing with the human spiritual process, have themselves a dominant spatial mode of consciousness as regards the universe itself. Biblical religions provide for the progress of the divine kingdom within an established universe that participates in the historical process in only a marginal manner. They seem to have as much difficulty as any other tradition in dealing with the developmental character of the universe.

Although the antagonism toward an evolutionary universe has significantly diminished, our limitations as theologians in speaking the language of this new cosmology in our religious understanding is everywhere evident. If much has been done in process theology in terms of the conceptions of the divine and the relations of the divine to the phenomenal world, this has been more in the realm of speculative theology. Rather little has been done in the empirical study of the cosmos itself as religious expression.

To envisage the universe in its religious dimension requires that we speak of the religious aspect of the original flaming forth of the universe, the religious role of the elements, the religious functioning of the earth and all its components. Since the human in its religious capacities emerges out of this cosmological process, the universe itself can be considered as the primary bearer of religious experience.

This way of thinking about the emergent universe provides a context for the future development of all the various religious traditions. Indeed, all the various peoples of the world, insofar as they are being educated in a modern context, are coming to identify themselves in time and space in terms of the universe as this is presently described by our modern sciences, even though they are not learning the more profound spiritual and religious meaning that is indicated by this new sense of the universe.

This story of the universe is at one time scientific, mythic, and mystical. Most elaborate in its scientific statement, it is among the simplest of creation stories. Most of all, it is the story that the universe tells about itself. We are finally overcoming our isolation from the universe and beginning to listen to the universe in some depth. If until recently we were autistic in relation to its more spiritual communication, this is no longer entirely true. In this understanding we have an additional context for religious understanding for all the traditions that can complement and expand previous religious views, much as our more recent cosmologies do not negate but add to the Newtonian world view and enable us to deal with questions that cannot be dealt with in the Newtonian context. So now, through our listening to the universe, we have additional depths of spiritual understanding that were not available through our traditional insights. Just as we can no longer live simply within the physical universe of Newton, so we can no longer live spiritually within the limits of our earlier traditions.

The first great contribution this new perspective on the universe makes to religious consciousness is the sense of participating in the creation process itself. We bear within us the impress of every transformation through which the unvierse and the planet earth have passed. The elements out of which we are composed were shaped in the supernova implosions. We passed through the period of inter-stellar dust dispersion. We were integral with the attractive forces that brought all those particles together in the original shaping of the earth. Especially in the rounded form of the planet we felt the gathering of the components of the earthly community and experienced the self-organizing spontaneities within the megamolecules out of which came the earliest manifestations of the life process and the transition to cellular and organic living forms. These same forces that brought forth the genetic codings of all the various species were guiding the movement of life on toward its latest expression in human consciousness.

This journey, considered as the sacred journey of the universe, is the personal journey of each individual. We cannot but marvel at this amazing sequence of transformations. No other creation story is more fantastic in its account of how things came to be in the beginning and how they came to be as they are, or how each of us attained the special determinations that give to us our personal identity. That we have the reflexive consciousness to appreciate and to celebrate this story is the superb aspect of our present period of history. The universe is the larger self of each person since the entire sequence of events that has transpired since the beginning of the universe has been required to establish each of us in the precise structure of our own being and in the larger community context in which we function.

Earlier periods and traditions have also experienced their intimacy with the universe, especially in those moments of cosmic renewal that took place periodically, mostly in the springtime of the year. Through these grand rituals powerful energies flowed into the world. Yet it was the *renewal* of the world or the sustaining of an abiding universe, not the irreversible and non-repeatable *original* emergence of the world, that was taking place. Only such an irreversible self-organizing world such as that in which we live could provide this special mode of participation in the emergent creation itself. This irreversible sequence of transformations is taking shape through our own activities as well as through the activities of the multitude of component members of the universe community.

Yet it is not a straight line sequence since the component elements of the universe move in pulsations, in sequences of integration-disintegration, in spiral or circular patterns, especially on earth in seasonal expressions of life renewal. On earth especially, the basic tendencies of the universe seem to explode in an overwhelming display of geological, biological and human modes of expression, from the tiniest particles of matter and their movement to the shaping and the vast movements of the seas and continents, with the clash and rifting of tectonic plates, the immense hydrological cycles, the spinning of the earth on its own axis, its circling of the sun and the bursting forth of the millionfold variety of living forms.

Throughout this confused, disorderly, even chaotic process, we witness an enormous creativity. The quintessence of this great journey of the universe is the priority of disequilibrium over equilibrium. Although so much of the disequilibrium fails in its reaching toward a new and greater integration, the only way to consistent creativity is through the breakdown of exiting unities. That disturbed periods of history are the creative periods can be seen in the dark ages of Europe as well as in the period of breakdown of imperial order at the end of the Han period in China around the year 200 CE.

So too religiously the grand creativity is found in the stressful moments. It was in a period of spiritual confusion that Buddha appeared to establish a new spiritual discipline. The prophets appeared in the disastrous moments of Israel. Christianity established itself in the social and religious unsettlement of the late Roman period. So now we find ourselves in the greatest period of disturbance that the earth has ever known, a period when both the human and the natural worlds are severely threatened in their continued existence. The identity of our human fate with the destinies of the planet itself was never more clear.

This new context of thinking also establishes a new context for liturgy. Presently our liturgies give magnificent expression to the periods of seasonal renewal, and also at times to incidental historical events or personal achievements. Especially in these moments of renewal, in the springtime of the year, the psychic energies of the human community are renewed in their deepest sources by their participation in the deep changes within the natural world itself.

But now a new sequence of liturgical celebrations is needed, celebrations based on those stupendous moments when the great cosmological transformations took place. Even more than the great moments of seasonal renewal, these moments of cosmic transformation must be considered as sacred moments. Only by a proper celebration of these moments can our own human spiritual development take place in an integral manner. Indeed, these were the decisive moments in the shaping of human consciousness as well as in the shaping of our physical being.

First among these celebrations might be that of the emergent moment of the universe itself as a spiritual as well as a physical event. This was the beginning of religion just as it was the beginning of the world. The human mind and all its spiritual capacities began with this first shaping of what was to become the universe as we know it. As with origin moments generally, this moment is a supremely sacred moment carrying within it the high destinies of the universe in its intellectual and spiritual capacities as well as its physical shaping and living expression.

Of special import at this time is the rate of emergence of the universe and the curvature of space whereby all things hold together. The rate of emergence in those first instants had to be precise to the hundred billionth of a fraction. Otherwise the universe would have exploded or collapsed. The rate of emergence was such that the consequent curvature of the universe was sufficiently closed to hold the universe together within its gravitational bondings and yet open enough so that the creative process could continue through these billions of years and provide the guidance and the energies we need as we move through the dangers of the present on into a more creative if not into a more secure future.

This bonding of the universe whereby every reality of the universe attracts and is attracted to every other being in the universe was the condition for the rise of human affection. It was the beginning and most comprehensive expression of the divine love that pervades the universe in its every aspect and enables the creative processes of the universe to continue.

It might be appropriate, then, if this beginning moment of the universe were designated as the context for religious celebration, even for a special liturgy, available for all the peoples of the planet as they begin to sense their identity in time and space in terms of the evolutionary story of the universe.

A long list of other transformation moments might be selected for celebration since these moments establish both the spiritual and the

physical contours for further development of the entire world. At
first it seems difficult to appreciate that these moments are supreme
spiritual moments, for we are so accustomed to thinking of the
universe either in purely physical terms or in mythical modes of
expression.

Among these supreme moments of transformation we might list
the supernova explosions that took place as the first generation of
stars collapsed into themselves in some trillions of degrees of heat,
sufficient to bring into existence the heavier elements out of the
original hydrogen and helium atoms, and then exploded into the
stardust with which our own solar system and the planet earth
shaped themselves. This entire process can be considered as a
decisive spiritual moment as well as a decisive physical moment in
the story of the universe. New levels of subjectivity came into being,
new modalities of bonding, new possibilities for those inner spontaneities whereby the universe carries out its capacities for self-
organization. Along with all this came the magnificent array of
differentiated elements with the capacity for all the intricate associations that now became possible. Indeed the earth as we know it, in
all its spiritual as well as its physical aspects, became a possibility.

To ritualize this moment would provde that depth of appreciation
for ourselves and for the entire creative process that is needed just
now when the entire earthly process has become trivialized and we
have no established way of entering into the spiritual dimension of
the story that the universe is telling us about itself and the shaping
of the earth and of all living beings and finally of ourselves. Our role
is precisely to be that being in whom this total process reflects on
and celebrates itself and its numinous origins in a special mode of
conscious self-awareness. At our highest moments we fulfill this role
through the association of our liturgies with the supreme liturgy of
the universe itself. Awareness that the universe itself is the primary
liturgy has been recognized by the human community since the
earliest times of which we have information. The human personality
as well as the various types of human communities have always
sought to insert themselves into space and time through this integration with the great movement of the heavens and the cycles of the
seasons seen as celebratory events with profound numinous significance. What is needed now is integration with the new sequence of
liturgies related to the irreversible transformation sequence whereby
the world as we know it has come into being.

So we could go through the whole range of events whereby the universe took shape and inquire not simply into the physical reality but the religious meaning and direction of the entire process. A great many of the mysteries of the earth could be celebrated. The invention of photosynthesis is especially important in this context. Then the coming of the trees and later the coming of the flowers one hundred million years ago.

Only such a selective seqence of religious celebrations could enable the cosmology of religions to come into being. If the sacred history of the biblical world is celebrated with such reverence, how much more the sacred history of the universe and of the planet earth needs to be celebrated. In all of this we can observe the continuity of the human religious process with the emergent process of the universe itself, with the shaping of the planet earth, with the emergence of life and the appearance of the human.

We find this difficult because we are not accustomed to think of ourselves as integral with or subject to the universe, to the planet earth, or to the community of living beings—especially not in our religious or spiritual lives which identify the sacred precisely as that which is atemporal and unchanging even though it is experienced within the temporal and the changing. We think of ourselves as the primary referent and the universe as participatory in our own achievements. Only the present threats to the viability of the human as a species and to the life systems of the earth are finally causing us to reconsider our situation.

When we turn now to the question of theology in the context of religious pluralism we might best situate our inquiry within this same perspective of the universe and in those basic tendencies of the universe that govern its entire structure and functioning. These tendencies can be identified as differentiation, subjectivity, and communion. The universe by definition is a differentiating process. The universe is not homogenous smudge. It is composed of clearly articulated entities each of which is unique and irreplaceable. Secondly, each of the component members of the universe has its own interiority, its radiant intelligibility, its spontaneity, its subjectivity. Thirdly, each member of the universe community is bonded inseparably with every other member of the community. The entire universe is genetically related. Every individual being is cousin to every other being in the universe since everything emerges by an unbroken sequence from the same physical-spiritual source. This cousin relationship is especially valid in the relationship between the various forms of living beings. Biological studies of the present would not

be possible without drawing the genealogical tree of relatedness of
the various orders of life. But even in the non-living world nothing
is itself without everything else. Each member of the universe is
immediately present to and influencing every other being in the
universe.

The religious traditions of the world would seem to follow this
same pattern of differentiation, subjectivity and communion. If there
is to be religion it will be differentiated in its expression. Each will
be unique and irreplaceable. Secondly, each will have its own inner
spontaneities, its own subjective formation, its own communication
of the divine, its own spiritual discipline. Thirdly, each will be its
full self only in its bonding with the other traditions. Each will also
have a universal mission as well as its particular mission to its own
initiated members.

As Saint Thomas tells us, in diversity is "the perfection of the
universe."[2] If there is to be revelation, it will not be singular but
differentiated. If there is grace, it will be differentiated in its expression. If there are spiritual disciplines or sacraments or sacred communities, they will be differentiated. The greater the differentiation,
the greater the perfection of the whole, since perfection is in the
interacting diversity. The extent of the diversity is the measure of
the perfection so long as the diversity is integral with the larger
unity of the whole.

This requires a threefold sequence of emphasis in the various
traditions. First there is the primordial experience expressed in an
oral or written form, the scriptural period. This take place by an
isolation process. Secondly there is the deepening of the tradition, a
patristic period, when the implications of the original experience
are elaborated in contact with the larger life process. Thirdly there
is the period of expansion, of interaction with other traditions in
their more evolved phase. These three phases are not mutually
exclusive since some interaction of traditions is present from the
beginning both in assisting positively and in providing a polarity of
opposition.

The importance of the isolation and interior development phases
can be seen in each of the major traditions that have so powerfully
influenced the religious life of the human community. In India, for
instance, its profound mystical and metaphysical developments of
the early first millennium BCE required a special type of psychic
intensity. In China the focus of attention was much more cosmological. The divine was understood as Shang-ti, as T'ien, as the great

mystery presenting itself in the vast cosmological cycles in which the human was also a functional presence. The divine, the natural, and the human were thus present to each other in the grand sacrificial reality of the universe itself and in its rhythmic pulsations. So too with the Japanese and their sense of the aesthetic expression of the numinous in the natural world. Their cultivation of spiritual simplicity and spontaneity is unique in the human community. So with the presence of the Great Spirit throughout the natural world and in the depths of the human in the American Indian traditions. In every case these ultimate orientations toward reality and value originate in an interior depth so awesome that the experience is perceived as coming from a transphenomenal source, as revelatory of the ultimate mystery whence all things emerge into being.

All of these traditions were substantially complete in their earlier expression. Hinduism in its proper line of development will not likely go beyond its expression in the Hymns, the Upanishads, the Epics, the Bhagavadgita. Buddhism in its proper line of development will hardly go beyond its expression in the early dialogues, the Dhammapada, the Sutta Nipata, the Lotus Sutra, the verses of Nagarjuna, the Vimalakirti Story. So with the Confucian classics, the Four Books, the Tao Te Ching, the Writings of Chuang-tzu. These are all full and perfect in their own context although each is a vital expanding process with an ever-renewing series of transformations through the centuries.

The deepest values of each tradition have been in its own distinctive insights. It would not have been possible for India's experience of the transphenomenal world to be developed in its full intensity simultaneously with the biblical experience of the revelatory aspect of historical events. Nor could China have developed its insight into the mysterious Tao of the universe simultaneously with the high metaphysics of India. Nor would the experience of the Great Spirit manifested in the natural world had by the indigenous peoples of the North American continent be compatible with a simultaneous experience of the Buddhist doctrine of emptiness or the Neoplatonic doctrine of the Logos.

None of these experiences are rivals of the others. Each needs a certain isolation from the others for its own inner development. Each is supreme in its own order. Each is destined for universal diffusion throughout the human community. Each is needed by the others to constitute the perfection of the revelatory experience. Each has its microphase, its initiated institutional adherents, and its macrophase or universal presence throughout the human community. We are now living in the macrophase period of development of most religious traditions, the period of extensive influence without formal initiation. When the traditions are seen in their relations to each other, the full tapestry of the revelatory experience can be observed. In the fabric of the whole, the numinous quality of the universe reveals itself most fully. The traditions are, as it were, dimensions of each other.

This leads us to a final question in our consideration of the various religious traditions, the question of the religious role of the human as species. History is being made now in every aspect of the human endeavor not within or between nations, or ethnic groups, or cultures, but between humans as species and the larger earth community. We have been too concerned with ourselves as nations, ethnic groups, cultures, religions. We are presently in need of a species and inter-species orientation in law, economics, politics, education, medicine, religion, and whatever else concerns the human.

If until recently we could be unconcerned with the species level of human activities, this is no longer the situation. We need now not a national or international economy or even a global economy; we need a species economy, an economy that will relate the human as species to the community of species on the planet, an economy that will ultimately be an integral earth economy. Already this is beginning in the awareness that the human is overwhelming the entire productivity of the earth with its excessive demands. The human is using up some forty percent of the entire productivity of the earth. This leaves an inadequate resource base for the larger community of life. The cycle of renewal is overburdened, to such an extent that even the renewable life systems are being extinguished.

We could in a corresponding manner outline the need for a species, an inter-species, and even a planetary legal system as the only viable system that can be functionally effective in the present situation. We could say the same thing as regards medicine, for the issue of species health has come into view and beyond that the health of the planet. Human health on a toxic planet is a contradiction. Yet we are, apparently, trying to achieve just that. The primary objective of the medical profession must be to foster the integral health of the earth itself. Only afterwards can human health be adequately attended to.

In each of these cases—in economics, law, medicine—the planet itself constitutes the normative reference. There already exists a planetary economics. The proper role of the human is to foster the economics of the earth and to see that our human economics functions in relation to and subordinate to the planetary economy. The same thing could be said for the realms of law and governance. There exists a comprehensive participatory governance of the planet. Every member of the earth community rules and is ruled by the other members of the community in such a remarkable manner that the community as a whole and its individual members have prospered remarkably well over the centuries and even the millennia. The proper role for the human is to articulate its own governance within this planetary governance.

What we have not discussed so extensively has been a religion of the human as species. This is an extremely difficult idea to articulate clearly. This concept implies a prior sense of the religious dimension of the natural world. If the earth is an economic mode of being as well as a biological mode of being, then it might not be too difficult to think of the earth as having a religious mode of being. This seems to be explicit in many of the scriptures of the world although this concept is yet to be articulated effectively in the context of our present understanding of the great story of the universe. In general, we think of the earth as joining in the religious expression of the human rather than the human joining in the religious expression of the earth. This has been the difficulty in most spheres of activity. We consistently think of the human as primary and the earth as derivative rather than thinking of the earth as primary and the human as derivative. Our best model for this new vision within the context of a spatial model of consciousness is probably found in the classical traditions of China. So far, within the perspective of a time-developmental mode of consciousness there is as yet no model.

NOTES

1. Tropical Forests and Their Species: Going, Going. . . ?" in *Biodiversity*, E. O. Wilson, ed. (Washington, D.C.: National Academy Press, 1988), pp. 33–34.

2. *Summa Theologica*, I, q. 47, art. 1: "Therefore, the perfection of the universe, which consists of the diversity of things, would thus be a thing of chance, which is impossible."

VISION AND PRACTICALITY
A RESPONSE TO THOMAS BERRY

Rita M. Gross

My task is to respond, from a Buddhist point of view, to Thomas Berry's vision of "a new revelatory experience . . . taking place in our times through our new story of the universe as known by our observational sciences." Obviously, as is appropriate for theology in an age of pluralism, I speak as a Buddhist who also has roots in Jewish and Christian spirituality, and who has been deeply moved by the most potent spiritual movement within those religions to-day—feminism.

I can find no basis in Buddhism, or any other religion, for any response other than gratitude for and deep agreement with Thomas Berry's vision of planetary religion and our species' place within it. Therefore, I will take as my task mainly to make some comments on Buddhist affinities with his vision and to tease out some practicalities, drawn from both Buddhism and feminism, that could ground his vision more firmly on earth.

In my first set of comments, I will focus on three points in Berry's essay which strike me as especially important and for which I see significant Buddhist affinities. These affinities revolve around key

Rita M. Gross, Associate Professor of Comparative Studies in Religion at the University of Wisconsin at Eau Claire, is well-known for her articles on Buddhism and feminism and for her involvement in Buddhist-Christian dialogue. Her most recent publication is Unspoken Worlds: Women's Religious Lives, published by Wadsworth Press. She is Vice-President of the Society for Buddhist-Christian Studies and is a judge for annual book awards presented by the American Academy of Religion. She also serves on the editorial board of several journal and lectures widely on topics related to feminism, Buddhism, and inter-faith dialogue.

traditional points of Buddhist teaching that certainly provide a firm basis for Berry's statements, even though they have not been articulated and spun out in the modern framework of observational sciences and an evolutionary perspective.

The single overriding insight of Berry's vision, at least as I understand it, is that we must see ourselves, in my words not his, as *within the cosmos, not above* it or *separate* from it. He speaks of "participating in the creation process itself" and of ourselves as "integral with or subject to the universe, to the planet earth [and] to the community of living beings . . . in our religious or spiritual lives. . . ." Though perhaps not with the same celebratory understanding, Buddhism has always seen humanity as *part of* the planetary and even extra-planetary cosmic system, not separate from it to superior to it. The basic teaching about cause and effect—*pratitya-samutpada* or co-dependent co-origination—articulates this sense of a vast web of interdependence, human and non-human. Perhaps the best known indication of this Buddhist at-homeness in the world is found in the Zen tradition, with its famous gardens and its respect for simple daily life-tasks. Less well-known, but theoretically as important, are Vajrayana teachings about the sacredness of the phenomenal world.

Nevertheless, in certain ways, traditional Buddhist ways of verbalizing this vision of interdependence are perhaps too homocentric; though the human is clearly *within* this world system, nevertheless, within this cosmos, a human birth is evaluated as the most fortunate (but not the more privileged or powerful) of rebirths because it alone contains the potential for enlightenment. Furthermore, like Christianity with its emphasis on redemption, Buddhism often presents itself as a discipline leading to *freedom from* the world process and painful entanglement within it. It is important to note, however, that though the quest for *freedom from* the world process is an important interpretation in Buddhism, there is as much emphasis on *freedom within* the world process as freedom from it, especially in Zen and Vajrayana forms of Buddhism.

Berry's vision depends upon an appreciation of change and impermanence in an evolving universe. He sees this as contrasting with conventional religions ". . . which identify the sacred precisely as that which is atemporal and unchanging." On this point traditional Buddhism does not conform to Berry's norm for a conventional religion, but is much closer to his vision. According to many traditional teachers, the fulcrum of Buddhist teaching is all-pervading impermanence. When we try to fight it, we mire ourselves in suffering; when we find our ease in impermanence, we also experience freedom within the world process.

Furthermore, Berry's vision depends not only on appreciation of change but also on an evolutionary perspective—an understanding of "the developmental character of the universe." He especially emphasizes that "our religious traditions must emerge from our perception of the universe, how it came to be in the beginning, how it came to be as it is . . ." On this point, Buddhism offers an interesting contrast, since, though its vision of the cosmos is at least as vast spatially and temporary as the cosmos of evolutionary mythology and Berry's understanding, Buddhism has always eschewed creation mythologies. This lack of interest is not because the problem is unimportant but because it is insoluble and detracts energy from more immediate, central, and practical religious problems and discoveries. From this contrast we might learn the extent to which even evolutionary mythology is still within the linear rather than cyclical, within the progressive rather than karmic, views of time that characterize western rather than Indian modes of spirituality. I am not suggesting that this represents a problem with Berry's vision; I am simply pointing out that while it may be helpful to ground a vision of our existence as citizens within the cosmos in an evolutionary perspective, it is not necessary to do so.

The Buddhist problem with creation myths has always been their inevitably theoretical and speculative character, which seduces one from attention to the present situation. A reasonable response might be that *if* we really understood our place within and our current responsibility for the planetary process, we would inevitably want to act in accord with that understanding. A Buddhist reply might well be that such understanding, such vision, by itself, accomplishes little. It is important, even crucial, to link vision with practicality.

In Buddhism, especially Vajrayana Buddhism, there are many linked dyadic unities, such as vision and practicality. They convey the sense that reality is multi-faceted, dynamic and plural, yet coherent, in perhaps much the same way that polytheism conveys the same message. They also indicate that to achieve one's potential, one cannot focus monolithically on a single ideal but must balance often opposing but complementary ideals. Symbolically, all these dyadic unities can be assimilated with and perhaps derived from the polarity of masculine and feminine principles (which are not especially linked with or limited to women and men). "Vision and practicality" is one such important dyadic unity—in which, incidentally, vision is linked with the masculine pole and practicality with the feminine.

In my middle set of comments, I want to turn from vision to practicality, for if there is an arena in which Buddhism can add to, rather than merely confirm, Berry's vision, it is in the realm of practicality, in the insight that vision and practicality are a dyadic unit and all the vision in the world accomplishes little without practicality. Furthermore, if I wanted to hear more from Berry as I read his exciting essay, it was not in the realm of vision but in the realm of practicality.

My suggestions for practicality rely not only on Buddhist tradition, but on feminism, since feminism, especially religious feminism, has always articulated concerns similar to Berry's for our kinship with all that lives on earth and for the earth as a living organism. In fact, among contemporary theologies, none is more consonant with Berry's vision than feminism. Especially noteworthy for their affinity with feminism are his statements that those species most fit to survive are those that can exist in cooperation rather than antagonism with other species, and his implication that we should think of humans as joining in the religious expression of the earth rather than vice versa.

The issue at the level of practicality, I suggest, is to turn from the macro-level of planetary religion in which we participate as a species to the micro-micro level of the realm of familiar and immediate everyday interactions and reactions. We need to understand, in a very practical way, why people are so out of sync with the world, so aggressive and acquisitive towards it, so dangerous to the global system and to themselves, so ready to engage in an "extinction spasm," affecting not only other life forms but also ourselves. I believe that important answers to such questions are to be found on the micro-micro level world of everyday relationships and that without attention to this mundane and yet all-pervasive practical realm of existence, no vision of our co-dependent place within the world system will encourage appropriate and necessary changes in our behavior.

In this middle set of comments, I want especially to look at two interlocking and intensely practical reasons why we are so dangerous to the planet and to ourselves, and also to try to point to some practical remedies in each case. The first reason why we become so dangerous is ego, classically defined by Buddhism and amplified in feminist understanding, as dis-ease with impermanence and desire to secure territory and dominate others in the futile attempt for security. The second explanation for our dangerous proclivities could be seen as alienation, defined by feminism, in agreement with Buddhist understandings, as dis-ease in our day-to-day interactions; such alienation is manifested in oppression and loneliness.

This is critical because when people are trying to secure territory/ ego or when they experience alienation and oppression, they *will be* aggressive, self-aggrandizing, and destructive. The vision of a peaceful world in which we take our rightful *humble* place *among* the many species *within* the world system cannot be achieved under such conditions. Thus the Buddhist and feminist explanations for our destructive and self-destructive tendencies are thoroughly enmeshed.

In Buddhist psychology, ego is a short-hand term for many conventional psychological and spiritual tendencies that cause harm both to ourselves and to others. Fundamentally, ego is uncomfortableness with the all-pervasive impermanence that characterizes our existence. It is the always futile attempt to stop the flow of experience, to find permanent ease, security, and bliss. That effort, of course, fails; the failure is not so serious as the suffering caused by the attempt to escape impermanence. The suffering covers the range from personal psychological trauma and distress to planetary disaster.

The virtue of locating such a practical cause for our self-destruction and our geocide is that, knowing the cause of things, we have some possibility of behaving differently. Buddhism has long devoted itself to exploring how we might behave differently. Two recommendations stand out. The first is a contemplative exercise. One thinks that the reason one is doing what one does is to avoid suffering. From this one can realize that all sentient beings, likewise, do not want to suffer. Therefore, one tries to avoid being the cause of suffering. But to bring this contemplative exercise into reality in everyday life, most people find a spiritual discipline, an actual meditation discipline to be quite useful, even necessary. Buddhist meditation practices involving mindfulness and awareness, ground one sufficiently and slow one down enough to be able to notice one's acts and their consequences. Having the proper vision is insufficient. One also needs a practical method to enable one to realize the vision.

Perhaps, if Buddhist practicality has a limitation, it is that it has not explored sufficiently some of the basic interpersonal causes of destructiveness on all levels from self-destruction to geocide. Feminist thought would locate the primary cause of such destruction in alienation. Alienation is another short-hand term, fundamentally pointing to inadequacy in everyday, face-to-face interactions. This basic inadequacy results in oppression and loneliness.

Alienation and oppression are catch-phrases that easily cover a multitude of sins. Let me point the finger more specifically. Though there may be a depth cause, analyzed by Buddhist psychology, in the processes leading to alienation and oppression, the fundamental sociological and empirical problem is, in my view, easily located. A patriarchal society—and almost all or all non-tribal societies are patriarchal—is a society characterized by relationships of power over, and therefore, unable to produce anything except alienation and oppression—for men as well as for women in the long run, though not always in the short run. For generations feminists have, correctly in my view, hypothesized that the sexual alienation between male and female is the most basic form of alienation, the alienation that leads to relationships characterized by power over another. The links between this sexual alienation and consequent economic, political, and sociological alienations have often been demonstrated. The link between patriarchy and ecological alienation and oppression is perhaps less well known, but it too has often been traced.

So, rather than the problems of patriarchy being a small corner that is of optional concern, not too urgent, something that can be worked on when "bigger" problems have been solved—if even then—the sexual alienation and oppression, so minute and routine, so day-to-day and omnipresent, may be the cornerstone of the whole edifice needing to be dismantled. It is obvious in a way. If women lack freedom regarding their sexuality, their bodies, their very persons and lives; if men compete relentlessly with each other in economic and political arenas, even to the point of economic disaster and nuclear warfare, and if children are socialized to fill those roles, while also being taught cultural and religious chauvinism, the fear of differences, and the love of competition and hierarchy, then people will hardly have an inclination to love Earth as our own bodies and treat her as such.

These causes may seem to be insurmountable, part of "nature" itself. Yet teaching people that patriarchy and power over are inevitable is only part of patriarchy's self-perpetuation mechanism. It is, therefore, instructive to study pre-patriarchal societies and the emergence of patriarchy into history. We can also analyze what kind of society requires and benefits from patriarchal gender roles. From such a study, we can learn that patriarchy is not inevitable and, furthermore, that patriarchal gender roles and values are obsolete, dysfunctional, and irrelevant in current conditions. So one very practical measure to be taken involves recognizing the irrelevance of gender roles and acting accordingly, both in personal life and in terms of public policy.

This transformation will involve working with the feminine and feminist value of attention to relationships as primary in human life. Unsatisfactory intimate relationships, fear of intimacy and vulnerability, and shallow or superficial friendships are the chief reasons why people become involved in relationships of power over—over other people, other species, or the earth itself. Serious, concerted, deep attention to relationship as a primary concern and value, not merely in private life, but also in public life, will be healing. We need to live lives in which, whether we are women or men, relationship is as important as work, scholarship, prestige, and economic success. We also need to recognize the deep spiritual significance of relationship and friendship. If we truly understand the spiritually and personally transformative quality of relationship, then we will train ourselves in relationship as seriously as we train ourselves in scholarship and in spiritual disciplines. Imagine a world in which people, men as well as women, were as concerned about caring for each other, and spent as much time doing it, as is currently invested in scholarship, various religious practices, and making money!

In concluding this section of my comments, I want to reiterate that attention to this micro-micro level of intimate relationships and friendships is critical to being able to realize the kind of vision Berry talks about. These are not *trivial* or *merely private* and *personal* concerns, as so many of us were taught to believe under patriarchy's tutelage. Just as much as we have not seen ourselves *within* the cosmos, so we have not learned how to befriend humans or to see people instead of roles. The two are linked. Ecological health is not possible without psychological and spiritual health. That statement is also true for all the economic, political, and social steps between the planetary macro-level and the micro-micro level.

My final set of comments deals with some rather controversial issues with which most or all world religions have not come to terms. Essentially, all religions need to rethink the phrase "reverence for life." Though my suggestions may seem radical, I see no way to realize Berry's vision with less radical means.

He points out that planetary disaster is resulting from "misuse of that same scientific vision" that is the source of the new relevatory experience he points to in his opening sentence. He also points out provocatively that "the direction of the earth which in former times was so completely controlled by natural forces has been extensively given over to the human community . . ."

With science and technology, we have entered into the world process in ways that are often destructive for the ecological process precisely because, at the level of the human, we use science mainly to promote, often mindlessly, the simple quantification of human life—more lives, lived longer, consuming more. But we know from all religious mythologies that there is a necessary balance between finite life and finite death. If we want to intervene on one side of the equation as human co-creators, we must also be willing to intervene on the other side of the equation. If we are unwilling to limit as well as to expand the quantity of life, it will eventually be done for us— through warfare and famine, or possibly new uncontrollable disease, incredibly painful methods of balancing the equation.

But traditional religions seem willing to intervene in the "natural forces" only to create more quantity of human life and then naively claim that obedience to divine command prohibits them from using those same interventions in "natural process" to control the quantity of human life. If divine command is the issue, one would think that divine command prohibited intervention in natural processes altogether, not merely intervention only when it counterbalances previous interventions! If we want to take the initiative to be co-creators of the world, as we have, then we have to be willing to be fully co-creators, not merely co-creators of quantity of human life.

Some familiar examples will demonstrate how thoroughly we pursue the perverse logic involved in selective intervention in "natural processes." We create life-saving technology, but then don't want to think about turning it off. We engage in fertility research in an over-populated world. People constantly seek to limit sex education, birth control, and access to abortion in an over-populated planet. My health insurance—a good insurance paid for by my employer, the University of Wisconsin—will not pay for my simple inexpensive birth control device, though it would pay full costs for pregnancy and childbirth. Do we need a more obvious example of the ludicrous extent to which we want to intervene in nature only to promote quantity of human life!

Clearly, many very difficult and painful ethical problcms are brought up by this obvious misuse of scientific knowledge. But the basic demands are inescapable and obvious. If humanity is overburdening the planet, which is obvious, and if the planet will eventually, perhaps soon, disintegrate under this burdne, then the human overburden needs to be lessened. There are clear implications about levels of per capita consumption required to lessen the human destruction of the planet. But equally obvious is the need to discourage rather than encourage growth in the sheer numbers of humans. It is critical to reverse the totally out-of-control and self-destructive rate of population growth that has wrought such havoc with the planet for the last few centuries. For only in the last few centuries, since we have so successfully intervened in "natural processes" with science and modern medicine, has run-away population growth become so problematic. Before that, the population remained relatively stable, due to natural processes. How much more sane and humane to limit population culturally through discouragement rather than the current encouragement of excessive reproduction. Our other option is to "leave it to Providence" in the form of famine, warfare, and new forms of disease.

When we intervene in the planetary process to create mere quantity of life, which ultimately produced painful lives and wretched deaths, we do so because we do not really recognize and embrace our finitude, our kinship and community *within* the world system. Rather, we still identify ourselves with an infinite transcedent entity and think we can live by its rules and values rather than with the demands of completely being part of an interdependent and impermanent matrix of life. The havoc wrought by this misidentification argues forcefully against the whole traditional theological system— but that's another topic.

Reverence for life is consonant with appreciating our finitude and may be dependent upon it, a point that has been well-articulated in much feminist theology, especially in recent work exploring goddess theology. The link between reverence for life and really embracing our finitude and interdependence within a planetary system that admits of no transcedent infinite entity is also commonplace in Buddhism. Thus, I suggest that Dr. Berry's wonderful vision be grounded in these practicalities.

EXAMINING GENDER ISSUES IN INTERRELIGIOUS DIALOGUE

Maura O'Neill

Among the goals of interreligious dialogue are the elimination of prejudice and conflict and the promotion of peace. In order for dialogue to be effective, however, it must take place in an open and nonjudgmental manner among leaders and practitioners of various religious perspectives. My concern in this paper is to raise the question: How can such a dialogue take place if a major perspective in each tradition, that of women, continues to be ignored?

Besides the noticeable absence of women from both the literature and the conversation, there exists an androcentric bias which permeates both the content and procedure of interreligious dialogue. This fact became clear to me after attending three dialogues at Claremont, California. Those engaged in these particular exchanges were not taking into account women's studies or women's experiences in any of the world religions. Because of this omission, important ideas were either being ignored or being presented as if for the first time. For example, Christians engaged in dialogue recognize that they have to work on a Christology which is far less

Maura O'Neill is an Associate Professor of Philosophy at Chaffey Community College (Alta Loma, CA). She received her M.A. in Theology at St. Michael's College (Winooski, VT), and is presently finishing her doctoral dissertation in Philosophy of Religion at the Claremont Graduate School (Claremont, CA). Active in the Women's Ordination Conference, she has also worked in Roman Catholic adult education programs and campus ministry. She is also a member of a Trialogue group in Southern California consisting of Jews, Christians, and Muslims. In 1988 she organized an interreligious dialogue among women which met in Claremont and brought together nine women participants from five religious traditions. This present essay is a reflection of the proceedings of that conference.

exclusive than that of the past. The belief that Jesus Christ is the only way to salvation or liberation needs to be reexamined as indeed it is by people such as John Hick and Raimundo Panikkar. But the question of the uniqueness of Jesus Christ is also being seriously considered by scholars such as Rosemary Ruether and others doing Christology from a feminist perspective. Shouldn't all the alternative Christologies be brought to the dialogue table and not just selective ones?

Also, much of the current dialogue centers around a search for commonality. This search has led some theologians to speculate that the common element in all world religions is the struggle for justice. Paul Knitter writes, "the preferential option for the oppressed serves as the condition for the possibility of dialogue—that which makes it possible for different religions to speak to and understand each other."[1] He sees justice as "the arena where Hindus and Muslims, Buddhists and Christians and Jews, can sense, and begin to speak about, that which unites them."[2] It seems to me that such a starting point requires attention to the injustices that have characterized women's experience and women's social status in the religions of the world. If justice is the common ground, should not women's voices, which are being raised around the world, be heard, and their quest for a more just participation in life be a major issue? Admittedly not all religions contain the same types of oppressive attitudes toward women, and women in these religions often view both the type and the extent of oppression differently from one another. It is much easier to define economic poverty and human rights violations than it is to define sexism in a particular religion. Perhaps this ambiquity of meaning has been one of the causes of the silence about women and also a reason why opening the discussion is such a challenge.

Perhaps, also, there are other reasons for the absence of women's issues at the dialogue table. Perhaps they, the issues as well as the women themselves, are too peripheral. What place would a woman's experience of oppression have in a very academic discussion of the theories of the personal vs. non-personal ultimate reality? Perhaps, too, the way they speak as well as what they speak about is too out of character for "real" academic discussion. Could we really consider personal accounts and self-revelations crucial for the exchange of information about belief systems? If any of these questions are raised as reasons for excluding women, then they indicate that the paternalistic attitude prevalent in so much of the academic work done today is also present in the arena of interreligious dialogue. This scepticism about the inclusiveness of dialogue was underlined when I witnessed the presence of two token women at the Claremont conferences and recall specific incidents in which their contributions were dismissed.

Initially it was my purpose to examine the effects that women's participation would have on the current interreligious dialogue. A closer examination and experience of the process of interreligious dialogue among women, however, made it clear to me how deeply rooted and complex are gender issues within the conversation among different religious believers. Because of the nature of these issues, I contend that there is a need for women to talk first among themselves and to address some of the unique problems peculiar to their situation and hence to their discussion. Only after this has been accomplished can a meeting of women and men be effective and enriching. Therefore, the issues to be examined at this point are (1) why women need to engage in their own dialogue and (2) how this dialogue could proceed most effectively.

I. Women Must Talk to Women

In an effort to explore some of the answers to these questions, I convened a group of nine women representing five major world religions for a conference in Claremont, California on April 16–17, 1988. The results of this meeting were not only extremely fruitful and interesting but taught me much about the content and method, advantages and problems of dialogue among women. It is mostly from this experience that I now offer some reflections.

The conference was spearheaded by remarks made by L. J. "Tess" Tessier who also attended those same three conferences that I did in Claremont. She observed that personal, embodied experiences tend to be devalued in an academic discussion of the disembodied ultimate in order to focus on a common oneness, or, as John Hick would term it, the "one infinite reality."[3] If we concentrated on the embodied particularities, we would have to consider too many specific cultural and personal differences. A commonality, therefore, could be achieved only on the level of the abstract. This situation lead Dr. Tessier to ask, "Is the very process of interreligious dialogue as it is currently conceived a patriarchal process in which we necessarily participate by accepting the process?"[4] If the answer to this question is yes, then we must put aside this process. The Muslim scholar

Riffat Hassan, expressed disturbance at the fact that men's thoughts, for example those of Huston Smith, Wilfred Cantwell Smith, and John Hick, have structured so much of the interreligious dialogue, and she stated, "I am personally not very interested in discussing my feminist research or my feminist experience in response to or in terms of what these men have thought."[5]

These words expressed what grew to be the consensus of the group, one which convinced me that women must meet among themselves, dialogue, reflect, write and publish. They must set their own agenda. They must work on the content and method of dialogue. They must agree, disagree, sift, sort and develop a body of experiences and write about them. Once this is done, perhaps then we can enter into another dialogue in order to understand not just the differences between the traditions but to understand the gender differences that exist both within each tradition and across traditional lines.

II. Problems in a Women's Dialogue

Once we've established the value of conducting a dialogue of women only, it is necessary to examine how to approach such a meeting so that the maximum benefit can be obtained. What type of format would produce the mutual support and understanding that have been named as the aims of dialogue? Some reflection on the meeting at Claremont can help answer this question.

The fruits of the meeting consisted mainly in the awesome sense of being in touch with a global perspective. The commonality was evident in that we were all women and, as one speaker termed it, we were all considered "other" in our own traditions. Yet, there was also a good amount of confrontation regarding the tremendous difference between us. In physical appearance alone, the effect was striking. Riffat Hassan in her native dress of Pakistan, the Roshi in her brown Zen robes and shaved head, and Pravrajika Bhaktiprana in her saffron sari offered marked contrasts to those of us in very modern western dress. As the meeting progressed, a strong contrast also emerged between two levels of discussion. One was focused on the goal of religion: enlightenment, contemplation, eschatology. I label this view transcendent, in the sense of being deeper or beyond the everyday appearances of things, of being ahistorical. The other concerned the immanent—i.e., the tangible, empirical world in which embodied persons struggle in time and space.

On the one hand, when we speak of the objects of our dedication such as a personal God, Brahman or Enlightenment, we can avoid the issue of sexual differences. Even the monotheistic faiths admit, at least theoretically, that the personal God transcends sexuality. Yet the languages, images or practices used by the cultures to express this ultimate reality have been plagued with misogyny such that even the most monistic traditions have had their share of problems with the male-female dichotomy. Thus, our problem: what is or should be the focus of sharing among such a diverse group of women? If the answer is the former—i.e., the ahistorical objective of our devotion, we can engage in dialogue in the same abstract and impersonal manner as do our male colleagues to the exclusion of personal experiences.

On the other hand, since the oppression of women takes place in concrete rather than abstract situations, shouldn't the specific political and social circumstances of women's lives be the real focal point of dialogue? A meeting held at Harvard University in 1983 had such a focus. Diana Eck and Devaki Jain have edited the proceedings of this meeting in which twenty-seven participants from all over the globe were asked to consider the question "What is the relation of religion to the kinds of social change projects and struggles in which women are engaged around the world?"[6] The presentations were "case-studies, which considered the particular questions and ways of thinking specific to the experience of women as they work for social change in their own cultures and religious traditions."[7] Here, where the focus was clearly on social and cultural ramifications of women's roles, we hear about specific situations in specific countries and the relevance of religion to those situations. It was the contention of the conveners of this Harvard conference that religion shapes the world view of societies and is in large part responsible for the oppression of women. By dealing with the oppression we are dealing with religions, albeit indirectly.

While this is true, I also believe that the social situation affects the shape of religion, and that from examining only one or two specific cases, we are unable to make any generalizations about the religion as a whole. A brief glance at religion in America could serve to illustrate this point. Consider the effects of the foundation of a new nation on the traditional beliefs of Christianity, especially in regard to indigenous groups such as Mormons, Seventh Day Aventists and Jehovah's Witnesses. Historians have a vast field of material to draw on when studying the specific experiences that brought forth the different interpretations of the Christian message embodied in these movements of nineteenth-century America. Similarly, one's cultural environment will affect the mode of one's religious belief and practice. Women from different countries and especially from different family or economic status will view their religion, particularly its teachings on women, differently. For instance, women with more liberal or egalitarian backgrounds are inclined to view their religion as more liberating than are women from more disadvantaged backgrounds.

Trying to understand the place of women in Buddhism, for example, is a very complex endeavor when confronted with both Japanese and American perspectives and with differing traditions within each of those cultures. One presentation given on the subject at Harvard was by Kumiko Uchino, a Japanese scholar with a doctorate in sociology from Keio University in Japan. In discussing the status of Soto nuns in Japan, she recalled that "In the Buddhist tradition, women are regarded as impure, having a more sinful *karma* than men and unable to attain Buddhahood."[8] The author then went on to explain how nuns worked in an equality movement to obtain educational opportunities in the early part of this century. Thus, from her point of view, Buddhism itself is not very egalitarian, but women within it have been able to work for change.

Attending the Claremont conference was Eiko Kawamura, a professor at Hanazono University in Kyoto who spoke of Buddhism from a different perspective. Her perception of Zen Buddhism is that it is inherently egalitarian in that the "Buddha-nature is intrinsic to all beings."[9] She expounded on this point in a working paper which was discussed in preparation for the conference. In it she wrote, "If the feminist movement were to base itself upon the kind of elucidation of the self as is carried out in Zen, then a completely new dimension would unfold at the fundamental locus of openness, and the many directions of the feminist movement would take on a new vitality fueled by the integrity of truth."[10] Here we have Zen Buddhism viewed by a Japanese woman in a very positive way, as a vehicle of liberation from the perspective of Zen's goal and meditative practice. According to Ms. Kawamura, women would not consider themselves oppressed nor, in fact, be oppressed if they were able to give themselves to meditation. If they did so, women would be able to understand that their identity is found "not only in [themselves] but also in nature and in the absolutely opened openness,"[11]—that is, they would be able to transcend the bondage of the substance of sexuality.

American Buddhist women also see Buddhism as a liberating philosophy but bring to it yet another perspective which is gaining prominence in the American religious community. A recent compilation of talks by American Buddhist women, A Gathering of Spirit, has been edited by Ellen S. Sidor, who writes about a "new spiritual culture: women practicing and teaching Buddhism in America. Never before in the history of Buddhism, and probably not since the long-ago days at the height of Goddess worship, have women played so prominent a role in directing their own spiritual lives."[12] Not only do American Buddhists share the positive view of this religion but "Under the powerful influence of the Buddha's teaching of 'no discrimination', women [in America] began to take and be given leadership roles, to define their own issues."[13] Buddhism in an American context, therefore, will find more women in leadership and will find more women struggling with what Eiko Kawamura called the horizontal dimension. In the words of another American Buddhist, Jacqueline Schwartz Mandell, "Today one may actually be fulfilled in every way, as a woman or a man, not just a non-gender being."[14] Sexuality, according to these Americans, is to be lived, not transcended.

Thus we begin to understand that Buddhism has both positive and negative attitudes towards women and women's role in its various manifestations. Therefore, to hear one voice speak might give us only one perspective or a limited and partial understanding. A concise overview of diverse attitudes toward women in Buddhist scriptures can be found in Diana Paul's book, Women in Buddhism.[15]

This same problem of diversity of views from within a tradition is also seen in Islam. There are Islamic feminists who hold that the Qur'an itself is really egalitarian, and that it is the interpretations that have been misogynistic. Riffat Hassan has written, "It is a clear teaching of the Qur'an that man and woman are equal in the sight of God . . . But the interpretations . . . by men . . . have distorted the truth almost beyond recognition."[16] There are others who uphold veiling and other apparently oppressive practices, not because they are submissive, but because, as Jane I. Smith has written, "women's liberation in the Muslim world is often seen as another concession to the influences of the West which has already done so much to undermine Islam."[17] Valerie Hoffman-Ladd in an article in International Journal of Middle East Studies says that Islamic dress is "most

popular among highly educated university students and profession-
als . . . [because] it enables them to be modern and Muslim at the
same time."[18] How should we view Isalm and women?

There are yet other Muslim women who are American converts,
and, for them, Islamic law is more liberating than are the norms of
American society. These women describe their complementary roles
in family and society as equal to men's and suited to the physical
and psychological differences given them by God. They consider
keeping their own names and own monies to be more liberating than
many American customs.[19]

Therefore, we approach dialogue knowing that each tradition
contains a gamut of attitudes and that the women before us will
represent partial perspectives of a given tradition. This understanding is essential to the exchanges that will take place among the
participants especially if the dialogue is in conversational form
rather than a series of papers.

Because so many different perspectives will be confronting each
other in so many different combinations, it is necessary to structure
the discussion in such a way that the participants will not be
swatting at invisible flies or passing one another in linguistic eleva-
tors. What kind of structure or method should be employed to
guarantee the maximum effectiveness of interreligious dialogue?

A Practical Problem

To address this question, we can examine some of the dynamics
of the Claremont conference. Attending was a woman who is the
director of the International Zen Institute of America, Roshi Gesshin
Prabhasa Dharma. The Roshi was born and raised in Germany but
has lived in the United States most of her life. She spoke often at the
conference and attempted to demonstrate that if we reflect on the
way of Zen "we are beyond the discrimination of man and woman"[20]
and could eliminate the effects of thinking in terms of male and
female. Now, at this point the dialogue could have concentrated on
the meaning of enlightenment in Buddhism, in which case we would
then have a very profound theological discussion. But the women at
the dialogue did not pursue this path.

Someone asked about battered women! The Roshi responded to
this concern with an explanation of the Buddhist teaching on suffering, that it comes from within, that it comes from our own "battered
mind. . . . When consciousness is at rest the same battering mind . . .

is clear and calm, and that mind alone clearly sees reality."[21] We see in this response, a solution that requires taking leave of the outwardly physical characteristics of the problem and opting for a more introspective and transcendent solution. We have met a chasm.

In a similar manner, Pravrajika Bhaktiprana, a nun of the Ramakrishna sect, spoke of the divine within the human soul which is manifested in the four yogas. She explained that all women are the symbol of the divine mother and all men are called son. While she did mention some inequalities of women and men in Vedanta, she saw the original teachings of Ramakrishna as being very egalitarian.

The problem: are we not dealing with two different levels of discourse here? One is discussion of the transcendent or the ahistorical and the other is the empirical world of time and space. To speak of enlightenment and divinity as did the Buddhist and Hindu women, is not to respond to the historical problem of oppression as it was presented by the questioner. Therefore, the sense of being heard and understood that is essential to dialogue is sacrificed. When women who have either experienced or witnessed oppression come together, they must be heard, and this can only happen when an empathy and understanding of the practical situation is displayed by the partners in dialogue.

This second level was illustrated by other participants who did speak in a more historical perspective about the restrictions put upon women by a male-dominated religious structure and the effect this structure had on their lives. The content of the remarks made by Riffat Hassan on Islam, Drorah Setel on Judaism, June O'Connor and Karen Torjesen on Christianity addressed the questions that feminists raise about the basic teachings of these religions: the exclusion of women from decision making positions, the androcentrism of prayer and worship, the problematic of designating a personal God as male. These women were able to share the practical approaches to the struggle against such patriarchal aspects of their traditions. These issues, however, highlighted the dilemma of dialoguing on two different, albeit important, levels.

Some Practical Suggestions

I believe that both perspectives, the ahistorical or transcendent and the historical or embodied, are necessary in a discussion of women and religion. The difficult question, however, is how to include both without creating an impasse in the dialogue. In one of the planning sessions for the conference, June O'Conner suggested that it would be advantageous for each participant to identify the positive and negative impact that her religion had on her life as a woman. This suggestion was implemented and found to be extremely helpful. In view of its success, I propose that a solution to the problem of multi-level communication would be to include a two-pronged focus: (1) How has your religion helped you develop your identity as a woman and (2) how has your religion hindered or confined your growth as a woman?

The first question regarding the positive aspects might bring forth responses dealing with the more philosophical and theological concepts to which those women who are practicing devotees could relate. The Roshi could then speak of the Buddhist experience of emptiness in which all differences disappear; Ms. Lina Gupta could relate the stories of the Hindu goddesses which give her both precedent and the strength to follow that precedent; Karen Torjesen, speaking from a Christian perspective, could point out feminine images of God. Answers to this first question could contain the transcendent or ahistorical aspects mentioned above, and the discussion could take place on that level.

The second question, that of the negative aspects, might deal with the more practical, experiential level because it is here that misogyny is most immediately evident. Pravajika Bhaktiprana, who has lived as a Vendanta nun in Sarada Convent in Hollywood for the last thirty years, spoke very eloquently about the egalitarian philosophy of the Vedanta Society. Yet at the same time she did mention attitudes that are held by the Indian swami towards the American women with whom he associates in the society. This type of problematic, the coexistence of both egalitarianism and sexism, was one with which women around the table were able to empathize because they could relate to similar circumstances. Therefore, a good springboard for dialogue was established.

Creating the proper atmosphere for asking questions is essential to any methodology for dialogue. Personal introductions must precede any attempt at dialogue, for it is imperative that the women know not only each other's names but also each other's stories. If the dialogue is purely theoretical, such introductions may not be terribly important, but if personal experiences are to be considered, knowing these narratives is essential for several reasons. First, telling them creates an atmosphere of trust without which a dialogue about religion and religious experiences cannot take place. Second, the

clarification of the particular perspective represented by the participant is important since such a perspective, as was noted above, plays
a determinative role in one's view of religion. A third reason is
presented by Emily Culpepper when she writes that, "including
personal information is an important safeguard against feminist
theory becoming too abstract and unconnected with the actual
diverse situations in which women live."[22]

Still a fourth consideration is the fact that what may be assumed
to be shared by all women—for example, oppression or feminism—
is in fact very complex and only by the relating of personal stories
can we discover that which we do or do not have in common. All
the women at the Claremont conference defined feminism, and,
while the definitions differed, the general field was the same. It
wasn't until personal stories were told that we realized we had less
in common than we thought we did. This point is well made by
Marjorie Suchocki in a paper delivered at a conference held in 1986.
She states that "Interreligious dialogue at the societal/personal levels
of justice will discover that what constitutes dignity will be defined
differently in various cultures. There may be no single standard."[23]
A dramatic example of this was given when Riffat Hassan warned
non-Islamic women against assuming that they know what Islamic
women want. She said, "I get very tired of western women who tell
me they sympathize with Islamic women without even knowing
what Islamic feminists want."[24] Hassan said that most Islamic
women hope to combine marriage and a family with a job and a
chance to participate in the policy-making process. "But western
feminists keep telling them that what they *should* want is autonomy
in a non-patriarchal society and freedom from child bearing."[25]

The telling of stories does indeed point out that even the concepts
of justice, oppression and feminism are not to be taken for granted
or assigned a universal meaning. It serves all women well to realize
that liberation in one culture may be very different from liberation
in another. Regardless of how much oppression each participant has
experienced, it cannot be assumed that the type of oppression or the
reaction to that oppression is similar in a crosscultural discussion.

If these very significant differences are realized in discussion of
the personal, it becomes clear how this method severely challenges
the pluralism presented by John Hick and others who look for an
abstract idea that can be held in common by all religions. Can any
umbrella idea actually cover the kind of basic differences that appear

once the participants from all traditions really start talking to each other?

One other issue of methodology needs to be considered: that of conflict resolution. What happens when two or more participants disagree and find themselves in front of an irremoveable difference? In one debriefing session held after the Claremont conference, a communications instructor explained that in the secular world men are generally more comfortable with confrontation than are women. Indeed, one text on gender and communication states that "Many females find the argumentative style not only difficult to use, but inhibiting when it is used against them."[26] American feminists are also raising the issue of the double standard with regard to anger. For men anger is not only justifiable but a sign of conviction and strength, whereas for a woman, it is a taboo labeling her as emotional and irrational. Hence, many women are usually demure or depressed rather than angry.

In interreligious dialogue, however, according to the experience of my colleagues as well as the literature on the subject, the situation is just the opposite. In the dialogues mentioned above, male participants came together to discuss religious matters with great civility and mutual agreement even in the midst of ideological challenges. This does not appear to be the case of those dialogues which have been among women. Of the Harvard conference, Diana Eck and Devaki Jain write, "It is clear that conflict in inter-cultural dialogue is unavoidable in the microcosm of an international conference addressing sensitive issues; it is equally clear that such conflict is vitally important. It is precisely conflict that reveals the faultlines where world understanding cracks . . . [and this conflict] was not only possible but constructive."[27] Likewise, some of the most intense and enlightening moments of the Claremont conference were ones of conflict. Riffat Hassan challenged Lina Gupta in her interpretation of the Hindu Goddess Shakti, the dutiful wife of the god, Siva: how can she possibly serve as a model of liberation? Drorah Setel brought a heightened awareness in her very direct challenge to us to be conscious of the use of words: did we really mean Christian when we said western? And many present questioned the Roshi's answers to the anger and oppression which many women are experiencing: Can the practice of Zen and the achievement of enlightenment really solve so many injustices?

These challenges and the discussion they provoked caused the participants to touch real problems that different traditions have with one another and thereby served to present vividly the nature of the task before us when we attempt to engage in dialogue. The task includes working through such conflicts instead of trying to still them and pretend they are insignificant: staying with them, defining terms, questioning comments, supporting opinions and listening to the other. Only through this type of ardent effort will conflicts be worked out rather than brushed aside and ignored only to surface, unexpected and undesired, somewhere else. It should also be recognized that the so called "working out" of conflicts does not necessarily mean the resolution of them into an agreement but rather an acknowledgement of the other's viewpoint and a respect for the feelings of oppression or injustice experienced by her. Only through this kind of confrontation will conflict be constructive rather than destructive.

Our conclusion reconfirms our opening remarks: if understanding among peoples is to be a reality, dialogue—especially interreligious dialogue—must take place. Yet such dialogue will not be effective and fruitful unless women are part of it. And for women to play their needed role in dialogue, they must seriously attempt to know and appreciate each other's differences and similarities. Perhaps the course of action proposed here can be a first step in facilitating mutual knowledge and understanding. As more and more women from diverse cultures and backgrounds come together, their dialogue will become increasingly fruitful. Only then will women find the mutual support and energy to cross both cultural and sexual barriers. Finally, it is when these barriers have been broken that the differences of cultures, religions and sex will be causes for mutual respect and enrichment rather than for oppression and conflict.

NOTES

1. Paul Knitter, "Towards a Liberation Theology of Religions," *The Myth of Christian Uniqueness*, John Hick and Paul F. Knitter, eds. (Maryknoll, Orbis Books, 1987), p. 186.

2. Ibid.

3. John Hick, *God and the Universe of Faiths* (London: The Macmillan Press, 1973), p. 138.

4. Linda "Tess" Tessier, opening remarks at conference "The Sound of Women's Voices Heard 'Round the World," April 16–17, 1988.

5. Transcript of proceedings of Claremont conference, "The Sound of Women's Voices," April 16, 1988.

6. Diana Eck and Devaki Jain, eds., *Speaking of Faith: Cross-cultural Perspectives on Women, Religion and Social Change* (London: The Women's Press, 1986), p. 1.

7. Ibid.

8. Kumiko Uchino, "The Status Elevation Process of Soto Sect Nuns in Modern Japan," in *Speaking of Faith*, p. 149.

9. Eiko Kawamura, "What Is It To Be Human?: The Zen Perspective on Women's Liberation," a paper discussed in preparation for the Claremont conference.

10. Ibid.

11. Transcript of Proceedings

12. Ellen S. Sidor, ed., *A Gathering of Spirit: Women Teaching in American Buddhism* (Cumberland: Primary Point Press, 1987), p. 4.

13. Ibid.

14. Jacqueline Schwartz Mandell, "Politics of the Heart," in *A Gathering of Spirit*, p. 22.

15. Diana Paul, *Women in Buddhism* (Berkeley: University of California Press, 1979).

16. Riffat Hassan, "On Human Rights and the Qur'anic Perspective," *Journal of Ecumenical Studies*, 19 (1982) 61–55.

17. Jane I. Smith, "Woman in Islam: Equity, Equality and the Search for the Natural Order," *Journal of the American Academy of Religion*, 47 (1979) 529.

18. Valerie Hoffman-Ladd, "Polemics on the Modesty and Segregation of Women in Contemporary Egypt," *International Journal of Middle East Studies*, 19 (1987) 23–50.

19. These attitudes were encountered in some of the meetings of the Trialogue—the encounter of Jews, Christians and Muslims in Southern California.

20. Presentation of Roshi Gesshin Prabhasa Dharma given at Claremont on April 17, 1988.

21. Ibid.

22. Emily Erwin Culpepper, "Philosophia: Feminist Methodology for Constructing a Female Train of Thought," *Journal of Feminist Studies in Religion*, 3 (1987) 15.

23. Marjorie Suchocki, "Religious Pluralism from a Feminist Perspective," *The Myth of Christian Uniqueness*, p. 160.

24. Transcript of conference, "The Sound of Women's Voices," Claremont.

25. Ibid.

26. Barbara Westbrook Eakins and R. Gene Eakins, *Sex Differences in Human Communication* (Boston: Houghton Mifflin Co., 1978), p. 49.

27. Eck and Jain, *Speaking of Faith*, p. 12.

JESUS AS SAVIOUR OF THE WORLD

Gerald F. Finnegan, S.J.

There is a move afoot today in Christian theology which is of massive importance for Christian faith. It is the move away from what is called an inclusivist position with respect to other world religions to one called pluralist. An inclusivist position admits that grace and salvation are to be found in the other world religions, but it also insists that their fulness belongs to Christian faith and revelation. It therefore uses the latter as its norm in evaluating these other religious traditions. The pluralist position, on the other hand, denies Christianity this normative role and prefers to approach all faiths with a greater openness. In doing so it calls upon fact and argument. It is a fact that God has spoken at different times and places and in different ways to different peoples. And it can be argued that it does not seem just to bring all these different religious families under one religious umbrella, a Christian one.

Despite its tolerance and fairness, this pluralist position gives rise to suspicion and fear in some Christians. Why? One explanation could be that it seems to fit too nicely the "Zeitgeist" of our liberal, western First World. In his *Closing of the American Mind* Alan Bloom describes this contemporary spirit in its American form as openness and as the one "virtue" which a professor can count on finding in his or her students, for it has been drilled into them by

Gerald F. Finnegan, S. J., is Assistant Professor of Theology at St. Joseph's University in Philadelphia, PA. He holds a Roman licentiate in theology from Sankt Georgen Hochschule in Frankfurt, W. Germany, and a doctorate in theology from Union Theological Seminary, New York, N.Y. He has published two articles in Review for Religious *on the ministerial priesthood in the theologies of Karl Rahner and Yves Congar.*

the American system of education.[1] Openness insists on the equality of every opinion or idea, and its sinful opposition is intolerance or discrimination. One falls into this sin if one judges one idea or position as superior to others. Bloom labels this understanding of openness as "paralysis of the mind." If he is right, if this uncritical understanding of openness characterizes the American mind at this moment, it could be argued that theological pluralism is little more than its theological expression. Those who would reject so negative an interpretation of theological pluralism would nevertheless admit that it is very much a child of its time.[2] Such an admission might seem unnecessary in today's academic world which is so strongly aware of the transition from classicist to historical consciousness. But there is a point in stressing the obvious in this case, for the pluralist position is so open, so tolerant, that it could almost appear to transcend all limitations and reach a kind of universal *niveau*. But that is not the case. It is very much a twentieth century position reflecting the consciousness of those who take seriously the present religious diversity of the world, even after centuries of Christian missionary efforts, and who are aware that in the past the superiority of the Christian revelation was very much tied to the political and economic superiority of those nations which were nominally Christian.

For those of us who are Roman Catholic and often presume that our church is the last to lay off the old, it comes as a surprise to discover that it is precisely the Catholic Church of all the Christian churches which comes closest to accepting the pluralist position. After almost two millennia of defending an exclusivist position with respect to salvation—i.e., that salvation can be found only through membership in the church—Vatican II moved to an inclusivist position which claims that every person who follows his or her conscience will be saved.[3]

If Vatican II had been content to say only that, its position on salvation would have rivaled any other position, even that of pluralism, for universality and openness; but it was not. It went on to talk about categorical revelation and salvation—i.e., about the way people are led to God concretely in the histories of their lives. Thus it had to talk about the different religions of the world and their salvific character. The verdict was positive. These religions are revelations of God (or at least can be) and therefore means of salvation for those who embrace them.[4] But here Vatican II parted company with pluralism, for it stated that compared to Christian revelation and the salvation it offers, the revelation and salvation offered by the other faiths of the world were partial and dependent on Christian faith for their fulfillment.[5] The question therefore is: What are the reasons which Christian faith can muster to defend this assertion of its greater fullness, and what are the reasons which pluralism can give to deny it?

The Vatican II position seems to rest on three major presuppositions, all of which have to do with unity. They are: there is one God, one plan of salvation, and one human race. Given this threefold unity, it is impossible for this position to leave all the religions of the world uncompared. Somehow they must all be part of the one divine plan. Nor can the plan's unity be restricted to God either as the beginning or as the end and goal of the plan. It must also be part of the plan's actual development or unfolding in human history. Why? Not because of God's arbitrary decision that so it must be, but because of God's willed unity of the human race. The plan's unfolding must reveal a unity because the human race and its history are a unity.

What also seems to be presupposed by Vatican II's position is the linear or one-directional quality of history. Human history, which had a beginning and will have an end, moves in one direction, forward. This movement can be varied in speed and intensity and includes within itself a vast amount of diversity, but it is nevertheless one movement forward. Thus everything within it is related to everything else, and what comes first serves in some way, direct or indirect, as a cause or condition for what follows. In short, human history is a stream or river with an irreversible current.

Where is the fly in the ointment? Is it in the assertion that God's plan, to maintain its historical unity, must be revealed at one time and place? Is this rippling process the only one available to God because of the human race's unity? Could not God, while having one plan for the human race, actualize this plan in a multiplicity of forms, none of which would be superior to the others? Or is such an idea, attractive as it may be because of its common sense quality, reality not true to history, to the way things happen, namely, that ideas and things and perhaps even the human race—certainly individuals!—originate at one point and then spread out from there?

Even if it were granted that the rippling effect must be accepted as the way in which God's plan expresses its unity in history, what justifies the choice of Christian faith as the single point from which the ripples of salvation spread out to the rest of the world? What happens when and if other religions share similar presuppositions and therefore claim for themselves the position of centrality in historical salvation? Whose claim can be believed, and on what grounds? Can there be rational grounds for such a claim, or is the best one can offer a kind of subjective reasoning in which one supports *post factum* the fact whose existence one is supposed to explain? And on the empirical level of everyday life, is it not true to say that for most people the faith in which they are nurtured is found to be complete and therefore central because it has formed their religious tastes from infancy, and only a sustained, intense, and rather early exposure to another faith can make them question their own faith's centrality? In this perspective a faith's centrality is a matter of culture, and only those religions that succeed in forming a massive culture can claim centrality for themselves with any kind of plausibility. In the end the name of the game seems to be numbers and cultural sovereignty, the very realities which many now feel Christianity used in the past to justify its own centrality.

If there are other reasons to justify the claim to centrality for a religion, they must come from its insides, from beliefs which can be offered to people for evaluation. What Christian faith offers in this way is the person of Jesus. It claims centrality for itself because it claims it first for him. Thus the question is: Why does Christian faith see Jesus as central to salvation? One primary argument offered by contemporary Christian theologians to justify this claim can be briefly described in this way. Jesus is the central point of the salvific process because he fulfills, even within the process, its aim or goal which is the deification of the human race. In Jesus the human race comes home to God, reaches a union with God which must be described as indescribable because we cannot understand how one becomes one with God without ceasing to be oneself, how instead one finds one's full and true self by losing one's self in God. Left to themselves people cannot achieve this union. They are unable to transcend themselves in order to make God the center of their lives. Therefore, when this happens, as Christianity believes it did in Jesus, it is due to the extraordinary presence of the divine in the human. Thus Christianity speaks of Jesus as God made present in the human, as the Son or incarnate Word of God, and as such he is seen to be central to the rest of humanity's efforts to achieve this union with God.[6] As the one who by grace has achieved this union, Jesus is the center of the entire salvific process. Indeed he is its goal already realized even within the process itself. The rest of history is simply a matter of letting what happened in him achieve its full effect. The ripples must multiply.

According to Knitter, the reasons which these theologians have given to explain Jesus' centrality now raise other questions. If Jesus is the center of the process of salvation because he is humanity brought to perfection, why is this perfection restricted to him?[7] The Christian answer is that it is not restricted to him. Indeed it has happened to him so that it can happen to all others. But then the more difficult question arises: If it is meant for all, why does its happening in others depend on its happening in Jesus? Confronted with this question, Christian faith could resort to the ideas we have identified as the presuppositions of Vatican II's teachings. It is the oneness of history and the human race which preclude multiple incarnations independent of Jesus. The incarnation is a break-through in a single process. There must be preparations for such a breakthrough, but when it happens it happens at one time and place and then influences everything else that happens in this continuing process. Thus in this understanding, all so-called incarnations prior to Jesus would have to be judged as mere preparations for his, and all those subsequent to his as repetitions only possible on the basis of his own.

In Knitter's opinion theologians like Rahner and those of the process school who explain the incarnation as the fulfillment of human possibility are inconsistent when they attempt to limit the possibility of an incarnation to Jesus.[8] Their answers do not satisfy him. For example, Rahner claims that the "what" which is expressed in Jesus is identical with the "what" expressed in us, but the difference between this "what" in him and us is that in him it is the expression of the divine Logos. But what is to prevent the Logos from becoming the self-expression of someone other than Jesus? Does not the Chalcedonian insistence that the two natures are both joined and distinct lead us in the direction of the possibility of many incarnations? As for the adjectives so often used by Rahner to describe the incarnation—irreversible, irrevocable—why, Knitter asks, should they mean that it is unique and once and for all? Don't they really mean that God has committed God's self to us irrevocably and irreversibly. But can't such a commitment be reaffirmed. It would be the same commitment *a parte Dei*, but it would be different historically. Indeed the diversity of history would seem to demand such diverse affirmations.[9]

The abstract quality of such approaches makes one want to turn to more empirical ways of handling the problem. For example, could we not suppose by way of hypothesis that there have been multiple incarnations and then ask for and examine the evidence given to substantiate such claims—namely, the lives and teachings of those singled out as incarnations of divinity? Even this way is not without its difficulties. For it would quickly become obvious that all such evidence would be prejudged to a great extent by the understanding of divinity held by the examiner. Unless one wishes to claim that in all of us there is an innate idea of God which can be distinguished from what we have been taught about the divinity historically, one will have to admit that neutrality in this matter would be almost non-existent. It would be hard, for example, for Christians to define God in terms other than those of unselfish love, and even harder for them to find a clearer incarnation of such love than that given by the crucified Jesus.

The dividing line between the inclusivist position of Vatican II and the pluralist position is to be found in their understandings of the unity of God's plan in its historical unfolding. It is the acceptance or denial of what I have called the ripple effect. The pluralist position insists on a plurality of independent ways or means of salvation in history and as a proof of its position offers the *de facto* plurality of religions in the world today even after two thousand years of Christian presence and missionary effort. God must will this plurality, this position would argue, at least for the present, and who are we to gainsay God? Why not accept this fact and attempt to understand it? Why build torturous theories to deny the historical fact that there are many independent means of salvation.

But what would the pluralist position say about the future of salvation history? Could there be a time in the future when the different religious phyla will merge into one? Is it not possible that one religious phylum will prove to be more powerful and attractive than the others and eventually absorb them into itself? Or if the different religions of the world are willing to dialogue, could not a new religion emerge from such a dialogue which would bear the traces of them all but not be identifiable with any one of them? The pluralist position, as I understand it, would accept such possibilities but would remind us that they are precisely that. They are possibilities. We don't know what will happen. Meanwhile we are confronted with many religions and the question of their relationships to each other.

There is a third possibility for the future of religions, a much less sanguine one. They could refuse to enter into dialogue. For the pluralists this possibility would be the worst of all, for they believe that God is calling the world to unite in its effort to improve human life, and the success of this effort depends in great part on the cooperation of all the world's religions. Religious energy is needed because it is the deepest and most massive energy in the world. To avoid this worst of all possibilities, the pluralists see the adoption of their own position as a necessity. There cannot be cooperation among the religions of the world if some of them continue to assume that they are superior to others. Such a presupposition destroys the very notion of cooperation.[10]

If Christians are to rid themselves of this superiority which makes cooperation impossible, they must reimage the unity of the religions in history. Marjorie Suchocki uses the traditional image of a mountain to describe one form of pluralism.[11] She imagines religious pilgrims climbing a mountain. When they reach the top, they discover that there are many other mountains as well, and there are groups of pilgrims on each of their peaks. All these different groups can do is shout hello to each other. Dianna Eck offers another mountain image from the Hindu tradition. This mountain is upside down, narrow at the bottom and broad at the top. The religious pilgrims who climb this mountain discover at the top that there is a wide area which includes all sorts of creatures and gods.[12]

Both images recognize the plurality of religions in history and if accepted could serve as a basis for dialogue and cooperation, but they lead, of necessity, to another question which pluralism must also deal with, indeed has already dealt with, that of the divine reality's unity. Is God one or many? Where, for example, is God to be found in these two mountain images? In the first image, is God to be found on each mountain peak? If so, then God is multiple. Or is God above all the peaks still higher up in the clouds. Then God could be one, or could be unknowable as to unity or multiplicity. In the second image we again have two possibilities. The different religions meeting on the broad top could discover that they have in fact been worshipping one God, and then they would join. Or they could discover that their Gods are ultimately different and therefore they must remain separate. The images therefore leave the question of God's unity or diversity open. Is that where pluralism necessarily leads us?

Although Christian faith holds to a triune concept of God, in terms of our images it would choose to say that God is one and is therefore to be found above the different peaks and as the one mystery worshipped in different ways by the different religions on the inverted mountain. But pluralists like Raimundo Panikkar are asking us to move beyond an understanding of God which is too exclusively tied to the western emphasis on God as Logos, as intelligible and intelligent. God is being, God is spirit, and being and spirit go beyond intelligibility. Intelligibility does not dictate to being, to reality, but follows it in its freedom. "There may be facets of reality opaque to the light of intellect,"[13] Panikkar tells us. If we accept his premises, we will no longer insist on God's being one, as we understand unity according to our own models of intelligibility, but will be open to the possibility that God may be multiple. Panikkar would also accept the understanding of God found in process thought which says that God's identity cannot be imagined to be something complete in itself but rather must be seen as open and completed in and through history. Since there are many histories in which God is involved, according to pluralist thought, it is clear that at least in this sense God must be said to be multiple. Using the mountain image, Panikkar tells us that there are different paths leading to the peak and that the peak would collapse if they disappeared. Thus the peak is itself the result of these different paths. Put more abstractly: "It is not that this reality *has* many names as if there were a reality outside the name. The reality *is* the many names and each name is a new aspect."[14]

Having questioned the unity of the divine plan in its historical unfolding, we end questioning the unity of God and reality itself. Pluralism has pushed us into metaphysics. But for many pluralists their position's heartbeat is not metaphysics but justice. Tom Driver writes that pluralism is a theological issue because it is an ethical issue.[15] To refuse to accept pluralism is to refuse to accept the validity of the other religions of the world. Such a refusal is the last gasp of the Christian *imperium*. It is religious colonialism, and its sinful character is now manifest in the evil which it, together with its other branches, economic, political and cultural colonialism, has produced. Moreover, it has expressed itself within Christian faith itself with respect to women and other minorities. The strategy is the same in both instances: the embrace which disarms by feigning equality or commonality, followed by the denial of actual equality.[16] Thus the first step in the removal of this evil is the freeing of oneself from the embrace through the assertion of one's own identity, one's otherness. Then and only then can justice and dialogue begin. Since

Christian faith holds that its mission is justice, it must accept pluralism for the sake of its own integrity, if for no other reason.

It might be hard to convince Driver and others that Catholicism's inclusivist position was not imperialist or colonial in intention but the very opposite of such an attitude, yet that is in fact the case. In extending the name *Christian* to non-Christians Rahner, for example, was saying that the same grace and salvation offered to Christians was also offered to all the people of the world. The theological alternatives at the time of this theory's origin were either to affirm the exclusivist position which denied salvation to all non-Christians or to claim for them a kind of natural happiness in the next life considered to be inferior to the happiness of Christian salvation. Theologians like Rahner, having worked their way out of the reification of the "natural state" of the world in which grace was something added externally to people through the sacraments, and only through them, now claimed that all men and women exist in the same order of grace and for that reason have a real though not historically expressed relationship with the person who gives or rather is the full historical expression of this grace. Even though Driver might call this bestowal of grace on the non-Christians a feigned embrace, it was not meant to be such by its proponents. When Rahner was asked by a famous Zen Buddhist how he would feel if the latter called him an anonymous Buddhist, Rahner said he would feel honored, although he would not recognize this interpretation of himself as correct.[17] But he recognized the fact that it was correct from the Zen Buddhist's viewpoint.

Unlike the inclusivist position of Vatican II, the pluralist position does not see Christian faith anonymously expressed in the other religions of the world, nor does it see the Christian light as somehow brighter or fuller than that provided by other religions, at least not at this moment. Perhaps in the future, after these religions have lived and dialogued together, a greater light will emerge, and perhaps it will then be recognized as belonging to Christian faith, but it is too early to make such a judgment. In the meantime it recommends modesty to all, especially to the Christians because of their imperial past. An image used by Driver catches this modesty very well: "The pluralist says to Christianity and to other religions, 'Put to sea in little boats. Cast your self, your faith, and your tradition upon the waters. See what happens.' "[18] Could it be that pluralism, which at first might have appeared to be a threat to faith, is in fact an appeal to greater faith? Could it be that we have hugged too close to shore and are now being called to put out into deeper waters? This is what those who accept this position claim.

What would the acceptance of Driver's invitation to cast one's faith upon the waters mean in terms of this article's understanding of the pluralist position? It would mean the abandonment of Jesus as the normative revelation of God and the premises which support his normativity: the historical unity of God's salvific plan for the human race, itself conceived as a unity, and the acceptance of Panikkar's view of God as mystery beyond human intelligibility. Then Christians would be able to enter into dialogue with non-Christians on an equal footing, for they would consider all religions as at least potentially equally valid ways to God—or even to gods.

What would happen in such dialogues? Would Christian pluralists inform their dialogue partners that their pluralist interpretation of Christianity is not the traditional one? If they did, might not their partners insist that they adopt a more traditional interpretation (whether exclusivist or inclusivist) not because it is more traditional but for the sake of dialogue itself. For how well can one dialogue with a pluralist? Once the realm of the absurd and humanly repulsive is superseded, all is conditionally acceptable, and nothing is finally normative. Moreover, in such dialogues pluralists might also discover that their premises are shared by relatively few others. The modern western roots of their position would be more clearly exposed.

Despite such difficulties in dialogue the pluralist position would survive, for its ultimate foundation is not its useful or non-useful character as a method of dialogue. This position exists primarily because those who adopt it do so because they find it to be the only valid way of interpreting Christianity. It is not a question of the validity of some other faith but of the invalidity of making any faith normative. The pluralist position is truly pluralist. All faiths are denied the right to claim normative validity. Of course some may see in this absolute claim by pluralism an intrinsic contradiction of its own character.

With respect to Christianity this means that the pluralist position can no longer accept the traditional Christian understanding of God as the one God whose mind and heart have been revealed in a plan which embraces all people of all time. And that is why it arouses such fear and suspicion among non-pluralist Christians. These Christians do not disagree with pluralism's claim that all religions must be treated seriously and respectfully. Nor do they claim that within history Christianity will be revealed as the normative way to God. But they do reject the presentation of Christianity as itself non-normative. For them the denial of Jesus' centrality in human salvation is an aberration from Christian doctrine and must be recognized as such. Thus, in their view, to be Christian and to be pluralist is a contradiction in terms.

Those who label the pluralist position so harshly have much work to do. The problem which seems so central to this position, the uniqueness of the incarnation of God in Jesus, must be examined and better and fuller explanations developed to defend it. Indeed the uniqueness of all things historical and the ability to distinguish and evaluate such realities may be the underlying question here. We return here to intuition and the ancient question of the one and the many. For those who favor pluralism seem to be opting for multiplicity over unity, whereas those who accept the traditional understanding of Christian faith seem to presume that unity exists at a deeper level of reality, indeed at the deepest level, and multiplicity is a phenomenon which arises from it and returns to it in the end.

For those who reject the pluralist position, the meaning of Driver's metaphor is reversed. To cast one's faith upon the waters in the pluralist sense is not an expression of too much but rather too little faith. Those who do this will, like Peter, sink into the waves because of a lack of faith in Christ.

NOTES

1. Alan Bloom, *The Closing of the American Mind* (New York: Simon and Schuster, 1987), pp. 25–43.

2. Paul F. Knitter, *No Other Name?* (Maryknoll: Orbis Books, 1985), pp. 1–20; Tom F. Driver, "The Case for Pluralism," in *The Myth of Christian Uniqueness*, John Hick and Paul F. Knitter, eds. (New York: Orbis Books, 1987), pp. 205–6, 217.

3. *Dogmatic Constitution on the Church*, no. 16.

4. *Declaration on the Relationship of the Church to Non-Christian Religions*, no. 2.

5. Ibid.; *Dogmatic Constitution on the Church*, chapters 1 and 2.

6. Knitter, *No Other Name?* pp. 188–92.

7. *Ibid.*, p. 191.

8. *Ibid.*

9. *Ibid.*

10. Ibid., pp. 205–31, and his "Toward a Liberation Theology of Religions," in *The Myth of Christian Uniqueness*, pp. 178–97.

11. Tom F. Driver, "The Case for Pluralism," in *The Myth of Christian Uniqueness*, p. 213.

12. *Ibid.*, p. 214.

13. Raimundo Panikkar, "The Jordan, the Tiber, and the Ganges," in *The Myth of Christian Uniqueness*, p. 103.

14. Knitter, *No Other Name?* p. 153.

15. Driver, *The Myth of Christian Uniqueness*, p. 213–15.

16. *Ibid.*, 209–10.

17. Karl Rahner, S. J., "The Universality of Salvation," in his *Theological Investigations* (New York: Crossroad, 1983), vol. 16, p. 219.

18. Driver, *The Myth of Christian Uniqueness*, p. 213.

Part Three

THEOLOGY IN A SUFFERING WORLD

THEOLOGY IN A SUFFERING WORLD: THEOLOGY AS *INTELLECTUS AMORIS*

Jon Sobrino
Translated by José Pedrozo and Paul F. Knitter

I. Introduction: Theology and Suffering

The intent of this 1988 annual volume of the College Theology Society is to situate the task of theology within the different realities that characterize and challenge today's world: theology *in* a culturally diverse world, *in* a religiously plural world, and *in* a suffering world.

In this essay I will develop the theme of theology in a suffering world. But first, I feel it is important to make a preliminary observation that will help fit my topic into the broader framework of our discussion. The themes that make up the three foci of this volume have an identical structure: "Theology in . . ." The intent, of course, is to recognize the necessity of doing theology in relationship with the actual, concrete realities of the world. The identical grammatical structure of the topics, however, would be misleading if one concluded that these three designations—a culturally diverse world, a religiously plural world, and a suffering world—represent three

Jon Sobrino, S. J. is Professor of Philosophy and Theology at the Universidad José Simeón Cañas in El Salvador. He was born in Barcelona into a Basque family during the Spanish Civil War. His studies took him to St. Louis University for a master's degree in Engineering Mechanics (1965) and then to the Hochschule Sankt Georgen in Frankfurt, West Germany for a doctorate in theology (1975). Besides his academic works in liberation theology—Christology at the Crossroads (1978), The True Church and the Poor (1984), Jesus in Latin America (1987), Spirituality of Liberation (1988) (all published by Orbis Books)—he edits the bi-weekly grassroots report on the church in El Salvador Carta a las Iglesias (available in North America as Letter to the Churches).

realities on the same level. Formally, what the three specified realities have in common is the demand that theology incarnate itself
within them. But in regard to their concrete content—if I may
simplify distinctions a bit—the first two refer to a suprastructural
reality that already presupposes a more fundamental reality,
whereas the third reality refers to the real world as such, to the
infrastructural world. In other words, I wish to assert from the very
start that the theme of theology in a suffering world has a methodological priority over the other two themes because it refers directly
to the reality of our world. That is to say, though cultural and
religious diversity are very important realities, they are secondary
with respect to the primary reality of the world as it is, characterized
by widespread suffering.

The various cultures and religions are, among other things, concrete ways of understanding and reacting to the primary reality and
its suffering. Because of this, the theme assigned to me is not
independent of the other two topics; it is in fact already present,
though implicitly, in them, since they likewise have to respond, and
are ways of responding, to the suffering of the world.

In what follows I would like to present a specific theology, the
theology of liberation, as a theology historically necessary in a
suffering world and systematically adequate for giving an account of
Christian faith in a suffering world. As is known, liberation theology
understands itself specifically as a theology of praxis—a praxis of
eliminating unjust suffering from the world. Consequently, I wish to
formally define liberation theology within the great theological tradition as *intellectus amoris*. As such, it integrates and retrieves—but
in a more radical way—what is contained in theology understood as
intellectus fidei and *intellectus spei*.

But before taking up these expressly theological considerations,
some preliminary reflections are necessary in order to situate the
theology of liberation in the larger theme of theology in a suffering
world.

The Relationship between Christian Theology and Suffering

Throughout history there have always existed many Christian
theologies and, of course, many forms of suffering; and the two
realities have been related. Suffering is a perennial question for
theology, to which theologians have attempted to give their various
responses. In this, Christian theologies are similar to other cultures

and to other religions and their theologies. Such efforts to relate theology and suffering are, of course, a positive sign, for suffering is one of the "hardest" facts of the reality with which all religions must contend and stands as a problem even before it is interpreted. (Interpretations, of course, especially when given by religion/theology, can themselves become a problem and a cause of greater suffering.)

In the different ways in which Christian theologies approach the problem of suffering, we can note a certain minimal and formal agreement: a) At the level of reality, all Christian theologians recognize the reality of suffering together with its natural and historical roots. b) At the level of meaning, they emphasize its negativity. c) At the level of specifically Christian revelation, they point out that suffering is unwanted by God and in one way or another is a consequence of sin; on the one hand they admit the absurdity and meaninglessness of suffering and on the other, its salvific possibilities. d) At the utopian level, all Christian theologies, in clearly different ways, hold up the possibility of doing away with suffering and propose precise formulas for doing so.

Besides these formal similarities among different Christian theologies, there are also clear differences in the concrete, actual ways in which theologians grapple with the reality of suffering in the world. Such differences tend to shape, consciously or unconsciously, the entire fabric of a particular theology and so make for radical contrasts between them. These differences are evident in two ways:

a) Theologies react to suffering by seeking to determine the *fundamental form of suffering*—that is, the form of suffering which, without denying other expressions of suffering, becomes a theology's focal concern. Such fundamental forms of suffering might be listed as follows: one's own suffering (centered on one's self), the suffering of others, the suffering of individuals (of the self or its equivalent, a close friend), collective suffering (of peoples, races, sexes, castes . . .), spiritual suffering (doubts, guilt, failure, meaninglessness), corporal-social suffering (serious problems in directing one's life or basic threats to life), historical suffering (the pain that occurs within historical process), metaphysical suffering (the absurdity of history).

b) The fundamental way in which a theology *reacts* to suffering may be to try to *clarify* its origin (in the human condition, sin, an etiology of historical sufferings) or its meaning; or to find some kind of *meaningful co-existence* with suffering (suffering as purifying or as meritorious); or to attempt to remove suffering (eschatologically and historically); or to discover some kind of theological "justification" for suffering (various types of theodicies).

Theology Confronts Suffering in Today's World

Every theology, therefore, must confront suffering, must determine the fundamental form of suffering, and must ask what can be done about it. I would suggest that the development of every Christian theology has been determined, explicitly or implicitly, by the way it has responded to suffering, for in one way or another all theology claims to be a form of soteriology. This makes sense insofar as salvation stands at the heart of Christian faith. Thus, all theologies today confront the challenge of detemining what is the fundamental form of suffering in our world and what to do about it. Unless a theology does this, its historical relevance and its integral development are in jeopardy.

Let me begin by stating my claim in the form of a thesis: for libertion theology, the major form of suffering in today's world is historical suffering—suffering unjustly inflicted on some by others. Historical suffering is massive, affecting the majority of humanity, making it practically impossible for people to direct their own lives, causing a poverty that brings death slowly and violently. In the presence of such suffering, theology must understand itself as an intellectual exercise whose primary purpose is to eliminate this kind of suffering. Briefly stated, suffering in today's world means primarily the sufferings of people who are being crucified; and the purpose of theology is to take these people down from the cross.

Though this thesis expresses the self-understanding and the task of liberation theology, it also has valuable implications, though in different forms, for any contemporary theology. This is so for two reasons:

a. From a historical perspective, the causes of sufferings in the Third World, are to a great extent, to be found in the First World. To admit this is a necessary condition for the First World to know itself truthfully. To decide to remove this suffering is essential if the First World is to carry out its fundamental ethical responsibiltiy. To actually do away with this suffering is the way of salvation for both Third and First Worlds.

b. From A Christian perspective, the type of suffering specific to the Third World is in fact the same form of suffering that appears at crucial moments of divine revelation (in the Exodus, the prophets, Jesus). Contrary to the claims of personalistic and intellectual types of theology, to ignore such suffering is to mutilate Christian revelation both quantitatively and qualitatively. It is to deprive theology of one of its central elements, for by closing one's eyes to the sufferings of the Third World, one ignores, annuls, and falsifies a pivotal part of Christian revelation. Furthermore, to decide concretely to remove the suffering of the Third World is to carry on divine revelation, for such efforts are the praxis of God's self and the praxis that God requires of human beings. If we do not take up this praxis of removing sin from the Third World, we essentially mutilate our Christian morality and our theological response to God.

Stated simply, the task of theology today, either in the First or Third Worlds, cannot be carried out if the massive, cruel, and mounting suffering that pervades our world is ignored. If a theology closes its eyes to suffering because such suffering is not occurring massively in "its" world, that theology would disassociate itself from the real historical humanity in which we all live and which, theologically, is God's own creation.[1]

In a world of suffering, therefore, what is at stake is the humanity of human beings and the faith of believers. And for these two foundational reasons, the relevance and the credibility of theology is also at stake. I would now like to lay out, in thesis form, just how a suffering world specifies the place, the purpose, and the self-understanding of theology.

II. The Option for the Suffering World as the Place of Theology

Thesis 1: Theology finds its place in a suffering world insofar as such a world is a mediation of the truth and the absoluteness of God. The determination of the suffering world as the place of theology is an option prior to theology, an option required of all believers and all persons.

Theology itself never comes first; it is always a "second act." From a theological point of view, what comes first is the reality of revelation and faith. From an historical and existential viewpoint, theology is preceded by the objective determination of its place and by the subjective decision to locate this place in a concrete way.

We must try to analyze, therefore, just what constitutes this "priority" over theology. In doing so, we recognize that such preliminary considerations are rife with divergent viewpoints and heated debates.

Theology and Its Place

Before one can theologize, one has to first be situated in a specific place. One's understanding of this place will determine how one understands theology and the theological task called for by one's place.

a. We can first review the different ways of understanding the place of theology and what it means for the theological task:

The place of theology can be understood in a physico-institutional sense—simply the ambient in which the theological endeavor is carried out (a community, seminary, university, etc.). Such places provide the immediate environment for the theological task, by their very materiality conditioning and making possible the method and purpose of theology. But such an understanding of place does not take up the question of how theology is supposed to relate to the broader reality in which one finds both these and many other "places" and where one is to find the real inspiration for the theological task.

The place of theology can also be considered the geographical-social situation, with its homogeneous cultural characteristics, which is to be served by theology. Here we have the pastoral dimension of theology, which gives special consideration to the addressees of theology. With such an understanding of place, there is the danger of thinking that theology bears a given, substantial self-constitution which simply needs to be applied in concrete ways.

Theology's place can also be understood by contrasting the historical and cultural differences between its present situation and that in which it originated and in which its faith was first formulated. This calls for hermeneutics as a means of bridging the historical and cultural distance between past and present. This view of place runs the danger of thinking that whereas in the past there were the dual realities of revelation-faith and of place, today we have to deal mainly with place and not so much with the present-day reality of revelation-faith.

Certainly, theology must inquire about its place in all these senses: What type of institution is most conducive to the theological endeavor? How to relate and apply the reality of faith to the present situation? How to understand what, in its origins, was experienced in a quite different world than ours today? I would argue, however, that with such considerations, we have not yet come to what is the fundamental place of theology.

The theology of liberation insists that its fundamental place must be that historical reality in which we can find a maximum of Truth and of the Absolute and which contains both the greatest demands to act within history and the greatest promise of salvation. In other words, the place of theology is the reality which provides the greatest historical mediation of God—where one can find the "signs of the times," understood in a strictly theological sense.

From this point of view, the title of this essay "Theology in a Suffering World" means that the preliminary task of theology is to find its place *in* the reality of this suffering world. This does not mean primarily to find a concrete "ubi" within a world that happens to be suffering but rather, to find a place within the very suffering of this world. Stated graphically, the place of theology is the suffering of the world, and to stand in its place means to stand within the actual suffering that racks this world. The place of theology, then, is much more a "quid" than an "ubi." An important problem, which we cannot take up presently, is how a concrete place (an "ubi") can make it easy or difficult to locate oneself within the reality of suffering as it really is (the "quid").[2] Insofar as theology is not done amid the world of suffering, as it actually exists, it has not yet found its proper place.

For the theology of liberation, theology has to be done within a suffering world because such a world is the most real world. In Latin America the hardest "fact" of reality is described as the "irruption of the poor" (G. Gutiérrez), with its capacity to reveal ("irruption" as a mediation of God's revelation) and with its historical mediation ("of the poor" signifying revelation through the reality of suffering).

The reason why the theology of liberation takes the irruption of the poor as the primary reality is, in the final analysis, an option, as we shall see. But in our contemporary world, it is an option that is eminently reasonable and comprehensible. In the first place, poverty is a massive reality for most people today—to the extent that it is practically a tautology to speak about a world of "suffering" and a world of "poverty." As Hugo Assmann already said many years ago, "If the yearly deaths of thirty million poor people do not keep theology busy, nothing will." Purely from a quantitative view, to do theology "in the world" is to do it in a de facto suffering world.

Second, the irruption of the poor can be considered our world's primary reality because of what this irruption contains. On the human-natural level, the greatest cause of massive, cruel, and intolerable suffering in today's world is the poverty found in the Third (and the Fourth) World. In these worlds, poverty is the instrument of death—either slowly through unjust structures that make it extremely difficult to meet the most basic needs of life, or rapidly and violently through the repression that brings forth and maintains these unjust structures.

At the human-social level, death-dealing poverty is what divides the world between poor and creators of poverty, between violated and violators, between victims and tyrants. Seen as a worldwide phenomenon, poverty is the nullification of the human and of human solidarity, and by keeping the peoples of the Third World poor, oppressed, marginalized, and crucified, poverty is the generator of conflict and war.

On the ethical level, death-dealing poverty, insofar as it is rooted in injustice, stands forth as the greatest of moral evils and expresses the fundamental sin of this world—the destruction of life.

On the level of praxis, death-dealing poverty cries out for its own eradication, for as long as it endures, so will a long train of other evils—physical, moral, spiritual.

On the level of meaning, death-dealing poverty, together with its causes and its consequences, poses the radical question of the meaning or the absurdity of history—the question whether life is to be lived with hope, resignation, or cynicism.

On the theological level (and analogously on the religious or ideological levels), death-dealing poverty triggers the question of God or of the Ultimate, of whether there is any truth to God or the Gods. Any theological answer must show how God or the Ultimate is opposed to human-made idols.

Two further considerations are of extreme contemporary importance for this analysis of poverty. First, death-dealing poverty is on the increase throughout the world. The Latin American Bishops Conference at Puebla in 1979 stated that the reality of poverty was even more widespread than at the time of the previous meeting in Medellin in 1968. In his latest encyclical of 1988 (*Solicitudo Rei Socialis*), John Paul II announced that the development of peoples throughout the world not only had not improved but had worsened since Paul VI's encyclical *Populorum Progressio* of 1967. Statistics for the year 2000 indicate that poverty in Latin American is on a galloping increase. Second, there is a growing awareness of many

other causes of massive poverty in our world: race, sex, caste . . .[3]
But to a great extent, those who suffer the indignity and pain of
racial or sexual or caste discrimination also belong to the world of
the poor, which sharpens their suffering and makes it all the more
difficult for them to liberate themselves from such indignity.

Determining the Place of Theology is an Option

To look upon death-dealing poverty as the *analogatum princeps*
of suffering and the most drastic expression of the pain of the world
is, in the final analysis, a pre-theological—even a pre-religious—
option. Theologians must ask themselves with utter seriousness—
without in any way preempting the answer—whether such poverty
is not the greatest challenge confronting them as theologians,
whether their most urgent theological task is to grapple with this
reality, try to understand it, and save people from it. Such an option
is logically prior to the so-called fundamental option for the poor in
all its ethical and pastoral dimensions. It is an option whether to
look at the truth of things or not.

a. The option is above all a creaturely option that puts theology
squarely in contact with the created order. It is an option that every
human being must make—whether Christian or religious or non-
religious. It is an option that cuts across and divides humanity into
two groups: those whose feelings are lacerated by the sufferings we
have described and those whose feelings are untouched.

It is an option that sees all reality from a preferential perspective—
that sees suffering from the partiality of those who suffer and not
from the (apparently) universal perspective of the metaphysical
suffering characterizing all finite being.

b. Though this option is pre-religious, it is related to revelation
within the hermeneutical circle. On the one hand, Christian revelation in itself does not seem sufficient to bring persons to view the
world of suffering as we have described it, for there are in fact many
readings of revelation that do not see such suffering or that interpret
it differently. Many of the post-war theologies have viewed the world
existentially or personalistically and so ignored, or not made central,
basic biblical passages in which the reality of suffering is recognized
and presented as a mediation of God's self-revelation (Consider, for
instance, how the exodus or the prophets or the kingdom of God or
the beatitudes have been understood.) On the other hand, the option
to view the world from the perspective of the suffering has been the

occasion of a revision of revelation that has done greater justice simultaneously both to the actual world of today and to biblical revelation itself. This has occurred at two fundamental levels.

On the level of content, persons have rediscovered that God has revealed God's self not only *for* but *through* the sufferings of oppressed peoples. They have discovered the transcendental correlation between "God" and the "oppressed" of this world—which means they have realized the partiality of divine revelation: through this partiality for the oppressed, God reveals God's self as universal—but not the other way around! Theologians have rediscovered the God of justice, the God of liberation, the God of life; and through these qualities the plenitude of God as a God of love is manifest—but again, not the other way around. (Similar discoveries have been made in other fundamental areas of theology: christology, pneumatology, ecclesiology, etc.)

On the anthropological-formal level, theologians have rediscovered that revelation is indeed salvific—that it becomes "eu-aggelion" when (methodologically) the I and We are decentralized and forgotten and the focus is shifted to the salvation of others. From a Christian perspective, it is evident that all theology must make manifest the salvific dimension of revelation. God is *pro hominibus*. But when this salvific "pro" is understood mainly as "pro me" or "pro nobis"—no matter how real, necessary, or convincing this understanding may be—it is utterly different from an understanding that sees the salvific "pro" as primarily "pro aliis," "pro pauperibus." Stated more simply, to find the most pressing aspect of reality not in what happens to me but in what is happening to the suffering people of this world is a way for theology to decentralize itself and so to render itself more Christian, according to the biblical admonition, "Those who find their lives will lose them and those who lose their lives for the sake of the gospel will gain them." (Mark 8:35)

c. The vision we have described is, therefore, an option that cannot be justified by anything outside the option itself. It is Bultmann's "Vorverständnis"—but with a distinct content. We have already pointed out that such an option is historically reasonable or plausible. That it is also a valid Christian option is clear from what happens when it is made: it sheds more light on revelation; it reveals God as Mystery and as Parent; more simply, it produces a way of life that bears greater resemblance to the life of Jesus in his actions, his words, his attitude, and his destiny.

The Option Overcomes the "Subjection of Truth by Injustice"

The option described above may be necessary, but it is not easy. Its difficulty is evident in the simple fact that many theologians do not make it, not even in Third World countries, much less in the First World. There are weighty reasons for this, the analysis of which can lead to overcoming them.

There is, first, the difficulty of simply not being able to *see* the world of suffering, for in the First World, images or concepts of this kind of poverty described above are not available. Furthermore—and this occurs also in the Third World—one can ignore such poverty by diverting one's attention from the facticity of suffering to the problematic of the ideological or political levels—claiming that here is where the worse evils are to be found. We are dealing with two very different approaches, for instance, when we view the situation of El Salvador or Nicaragua, on the one hand, as a "Marxist problem" or, on the other, as a problem of human suffering. Both approaches have their validity, but the first locates the "greater evil" (the evil that touches the greater number of people) on the level of ideology, whereas the second finds it on the level of real experience.

There is also the difficulty of *not wanting* to see the world as it is, for to look honestly at the sufferings of the world is at the same time to have to ask about their causes. And once we begin to grasp this world as the product of our own hands, we are overwhelmed with questions, uncertainties, self-incriminations. The sin of the world is unmasked, together with the lies and false values by which we seek to veil this sin.

There is also, finally, *human hybris*—the tendency to manipulate the truth and to suppress it for our own advantage. According to Paul's dialectic in Rom. 1:18ff., from the original act of oppressing the truth there results the darkening of the heart. Then the original lie leads to the institutionalized lie.

While all of this applies to every human being and believer, it also and especially touches the theologian. Theology is, after all, the product of an activity—an activity in the first place, intellectual and therefore subject to the laws of intelligence, but also a human-Christian activity and therefore subject to the laws of the human. As both human and intellectual activity, theology is exposed to both noble possibility and sinful corruption. Given the nature of things, theology's basic sinfulness is rooted in our primary tendency to subjugate truth—in our case, in the tendency not to see reality as it is: a world of suffering.

Therefore, the option to view the world of suffering honestly has to be made in oppostion to other options and powerful forces seeking to show there are other more "reasonable" (really more "interested") ways of looking at reality or other more important forms of suffering. More positively, the option to view the primary reality of the world as a world of suffering expresses a fundamental honesty—the kind of honesty that is necessary, though perhaps not sufficient, to find the truth of God in the truth of the world, to find the divine Ultimate in the ultimacy contained in human suffering, to find the scandalous Mystery of God in the *mysterium iniquitatis* of the world, and also, as we shall see below, to find whatever there is of promise and salvation in God within the hope and the praxis alive among the suffering people of this world.

At the end of this first part of our considerations, I would like to stress what is really at stake for theology. The problem of determining where theologians stand—that is, the reality in and from which they will develop and expand and interpret their data (revelation, scripture, tradtion, the magisterium, other theologies)—is a fundamental problem whose solution will determine all the subsequent concrete reflections that the theologians will be making. We are talking about the most fundamental truth of theology, for inasmuch as this truth is not accepted, all subsequent theological discourse will be vitiated.

From Latin America one hears the insistence that the fundamental truth of theology is the suffering of this world. As Ignacio Ellacuria states, "the primary sign of our times is our crucified people," for it is by honestly recognizing this sign or truth that the eyes of theologians can really be opened to the fulness of their task. In light of what we have been talking about, we can paraphrase Kant's questions and say: What can I know? We can know the enormous suffering of crucified peoples—and here, more than elsewhere, we can begin to grasp the fulness of truth. What am I permitted to hope for? The liberation of these people, which will lead us to the fulness of hope. What must I do? Liberate these people from their crosses— which will introduce us, more effectively than anything else can, to the kind of praxis required of all human beings: active mercy.

In short, the preliminary step of all theology is—as it is for Christology—an adequate incarnation into reality as it is. And as we know from the original option of God expressed in Christology, "reality as it is" is the reality of suffering and poverty.

III. Theology as Intellectus Amoris (Intellectus Justitiae)

Thesis 2: In the presence of a suffering world, one's primary reaction is that of a compassion intent on eliminating such suffering. Like any other human and Christian activity, theology participates in this primary reaction, though in its own specific way. Thus theology will become and an *intellectus amoris*, which will include the historical specifications that love assumes when confronted with a suffering people (love as justice).

Confronted with suffering, one reacts first of all with compassion (or with a lack of compassion); confronted with the sufferings of today's world, as described above, one will react with a compassion that seeks to eliminate such suffering. In contemporary terminology, compassion becomes liberation. I am thus affirming that there is something ultimate, pre-theological, and even pre-religious in such compassion, just as there is in the suffering of today's world.

Again, this is an option. To respond to suffering with the desire to eliminate it and to do so for no other reason than that someone else is suffering—that is an option. Liberation theology participates in this option. Insofar as this option is ultimate, pre-theological, and pre-religious, we can speak about it in terms of Bonhoeffer's "etsi Deus non daretur," an expression that in its time was extolled as a graphic and rhetorical recognition of humanity's autonomy and coming of age. I make reference to this expression in order to stress graphically and rhetorically the primacy and the ultimacy of compassion as a response to the suffering of this world. Even more, when this option for compassion is carried out and is experienced as an entirely correct option, it is rediscovered as a revelation of something truly ultimate that can have no other explanation than being from God.

God in God's very self is moved to compassion (parable of the prodigal son); Jesus is the one who performs miracles out of compassion; the good Samaritan, as an example of true humanity, is someone who acts out of compassion. The demand and the guidance for such compassion are found in the very exercise of compassion, not in anything outside of it. It is true that in the exodus God wanted to make a covenant with a people; but the liberation from Egypt did not take place for the sake of a future covenant but as a primary response to oppression. It is true that Jesus was saddened when the lepers did not give thanks to God, but the healing as such was solely the result of an act of compassion. It is true that the Samaritan fulfills the great commandment—indeed he is presented as an example of this commandment—but he acts not to fulfill a commandment but out of compassion.

Theology and Praxis

The purpose of the preceding reflections was to situate the theological task, together with all other human and Christian tasks, within the global response of compassion to suffering. More specifically, our intent was to clarify the fundamental meaning of the so-called theologies of praxis and, concretely, of the theology of liberation, and to grasp why every theology must be a theology of praxis. In other words, we now have to take up the question of what theology is really all about and how theology is affected by the fact that compassion is the primary response to suffering.

a) Liberation theology affirms that praxis is related to theology in two different but dialectically united ways. In the first place, the praxis (of liberation) in its historical reality is necessary in order to provide a liberative way of knowing—or more concretely, to make known the content of theology. Leonardo Boff puts it concisely: "A true theology of liberation can be developed only on the condition that the theologian make an unequivocal option for the poor and for their liberation." He explains this option explicitly in terms of "seeing" and "doing" (analysis of the causes of poverty and defense of the poor). In this the theology of liberation is in agreement with current epistemological theory that stresses the necessary and constitutive role of praxis in bringing about knowledge. More simply, one knows reality better when one is acting within it. Or, in more technical terms, one knows reality when one not only understands reality ["hacerse cargo de la realidad"] (the noetic moment) and takes responsibility for it ["cargar con la realidad"] (the ethical moment) but when one takes charge of reality ["se hace cargo de la realidad"] (the praxic moment) (I. Ellacuria) Or in biblical terms, one knows God when one does justice (Jeremias, Osea); one knows by loving (1 John.); one realizes what it means to be human when one serves those in need (although such knowledge may not be explicit) (Matt. 25).

b) Praxis—understood as love, service or justice—is a necessary, element in the constitution of all knowledge, including theological knowledge. But the theology of liberation also stresses that theology, insofar as it is already constituted—or more precisely, in process of constituting itself—is the noetic element in all praxis. Here we have an important difference between liberation theology and other theologics that understand themselves solely as carrying out a noetic-explanatory, or interpretative, or significative role. L. Boff asserts: "All praxis contains within itself its corresponding theory. This is what we see in liberation theology, which claims to be an adequate theory for the praxis of oppressed and believing peoples; it hopes to be the ingredient of clarification and animation for the road of popular liberation, under the inspiration of the Gospel." And with even sharper precision, I. Ellacuria states: ". . . theology is the ideological moment of ecclesial and historical praxis . . . the conscious and reflective element in this praxis."

The reasons why liberation theology understands theology as the theoretico-ideological moment of praxis are varied though convergent:

Liberation theology understands theology as a specific and autonomous undertaking insofar as it is an exercise of logos, but not as completely autonomous with regard to the fundamental human-Christian task. Within and alongside other historical activities (social, cultural, political, economic) and ecclesial tasks (pastoral, liturgical, prophetic, catechetical), the theology of liberation understands its purpose as the authentic liberation of crucified peoples. Liberation theology makes use of logos primarily in order to bring about the liberation of reality and not simply to further the clarity of theological or magisterial teaching (although such results are obtained).

Thus the end purpose of liberation theology is the liberation of reality, and this is a constant in all existing theologies of liberation. Granted that from its beginnings, liberation theologians have stressed the necessity of a *liberation of theology* (J. L. Segundo)— that is, that theology (and religion in general) must free itself from its contribution to oppression; granted that they have insisted on a *theology of liberation* (G. Gutiérrez, L. Boff, I. Ellacuria)—that is, the need to use the social force of the religious and of faith and the churches to further historical liberation—what remains fundamentally clear is that the end purpose of liberation theology is the liberation of the suffering world. Or, in the language we were using earlier, its end purpose is to bring to fulfillment, urgently and effectively, the compassion that is called forth by the crucified peoples of our world.

In view of such an end purpose, liberation theology makes the theological determination of its fundamental object as the reign of God; and it understands this object as something to be realized now (even though God's reign also remains an object of hope and, eschatologically, a gift of God). The purpose of liberation theology, therefore, is that the reign of God be realized in this world, and the specific role of the theological logos is to illuminate, promote, and direct the formation of this reign.

In understanding God as the primary object of theology, liberation theologians always view God within the totality of the reign and therefore they insist that God "is to be contemplated and practiced" (G. Gutiérrez). Again, the end purpose of theology is to clarify and promote this proper relationship between God and humanity in order to permit God to make known and make clear divine truth and (this is something new!) in order to realize within history the very reality of God (God's will, love for humanity, God's taking sides with the poor). In terms that I have developed elsewhere, the end purpose of theology is to clarify and facilitate how humanity is to *respond* and *correspond* to God within history.

The insistence of liberation theology on praxis and its self-understanding as a moment of praxis are rooted ultimately not in a theoretical discussion about the perennial question "what is theology?" (although liberation theologians raise and try to answer that question) but, in the two primary options analyzed above: before a world of suffering, the primary response must be a compassion that seeks to eliminate such suffering; and this response must be present in every human, religious, and Christian activity. Every activity will be carried out according to its specific nature, but what is specific in every activity, including theology, must be subordinated to, and directed toward (and later be illuminated by) the elimination of the world's suffering. What always holds priority, therefore, is the elimination of suffering from this world, which is a praxis to which every other activity will make its specific contribution.

Theology as Intellectus Amoris

Once it is asserted that liberation theology understands itself as the ideological moment of a praxis, it becomes necessary to clarify other matters. We are talking about a praxis of liberation from massive suffering that has deep structural and unjust roots; for this reason, our praxis must take the form of justice and our theology must find forms of historical mediation that will make it effective. We are talking about a dialectical praxis that can confront the injustice that sustains so much unjust suffering; but because the roots of this praxis are grounded in an originating compassion, this praxis must be, before all else, love—a praxis that acts both in favor of and—derivatively but necessarily—in opposition to. We are talking, also, about an ecumenical praxis that in principle is in communion with all persons who respond with compassion to human suffering—although within such ecumenism, theology, as Christian theology, will have to make its specific contributions. We are talking about a praxis that, to a great extent, originated in historical or church movements that preceded theology; but now theology must seek to clarify, enhance, purify, and energize this movements.

a) These and other problems need to be analyzed in detail; but for the moment I want to focus on the new theoretical insights contained in the way the theology of liberation understands itself as the ideological moment of praxis. We are dealing with a new insight—I would say the most radically new insight that liberation theology implants in the history of theology; it is an insight that touches not only the content of theology (insofar as liberation theology holds up the reign of God as its fundamental object) but also the very notion of what theology is and what makes up the theological task. It has rightly been said that "the definition of theology is in itself a theological task; one cannot say what theology is except by doing theology" (J. Alfaro); which is to say, the concrete way of doing theology already expresses in actu how the theos of theology is understood and how one responds and corresponds to this theos. I would say that the stated self-understanding of liberation theology breaks with a centuries-old way of thinking and reflects, better than other theological self-understandings, the content of revelation and faith. Let me explain.

b) There is a long tradition of understanding theology as intellectus fidei; and inversely, faith is understood as fides quaerens intellectum. This is not only entirely legitimate, for the inclination to know the mystery of God is innate in the human being; it is also necessary, since already from the beginnings of Christianity, the divine mystery has been viewed as rational and reasonable insofar as it is real and actual, not mythical. Therefore we must be ready to give reasons for God—"to give account of your hope" (1 Pet. 3:15). Even more, the concrete God who gives God's self to be known does so in a self-revelation by grace and not solely by way of a discovery by reason. And thus, as Henri de Lubac states, all theology can be, and must be, in the final analysis "apologetic"—a rational defense of something that has been given, not discovered as a human achievement. All this is clear. It means that revelation and faith are comprehensible and conceptualizable realities that can and must be shown to be true; and the responsibility for such an important task fails to theology. Theology becomes an "intellectus"—a knowing of the mystery of God and of the mystery of humanity and history before God.

But even though such an understanding of theology is clear and has been present throughout the history of theological reflection, what it really implies has not been entirely evident. What revelation seems to tell us and what theologians have recognized is that the end of God's revelation is the *real* fact of God's self-communication in history and the *real* fact that history can and must correspond to God. This real fact—naturally from the perspective of faith—is something true and therefore something able to be known and analyzed. But the fundamental announcement of revelation is that God wants this real fact *to take place*. Insofar as it does not take place, all attempts to conceptualize or comprehend God's truth will be in vain. Stated more simply, one cannot but be impressed at the way Scripture gives an absolute priority to the need for this real revelation of God to actually take place and for human beings to actually respond and correspond to God. Jesus asserts that what is ultimate and absolutely necessary is that persons follow him. Historically, he makes clear that what is most important is not to say "Lord, Lord," but to do the will of the Father; and eschatologically he makes clear that salvation—that is, the final realization of God's designs and of the purpose of revelation—is realized when love of those in need actually takes place, no matter the explicit awareness that accompanies such love. Paul unambiguously affirms the superiority of charity over faith and hope, as does John, who adds that without love there can be no knowledge of God's truth (1 John). It is clear that it is more important for Christianity that the Christian reality *take place* rather than that it be correctly understood and that what is most fundamental for Christians is that love happen in this world.

c) All this is well known, and we hear much about it from dogmatic, moral, and spiritual theologians; yet few draw any consequences for the self-understanding of the theological task. What I would like to propose here is the theoretical possibility of understanding theology according to the systematic triad of Paul. Theology can be understood as *intellectus fidei* in order to stress what in the mystery of God is the truth to be known and what in human nature is the means to know it. But theology can also be grasped as *intellectus spei* in order to stress what in the mystery of God there is of promise and of gifted love, salvation and Gospel, and what in human nature enables persons to correspond to this gift through the practice of love. In principle we cannot say that only God as mystery and only faith as acceptance of the mystery give rise to further thought, for also the realization of hope and love can and do give rise to thought and so possess their own "intellectus" or understanding, which then serves to clarify, foster, and energize hope and love.

If we can talk about a *fides quaerens intellectum*, we can also speak of a *spes* and a *caritas quaerens intellectum*. In his theology of hope, Moltmann asserts that hope is something that seeks understanding and that the logos of eschatology functions as an *intellectus spei*. Within his theological analysis of the future as ultimate and as radically new, this is entirely reasonable. But the theology of liberation affirms that it is love—the concrete liberation from suffering in the Third World and the transformation of this world into the reign of God—that seeks understanding. Within the practice of liberating love, then, theology becomes an *intellectus amoris*. This, too, is entirely reasonable in view of the horrible suffering of the Third World, on the one hand, and the essence of Christianity as consisting ultimately in the realization of love, on the other hand. I would say that it is the very essence of Christianity that requires theology to be, before all else, an *intellectus amoris* (scholars of comparative religion seem to agree with this when they note that Christianity is fundamentally a religion of love, though it does not ignore gnosis). But it is also the historical reality in which we are living that makes the same demand. So, we must also speak of an *amor, justitia, liberatio quaerens intellectum*.

One can ask what is it, in the final analysis, that gives rise to thought and that calls for reflection. Answers vary. Reality gives rise to thought insofar as it stirs admiration, or promises something radically new, or displays massive suffering that cries for liberation. Each of these stimuli for thought has its distinctive perspective on how and why we are to reflect. Confronted by a world of suffering, one's thinking is affected by this suffering and responds with compassion; one's thinking is directed toward eliminating suffering and transforming it into the reign of God.

Liberation theology, therefore, insofar as it is theology, is an *intellectus amoris,* which in our actual world is concretized as an *intellectus justitiae.* Or, in the language that we used earlier, it can also be called an *intellectus misericordiae.* But here, love and justice and mercy are not genetives that provide a content from which we develop doctrines; rather, they are the reality that engages the intellect and enables it to realize its own nature.

As a practical conclusion to these considerations, I would add the following: When theology understands itself as *intellectus fidei,* it tends to lay out the truth, explain it, communicate its meaning in different theological perspectives. This is surely a positive and necessary task; but, as history attests, it is also exposed to the danger of refraining from changing reality and of abandoning reality to itself. And when reality is that of a suffering world, to abandon it— in the name of theology's self-understanding—is catastrophic for the suffering world and for theology. When theology understands itself as *intellectus amoris,* it seeks to operate within reality in order to save it, incarnating itself within humanity as it is, responding from an original compassion. In this way theology realizes, in its very theological activity, the fundamental demand of God to love and save this world.

The Intellectus Amoris as Mystagogy for the Intellectus Fidei

Thesis 3: The practice of love and justice is not only something that theology must foster; it is also that which can become a mystagogical reality that gives access to the mystery of God. The *intellectus amoris (justitiae)* can function as a mystagogy for the *intellectus fidei.*

The fact that liberation theology understands itself as *intellectus amoris (justitiae)* does not mean that its contents are reduced to love, compassion, justice, liberation. Rather, the theology of liberation considers itself to be a wholistic theology which, from its particular locus and its specific self-understanding, embraces the whole of revelation. Elsewhere I have tried to show that by making the reign of God its central object, liberation theology naturally deals with the totality of theological concerns. Here I would like only to point out, very schematically, how faith, hope, and charity are interrelated as a response to the mystery of God and what difference it makes in our approach to God when we start with a theology that understands itself as *intellectus amoris*.

a) In my opinion, never in the past and certainly not today has the theological response to faith in God been a purely doctrinal matter—that is, purely an assent to God's truth. By this I certainly do not want to deny that we need doctrines about God to make clear just what God we believe in; but on a deeper level, doctrine is preceded by a mystagogical grasp of the divine Mystery. In systematic terms, we can say that mystagogy has the role of leading the human being into the reality of radical *otherness* that is found in God, whether it is called Absolute Mystery, or Origin of Origins, or Absolute Future. One effective way of maintaining what in God is mystery and the mystery of salvation is the realized *hope* or the unconditional, trusting openness to what is new, unexpected, unable to be manipulated, and salvific. But mystagogy also has the role of leading us into the reality of *affinity* with God—that is, humanity's "divinization"—which consists in corresponding to the reality of God within history. This affinity becomes real through love realized within history, through making present within the world God's love and justice and compassion.

Therefore, besides being part of theology's concrete and necessary content, hope and love are also the means of being introduced into the reality of God. From this perspective, then, the *intellectus fidei*, in order to be true "intellectus" or understanding and not just doctrine, needs help from the *intellectus spei* and the *intellectus amoris*.

b) Furthermore, I believe that realized love is what best introduces us to the total reality of faith, hope, and charity. There is an a priori, fundamental reason for this: love is what brings human beings close to the reality of God. Also, the practice of love is what makes faith and hope concretely Christian. What this means can better be grasped from considering the practice of love in a suffering world.

The practice of love—which, in a suffering world, is the practice of justice—enables us to "see" history's most pressing realities and questions: that sin in history is powerful and works against justice; that all too often, justice is impotent; that those who devote themselves to promoting life often are exposed to losing their own.

The practice of justice leads to many questions, and they are profound. Is hope meaningful? Or is it wiser to choose resignation, or epicureanism, or cynicism? Rather than hope, are we better off to embrace agnosticism or a protesting atheism? By stirring up such questions, the actual practice of justice demands that if hope and faith are to be real, they have to take concrete shape—they have to be fashioned into Christian hope and faith. On the other hand, the practice of love maintains believers in a fundamental honesty and thus in a fundamental truth; it allows them to experience personally that it is in giving that one receives and it enables them to realize— at least in the case of doing justice to the poor of Latin America— what it means to be evangelized: to know more clearly the truth of this world, to experience conversion as necessary and possible, to be pardoned, to be inspired to carry on the pursuit of justice, to be born forward by others.

The struggle to bring about justice, then, confronts the believer with what is ultimate—either as something to be questioned or as something to be accepted in Christian faith. Contrary to popular opinion, it is especially in the Third World that faith and hope are placed in question most radically, for it is here that the world appears to be most starkly opposed to God's will; it is here that the battle of the gods is taking place—and the idols are winning out over the true God!

On the other hand, the struggle for justice is, in fact, carried on, and this enables hope and faith to be made concrete and to take on Christian form. It is always possible to abandon hope and faith, but because this does not happen, hope becomes Christian—it becomes the hope of a people for a new heaven and a new earth (thus overcoming the egocentric individualism of other forms of hope). A people hopes against hope, not simply because of an anthropology that is open to a possible future good, but out of a historical process that continuously calls hope into question. Thus hope becomes the hope of the poor and oppressed.

Faith in the reality of the mystery of God, then, includes all those essential teachings of revelation, which are known doctrinally but which are so difficult to realize outside the practice of love-justice: that the God who is the highest and most valued good is the God of life; that God is essentially a liberator; that God is partial toward the oppressed; but also that God is impotent and crucified, not only close to but the victim of humanity. More simply, the praxis of love-justice which demands an absolute decentering of self to the point of giving one's life and which at times brings forth life in some only to see it lost in others or in oneself—such praxis can be a profound questioning of faith but it can also become (which is frequently the case) a way of concretizing and christianizing faith.

When the prophet Michah, in a solemn moment (6:8), announced what is good for humans and what they should strive to be, he urged two things: first, to practice justice and second, to walk humbly with God. Taken together, both admonitions summarize what it means to lead a Christian life. But the mystagogical element in the Christian life—what is absolutely necessary to do and maintain—is the practice of justice; in this practice, one moves forward in the process of understanding historical life as a journey with God and toward God. In other words, through such a practice of love-justice, we sustain (or we question) the reality of hope and faith.

c) In locating love-justice in the systematic center of the triad of faith, hope and charity, there is one more point to make. Insofar as love-justice is a matter of praxis (though it is a practice that has to be carried out with a definite spirit), it might seem to some that this praxis would not directly express—in fact, it might even obstruct or annul—an element that is essential to revelation: gratitude. Gratitude would be better preserved both by faith, which allows truth to be given, and by hope, which allows the ultimate and blessed end to be provided.

But there is no reason to reduce gratitude to a response to the gift of faith and hope. Gratitude can also imbue the praxis of love-justice; we feel overwhelmed with gratitude not only because of our "new ears" by which to hear or our "new eyes" by which to see, but also because of our "new hands" by which to do. In the spirituality of liberation, much attention is given to the gratitude that pervades the practice of liberation: we have been "freed in order to free," "loved in order to love" (G. Gutiérrez).

Conclusion

I would like to summarize everything I have tried to say in this essay. We live in a suffering world, whose suffering is rooted in a death-dealing poverty that is massive, mounting, unjust, and scandalous. Confronted with such a world of suffering, one's primary and ultimate response is—as it would be before any suffering—that of compassion; this response is an option that precedes the task of theology as it does any human or Christian task. Given this kind of massive and structural suffering that pervades the Third World, the response of mercy must be a response of justice that will bring about liberation. When Christians reflect on such compassion and such justice, the theology of liberation takes shape.

If suffering constitutes the fundamental reality of our world taken as a whole, then every theology—even though in the First World there are other serious issues that must be confronted—must in some way be a theology of liberation. This certainly does not mean that every theology must replicate the liberation theology of Latin America, but it does mean that every theology must have the same fundamental object as does Latin American theology. Yes, there needs to be a variety of theologies since there is variety in our world; but within this variety, the fundamental concern and object must be the reality of suffering that pervades our world. Every theology must seek to provide a response to such suffering.

Liberation theology is one theology; it is the historical form that responsible Christian reflection has taken when confronted by a suffering world. Although this theology may take different shape in the future, its central affirmation remains permanently valid: that the most truth-filled place for any Christian theology to carry out its task is always the suffering of our world, and that in the crucified people of our world theology receives a light that it can receive no where else. In the crucified peoples of our world, theology finds—as part of the Christian paradox—its own salvation, its proper direction, and the courage to carry out its task. As the Puebla Conference stated, the poor of this world are to evangelize us. This evangelization takes place for theologians insofar as the poor offer them the opportunity to realize (not just conceptualize) the realities fundamental to theology: real faith and hope, real Gospel values, and—something that has often required of the poor their very lives—real love. Here we have the ultimate mediation of the truth about God and the truth about humanity.

NOTES

1. I emphasize this here, in this volume, since the United States, in what it does and in what it should do, is related in a special way to the suffering of the Third World. Certainly the US is related to the other two themes of this volume—cultural and religious diversity—but its responsibility for Third World suffering is direct and immediate.

2. To carry out the usual task and teachings of theology properly, it is extremely important to determine whether and how the sufferings of the world are present in the conventional places of theological activity (universities, departments, seminaries, etc.); and inversely, it is essential to determine whether and how these places make it easy or difficult for theologians/students to stand within the actual reality of a suffering world. In general, the physical locales where theology is carried on and taught veil much more than make present the suffering taking place in our world. To overcome these impediments, the theologian must make a personal option to do theology "from within" the suffering of the poor—no matter what her/his actual place of theological study; such an option naturally requires a certain material proximity to the suffering of the poor.

3. The theology of liberation is becoming more aware of these other forms of structural oppression which do not always coincide with socio-economic oppression; thus there is more talk today of the indigenous peoples of Latin America and of poor women who suffer under a twofold form of impoverishment. Liberation for such groups, though it will have to be multiple, can still be simultaneous—at the same time, liberation from both socio-economic poverty and from cultural, religious, or sexual poverty.

SUFFERING: DIFFERENT FACES AND REACTIONS
RESPONSE TO JON SOBRINO

Susan Brooks Thistlethwaite

Part of the genius of Christianity is its proclamation that the word has become flesh. Yet in theological meetings and in volumes such as this, we often turn that around. We take flesh and turn it into words. One of these days, I'm going to have the courage to "respond" to the suffering of Latin America by telling us all to keep quiet. After reading Sobrino's essay, I seriously considered doing just that—I wanted to respond by urging us all to stop talking. Is there anyway, I ask myself, that we can evoke the flesh of the suffering of which this essay speaks? While you are reading these words, a thousand children will die, will starve to death.

Fiction can evoke the reality of suffering much more effectively than statistics. Successful fiction is able to take words and make them into flesh. I have recently finished a novel that succeeds in evoking something of the reality of suffering that Sobrino speaks about—Tony Morrison's *Beloved*. The book is about a black woman who escaped from slavery with her children, and as she is about to be recaptured, she slits her baby's throat rather than have it taken back into slavery. The novel consists of the baby's haunting of the woman. It contains a line about the "palsied fury" of this baby. I would like to evoke in our midst, not all the babies of the world, but

Susan Brooks Thistlethwaite is Associate Professor of Theology at Chicago Theological Seminary. She has written several books, the most recent of which is an introductory textbook on liberation theology for theology students, Lift Every Voice: Constructing Christian Theologies from the Underside (San Francisco: Harper & Row, 1989). (Portions of this response appear in that text.) She and her husband and three children live in Chicago.

just this one, just this suffering—this suffering which is part of our North American history and which has seeped down into this moment, forming part of the structures in which we go about our theological trade.

All around the world, the blood of other such babies—other such murdered children—cries out and will not be silent. In the novel, the baby's "palsied fury" shakes the house. Our houses, too, are being shaken. Our theological houses are shaking from the fury of the murdered people around the world. Language is so inadequate to evoke this reality. To try to do so academically is dangerous, for we think we known when we really don't. Yet in the course of the various projects of liberation around the world, there have been some who have become what I would call "organic intellectuals." They are theologians who have accepted as their task the articulation of the pain of the world. I understand Jon Sobrino to be one of these organic intellectuals. They are not armchair intelligentsia. Formally trained in the best schools of theology, they have taken it as their job to articulate the struggle for liberation of particular communities— and thus to be personally committed to this struggle as they apply their skills to help lead and clarify it.[1]

Sobrino argues that theology must be situated in a world in which millions of people are murdered. How can this not be our context? We are doing theology in a world in which the death of the poor and suffering is being *caused* by others. Their death is not natural or accidental; nor is it simply the result of sin. It is the concrete situation of structured injustice in the particular context of El Salvador. From the beginning, liberation theologians have argued that context is particularly important; the way we understand our context significantly shapes the method, the content, and the struc- tures of our theology. Because liberation theologians come out of different social, political, and economic contexts, there are profound differences among them. I stress these differences in light of my experience of trying to teach the theologies of liberation to North American students; this experience has made me an expert in the many ways of distorting the understanding of the theologies of liberation. This happens especially when students try to grasp and appreciate the differences among liberation theologians.

Certainly, all theologies are contextual; even so-called objective, traditional theologies are. Yet in seminary catalogues, we find the general heading "Theology," and under it, "Liberation Theology," "Feminist Theology," "Black Theology." To be accurate, one should formulate the general heading as "White North American Patriarchal Theology." In its present use, the term "Theology" is a code word suggesting that "this is theology and the rest of what you people do is contextual and limited." By stressing the importance of contextual differences, we can help correct a serious misunderstanding on the part of many white North American theologians about so-called liberation theology. There is a strong tendency to lump all these theologies together. The effects of doing so are similar to those resulting from the First World's creation of the term "Third World." It fashions a kind of bloodless universalism that robs individuals and societies of their particularity. In our concerns for clarity, we go forth and denude people and movements of their individuality and never come to see how different liberation theologies are from one another.

I might adapt the opening line from *Anna Karenina* and say that each society, like each family, is unhappy in its own way. The banner of Third Worldhood is therefore absurd and denigrating. It is, according to Shiva Naipul, a "flabby concept"—an ideological tool of the West with which we throw everyone else onto one pile dubbed "Third World."[2] There are very real differences among the Latin American theologies of liberation, and the same is true of North American white feminist liberation theologies, gay and lesbian liberation theologies, Black liberation theologies, Native American theologies. All of these are not clones of each other; nor are they interchangeable. Each has its own particular aims, emphases, viewpoints, analyses—depending on the demands of the social situation and context in which each is lodged. Latin American theologians have given special attention to developing the notions of human agency, freedom, history. Native American and feminist theologians have concentrated more on constructing new views of nature, while North American Black and Latin American theologians have contributed new understandings of sin and evil as structural and systemic. White feminists have proposed creative ways of understanding sin as self-denial, a point I will return to in a moment.

It is therefore important to speak of liberation theologies, rather than liberation theology. One of the greatest honors you can do someone is to recognize not only that they exist but that they exist in a specific way. Yet to say this, and to insist that liberation theologies are imbedded in different contexts, can still be completely misunderstood. This is what I have found so often to be the case with my North American seminary students; they interpret the different contexts as differing personal experiences—as "you do your thing and I'll do mine." This is not at all what Sobrino is talking about. The students miss the meaning of different contexts because they have no notion of structural economic and social analysis. They understand context intrapsychically.

And yet if, as Sobrino maintains, the suffering of the world is not an option to ignore, there is a point of connection among the differing theologies of liberation. It is important that all liberation theologians, no matter what their context, recognize and underline that they are connected by the reality of suffering. Though suffering may look different in different contexts, it is the same reality.

This issue has been the occasion for a good deal of discussion among theologians of liberation. Some of them have been blind to other forms of oppression within other contexts, even though these other contexts are connected with their own. In earlier years, for example, male Black liberation theologians ignored sexism until they heard from Black women; challenged by Black feminist liberation theologians, this theology has changed. For many years, also Latin American liberation theologians have ignored sexism, but they too are changing, having listened to the criticisms of women within these movements.[3] And speaking as a white North American feminist, I can recognize that my movement has long ignored classism and racism and focused on sexism only from a white northern middle-class perspective. There is a great danger, therefore, in the usually implicit assumption that one's description of problems and possibilities is inclusive of all the other forms of oppressions; this is not usually the case. When challenged, Black, Native American, and Hispanic women told us that we white women did not speak for them; in fact, we didn't even speak for all white women.

Almost all liberation theologians have ignored heterosexism and homophobia, and have failed to see sexual and domestic violence as significant forms of oppression. Fortunately, liberation theologians have begun to replace their arguments over which form of oppression is primary with the recognition that differemt forms of oppression are interlocking. I myself, in responding to Sobrino's essay, am uncertain as to how to relate what he says to the situation of white North American feminism, for I have to admit that as a white woman I have one foot in oppression and one foot in being oppressed: as white and as North American, I have privileges; yet as a woman I am also oppressed.

We First World people must therefore be careful of using the term "solidarity" too facilely. In this regard, I have found very useful Gail Peterson's study of the distinction between solidarity and alliance. Peterson is Dutch, and she included a large variety of women— Black, Hispanic, white Jewish, white Christian, lesbian, heterosexual—in her study of how these people understand solidarity. She came to the conclusion that *solidarity* signifies knowledge of, respect for, and unity with people whose identities are in important ways common to one's own—that is, among persons who are similar racially, economically, in sexual preference, religiously, in the concrete experience of oppression. It is a horizontal solidarity. *Alliances,* on the other hand, indicate knowledge of, respect for, and commitment with people who are in essential ways different but who have similar interests. Alliances consist of people who have chosen to work together for social reconstruction.[4]

I find it almost offensive—in myself as well—when I hear us First World people speaking of being in solidarity with Central Americans. We really don't have a clue to what kind of suffering they are enduring. As North Americans, our job is to figure out how we are contributing to this suffering and to stop it. This is *alliance.* I have stopped using the term solidarity.

The particular methodological perspective I bring to reading Sobrino's essay is that of feminism. But feminism, too, has its differences. Mary Daly has argued that patriarchy is everywhere; even outerspace and the future have been colonized by the patriarches.[5] And yet other feminists would argue that patriarchy does not look the same everywhere. While Daly does not acknowledge the particular permutations of patriarchy in different social, political, economic, and cultural contexts, most feminist liberation theologians break down their analyses of patriarchy and interface them with other modes of analysis such as that of race or class. Applied to Sobrino's essay, this means two things: 1) a Hispanic woman's reading of his essay would be very different from my own; 2) theologies of patriarchy are adaptable to different contexts, including that of liberation theology.

In reading Sobrino's essay in its original Spanish, I was struck by the expression *"los pobres."* I checked my Spanish dictionary and found that there is no feminine form—only the masculine noun *los pobres.* Even though the feminization of poverty is a reality, there is in Spanish no feminine form for the poor. Millions of the people throughout the world who are being murdered—who are starving to death—are women, particularly women with dependent children.

But the suffering Spanish-speaking woman does not even have a word for her poverty. And so I submit the term *"las pobras."* I just made that up. That's what one has to do—make up new expressions. Marcuse said that the success of a system depends on its ability to make alternatives unthinkable. One of the best ways of making something unthinkable is to make it unsayable. So where necessary, we have to make up new words. We must be able to think and talk about *las pobras*, for there are a lot of poor women, and they're dying.

Sobrino's stress on compassion and mercy as the primary response to suffering might also be seen differently in light of what feminist theologians have said about self-denial as women's primary sin. What constitutes the Christian virtues—humility, compassion, mercy, selflessness—becomes sin for women insofar as they are taught by the dominant culture not to assert themselves. This is also the analysis that Ada Maria Isasi-Diaz and Yolanda Tarango make in their new book on Hispanic women's liberation theology.[6] In my context—that is, in my situation as a North American white feminist—my besetting sin is not hubris, not pride, but self-denial. Therefore my response to massive suffering, which is the general context for all theology, is not best understood as compassion or mercy but as *anger*.

What is our problem as North Americans? One of the most seductive forces that hold us in our stance as oppressors is the cloying, almost cocoon-like seduction of consumerism. I find that I cannot resist this seduction unless I get angry enough at oppression to break through the things that hold me in the stance of oppressor—as well as of oppressed. This will give me the energy to make the break, to change.

Women's anger is considered particularly frightening. Some people say that one of the problems with the female image of God is that it does not express the anger of God. Anyone who says that never met my great-aunt. She was an organizer for the International Ladies Garment Workers' Union and had an incredible capacity to get angry at injustice. She just died this year at ninety-five, and I have been remembering how she spent many years of her life basically getting furious. I know her feelings; I share her anger. I believe that God is coming, and I think She is furious at injustice.

I want to end by lifting up what I think is Sobrino's "last word" on suffering—and what is certainly my own. Anyone who reads his essay—anyone who is in touch with the world he describes—cannot help but feel overwhelmed by the reality of suffering. Whether our response is one of compassion or anger, the experience of suffering must lead us to a further experience. Despite the fact that weekly I counsel women who are battered, who are abused, who are violently degraded, I believe and I contend that suffering is not the last word on the human condition. In fact, what moves people to cry out at injustice is their experience in their families and their communities that, despite the massive structures of injustice surrounding them, parents do care for their children. Every morning, a lot of people get up to prepare breakfast. This is real too. Husbands and wives can love each other; communities can pull together. This is what is felt in the base communities—the *reality of grace*. What is so offensive about suffering is that it contradicts the reality of grace.

Leonardo Boff's book *Liberating Grace* helped me grasp this more clearly. He states that we cannot ignore factors of biographical conditioning in our understanding of why Christian theologians have traditionally viewed grace as the unmerited bridge over which we can escape the experience of alienation and despair. He sees this especially in Paul, Augustine, and Martin Luther—three men who have set the context for western notions of grace. According to Boff, all of them suffered painful experiences of alienation and a deep inability to carry out the human project of holiness.[7] Also Paul Tillich's theology is characterized by a powerful experience of the alienation of despair. Sobrino speaks from a different experience of reality, and therefore a different experience of grace. Boff suggests that Paul, Augustine, and Luther, in their theology and piety, never took conscious note of the historical mediations of grace—of the gratuitous presence of grace in countless profane dimensions of their own daily lives. They missed the ordinariness of the reality of grace. In the writings of many liberation theologians such as Sobrino, on the other hand, I witness the recognition of the presence of grace in nature, in politics, in human interests, in human growth and development. His is a view of grace less estranged from the natural world and human life and work. According to liberation theologians, God's movement in the world is not so extraordinary after all.

Finally, a word of caution. Liberation theology does not tell you much if you enter it as a tourist. Learning the method of the theologies of liberation, understanding the commitment to doing

theology contextually, communally, concretely, means asking yourself where in your social location is justice struggling to be born and
how can you help. As Audre Lorde has written, "Survival is not an
academic skill."[8]

NOTES

1. Juan Luis Segundo, *Theology and the Church: A Response to Cardinal Ratzinger and a Warning to the Church* (Minneapolis: Seabury, 1985), p. 150. The notion of organic intellectual is Antonio Gramsci's.

2. Shiva Naipul, "The Third World" Does Not Exist," *Global Perspectives: A Newsletter of the Center for Global Education*, March–April, 1987, p. 1.

3. See, for example, Elsa Tamez, *Against Machismo: Interviews by Elsa Tamez* (Bloomington, IN: Meyer-Stone, 1987).

4. Gail Peterson, "Alliances between Women: Overcoming Internalized Oppression and Internalized Domination," *SIGNS: A Journal of Women in Culture and Society*, 12 (1986) 148.

5. Mary Daly, *Gyn-Ecology: The Metaethics of Radical Feminism* (Boston: Beacon, 1978), p. 1.

6. Ada Maria Isasi-Diaz and Yolanda Tarango, *Hispanic Women: Prophetic Voice in the Church* (San Francisco: Harper & Row, 1988).

7. *Liberating Grace*, John Drury, tr. (Maryknoll: Orbis Books, 1979), p. 23.

8. Audre Lorde, "The Master's Tools Will Never Dismantle the Master's House," in *This Bridge Called My Back: Writings by Radical Women of Color*, Cherie Moraga with Gloria Anadaldua, eds. (Watertown, MA: Persephone Press, 1981), p. 100.

LIBERATION AND MARXISM

Enrique Dussel

Translated by Irene B. Hodgson and José Pedrozo

A description of how liberation theology and Marxism are themat-
ically related should include at least four dimensions. First, the
presuppositions of praxis: the political dimension consisting of the
relationship of faith to recent Latin American historical reality.
Second, the epistemological dimension or the presuppositions of
theory: the relationship of faith and the social sciences in Latin
America. Third, the criticism, both from within the church and from
outside, of the linking of liberation theology and Marxism, especially since the *Instructions* (1984 and 1986) of the Congregation for
the Doctrine of the Faith. And, fourth, the paths that are presently
opening for a fruitful use of Marxism by liberation theology.

I. Latin American Historical Praxis: Faith and Politics

Theology emerges from Christian praxis, and, for that reason, we
should look at historical praxis, at the relationship between Christians and Marxists, in order to determine possibilities for the theoretical use of Marxism in liberation theology.

Enrique Dussel earned his doctorate in philosophy in Madrid and in history at the
Sorbonne. He studied church history in Mainz and then lived for two years with Paul
Gauthier in Israel. Once a political refugee from his native Argentina, Dussel now
lives and teaches in Mexico. He is a committee member of the theological review
Concilium and president of the Commission for Church History in Latin America.
Among his works recently published in English are Philosophy of Liberation (Orbis
Books, 1985) and Ethics and Community (Orbis Books, 1988).

Historical Lack of Encounter

The social doctrine of the church has prevented Christians from arriving at any real understanding of Marxism. From the early encyclical *Noscitis et nobiscum* (1849) to *Rerum Novarum* (1891), [1] in which Marxism was condemned because its followers "excite in the poor hatred of the rich, [and] intend to do away with private property and replace it with common ownership,"[2] and even later in *Quadragesimo Anno* (1931), the Vatican's position has remained unchanged: unmitigated condemnation.[3] In Latin America, in the same way, anticommunism was the general position of all Christians—remember that Chardin founded the JOC (Young Catholic Workers) to fight Marxism; Father Hurtado in Chile launched social action as an anticommunist crusade; also Bishop Franceschi in Argentina, and, even in the turbulent year 1968, in Mexico, Father P. Velázquez continued in the same line (and these are the most "progressive" figures). Perhaps no one criticized Marxism as passionately as Bishop Mariano Rossell y Arellano (1938–1964) in Guatemala who with his pastoral messages "On the Communist Menace" (1945) and "On the Excommunication of the Communists" (1949), encouraged the fall of the populist movement of J. Arbenz. Bishop Victor Sanábria (1899–1952) of Costa Rica, was a notable exception—creating ties between the church and the Communist Party in 1948.

Even so, the Marxists themselves (since the founding of the Communist parties in 1920) were not ready for any dialogue either, given their theoretical dogmatism (atheism and philosophical materialism) and their historical errors.[4] Christians who beginning in 1930 participated militantly in Catholic Action or in the Christian Democratic Party (after 1936 in Chile) concentrated much of their "apostolic" work in fighting Communist youth organizations (when these existed).[5] The confrontation had lasted a century and was total.

Initial Phase of Encounter (1959–1968)

In January of 1959, Pope John XXIII called for the Second Vatican Council, and in that same month Fidel Castro entered triumphantly into Havana. It was a new era. The worldwide, and especially Latin American, Catholic renewal, coincided with the death of Stalin and with the Twentieth Party Congress in Moscow (1956) under the leadership of Krushchev. The crisis of populism (Vargas, Perón,

Rojas Pinillas, etc.) also led to that of Catholic Action. The JOC (Young Catholic Workers) and the JUC (Catholic University Students), which were more specialized groups, had ears better tuned to the new developments. The Movement of Popular Education began in northeast Brazil. In 1959 a Christian university group founded *Popular Action* in Sao Paulo, the first to declare itself to be socialist-inspired.[6] Here we have the beginnings of radical Christian commitment to politics. The question of "faith and politics" became a central concern. It is true that many Christians, upon entering the political arena, "lost" their faith. The issue is: why did they "lose" their faith? Should there not have been some other expression of faith that could have survived the "test" of politics? The "foquist" experiment—to which many young people committed themselves during the 60s—ended with the total commitment of Camilo Torres and his death in 1966.[7] Another path had to be found.

Even so, dialogue with the Marxists was possible in praxis. The "new left" itself had lost much of its dogmatism and opened itself to new positions which allowed it to come to a better understanding of the "popular" problem. Shortly afterwards, Althusserianism would provide new motivation for post-Stalinist Marxism.

The failure of economic "development" (Kubitschek in Brazil; Frondizi in Argentina; Rómulo Betancourt in Venezuela; López Mateo in Mexico; Frei in Chile; Caldera, also in Venezuela) provided, in the same way, arguments for new kinds of Christian commitments. It was now the poor, the people, the historically oppressed, who were calling both Christians and Marxists to their service.

Convergence (1968–1979)

Events during the year 1968 profoundly affected Latin America. From Tlatelolco in Mexico (with the deaths of more than 400 students) to the Argentinian "cordobazo" (with the fall of Onganía), there were student and popular movements in all countries. Also of enormous historic importance was the success of the Conference of Latin American Bishops in Medellín, together with the failure of the Chilean Christian Democrats (1964–1970). For its part ISAL (tied to the World Council of Churches of Geneva) brought to Latin America the experience of revolutionary Christians of Africa and Asia.

The first significant instance of joint work of Christians and Marxists was carried out during the government of Salvador Allende (1970–1973), within the *Frente Popular* (Popular Front) itself by

MAPU (a Christian movement which grew out of the Christian Democrats). This movement was the fruit of two processes: the already emerging theology of liberation and the Christians for Socialism movement. The latter was not unrelated to the crisis that was produced in ILADES (Latin American Institute of Social Studies), when in 1969 the Bigo-Vekemans group opposed the Marxist-based analysis proposed by the Arroyo-Hinkelammert group.[8] University and labor Catholic action groups (JOC and JUC) followed these events closely and identified themselves with them throughout Latin American—from Mexico and Central America to the Caribbean and South America (even Brazil).

Furthermore, the kind of dialogue that took place between Christians and Marxists in France (which began during the "Weeks of the Intellectuals" in the 50s) and which also included the leaders of Catholic Action (such as Fathers Blanquart or Cardonnel), also occurred in Latin America. Such dialogue was popularized in the 70s by the Althusserian work of Marta Harnecker, who, although a structuralist Marxist, was president of the Chilean JUC. Around this time Fidel Castro declared: "I believe that we have arrived at a time in which religion can enter the political arena in response to people and their material needs."[9]

And in the declaration of Christians for Socialism, we read:

> Christians are clear that their political practice cannot be derived directly from their faith. Revolutionary Christians use the mediations of science and of revolutionary theory in order to open a historical path for action together with the working class and the Latin American people.[10]

In Argentina, because of the return of Peronist populism (1973), the theme of the "people" became central, and although not easily categorized as Marxist, was rapidly assimilated by liberation theology.[11] Luis Corvalán, Secretary of the Chilean Communist Party, wrote from exile:

> In these conditions religion loses its character of opiate of the people, and, on the contrary, in the measure in which the church commits itself to humanity, one can say that, instead of alienating, religion is a source of inspiration in the struggle for peace, liberty and justice.[12]

The year was somber: Allende fell and generalized repression spread through all of Latin America. Amid the darkness, the "base communities" would illuminate a path for the people, the poor, the oppressed. The dynamic we have been analyzing would grow stronger.

Beyond the Strategic Alliance (1979–1984)

The triumph of the Sandinista revolution provided the first historical test of the feasibility of the dialogue between Christians and Marxists. Theory became reality. In their declaration of October 7, 1980, the FSLN (National Sandinista Front for Liberation) clearly moved beyond the worldwide period of misunderstanding between Christians and postcapitalist revolution—and this lesson would be learned not only by Africa and Asia, but also by Cuba and the Soviet Union:

> We, the Sandinistas, affirm that *our experience demonstrates* that when Christians, *supported by their faith* are capable of responding to the necessities of the people and of history, their own beliefs impel them to revolutionary militancy. Our experience shows us that one can be a believer and at the same time a committed revolutionary and that there is no unresolvable contradiction between the two commitments.[13]

The use of social analysis by liberation theology allowed the Nicaraguan episcopate to write:

> If socialism means, as it should mean, preeminence of the interests of the Nicaraguan majority and a nationally planned economic model that is solidly and progressively participative, we have no objection.[14]

During the ensuing years, the deaths of hundreds of Latin American Christian martyrs, especially that of Archbishop Oscar A. Romero on March 24, 1980, sealed these affirmations. Although great progress was made in opening channels of communication between Christians and revolutionary movements, there were still clear tensions within the respective institutions themselves (that is, a traditionalist church opposed to the new openings, and dogmatic revolutionaries who continued to insist on atheism and materialism.)

New Contradictions Guaranteeing Past Achievements (Since 1984)

The criticism of liberation theology contained in the 1984 *Instruction* from the Congregation for the Doctrine of the Faith centered its argument on the fundamental Marxist contamination of that theology. This produced a new debate; but, at the same time, it basically convinced the Marxists (and the countries with "real socialism") [that is, avowed Communist countries] that liberation theology was not merely a fad, but rather, a deeply-rooted current within the church which could provide people with convictions that enabled them to defend themselves publicly, even before the highest tribunal of the church. The persecutions that liberation theology suffered after 1972, especially from figures within the Latin American Bishops Conference, were now coming from Rome. In response to criticism, liberation theology reaffirmed its basic principles: that the fundamental option for the poor and the oppressed demands of theological discourse instruments of analysis that permit it to carry out an authentic, pertinent, adequate reflection. The use of the social sciences (and of Marxism if necessary) is analogous to the need for a scientific instrument that has been felt by all schools of theology since the second century of the Christian era when the School of Alexandria used Platonism, which was also considered satanic by many Christians of the time.

We shall see that the use of Marxist analysis by liberation theology, in a manner fully consistent with the tradition and the doctrine of the Church, would continue and intensify.

II. Epistemological Dimension: Faith and the Social Sciences

We first want to establish that theology is a reflection that grows out of praxis and needs some form of theoretical analysis to carry out its own discourse. We will then have to take up three other issues: Why use Marxist analysis? Which Marxism are we talking about? How do liberation theologians make use of Marxism?[15] This last question merits particular consideration.

Theology and Scientific Discourse

Since the question of methodology has been amply treated in recent theological discussions, all we need to do here is review certain key ideas and situate them in the framework of our analysis.

All theology, in any given historical moment, uses some specific scientific discourse to construct its reflection.

Faith is the fundamental moment of theological discourse. But faith is an aspect of *praxis*: of *Christian* praxis. Christian action (praxis) includes the "light" that illuminates all action considered "Christian." That is, existential faith, ordinary or prophetic, illuminates the daily praxis of Christian living, as a following of Jesus of Nazareth. In the same way, praxis (which includes faith as its Christian base) is the constituent antecedent of theology. Theology is nothing but a theoretical discourse (for Thomas Aquinas, it is spiritual, sapiential and methodical, but, at the same time, practical) that starts from Christian praxis and uses the light of faith to reflect on, think about, and describe rationally the reality of the problems that such a praxis daily faces.

Whether as an ordinary or a prophetic reflection, theology characteristically seeks to provide a "methodical" reflection for the Christian life of any period both in that life's daily routine and in its extraordinary and innovative moments; and it seeks to elaborate this reflection according to the time's most developed rules or demands for rationality. In Babylonia during the sixth century BCE, the "Adamic myth" was a theological construct corresponding to the best of the symbolic rationalism of its time (for example, as compared to the myth of Gilgamesh). Jesus used the theological instruments of his time—those of the rabbinic and Pharisaic schools, etc.). Since the second century CE, with the appearance of the Greek Christian theological schools (first among the Apostolic Fathers and later the Apologists or the Alexandrines), Christian believers constructed a theological discourse with the "science" (*episteme*) of its time: Platonic philosophy (and theology).[16] Platonic "categories" allowed the construction of a Christian theology using instruments that in the first century had been considered part of the "pagan" culture and, as such, *intrinsically* perverted. In the twelfth century, Albert Magnus and Thomas Aquinas made use of Aristotle at a time when his philosophy was *explicitly condemned*. This resulted in a theological discourse that has dominated Catholic theology to our days.

In the nineteenth century, the German theologian Möhler used philosophical instruments of his time to profoundly renovate German Catholic theology which greatly lagged behind Protestant theology already using the best philosophical insights from the Enlightenment and Hegel. It would not be until the twentieth century that Rahner could make use of a Heideggerian existentialism and Metz could draw on the Frankfurt "critical school" to bring theology up to the level of the best contemporary philosophical thought.

So it is clear that theology has always needed a method of analysis (traditionally almost always a philosophical one) in order to fashion praxis and faith into a methodical, rational, scientific discourse. For Thomas, therefore, theology was a "science" (although a very special kind of science).

Why Use Marxist Analysis?

Liberation theology grows out of the experience of Christian praxis, out of faith. Juan Luis Segundo tells us that it was in 1953, with the help of Melevez in Louvain, that he came to this fundamental insight; in my case, it was during the years 1959–1961 that Paul Gauthier in Nazareth made me see the necessity of evangelizing *the poor*, since the Christian rule for life was based on *Isaiah* 61:1 (*Luke* 14:18): "The Spirit of the Lord God is upon me, because the Lord has anointed me to bring good tidings to *the afflicted*."[17] In 1959 Comblin wrote his *Fracaso de la Acción Católica*, which opened a new current of theological thought in Latin America. Gutiérrez remembers that already in 1964 he had his first intuitions into experience as spirituality, and theology as wisdom.[18]

Historically speaking, before the formation of liberation theology as theology, it existed in the praxis and faith of the church, that is, in Christian communities, and in those who would later shape it as a theology. In order to serve militant Christians, this Latin American theology, from its beginnings, had to explain the theological justification for the "*political* commitment" of these Christians. But, why should Christians commit themselves politically in the first place? The answer is evident: in order to effect social, economic, and political changes that would allow the exploited classes (on a first level), the poor (on a theological level) and the Latin American people (ultimately) to achieve a just, human, fulfilled life.[19] It was this double necessity of thinking theologically about the "political commitment" to serve the oppressed, the poor, the people, that required the nascent theology to use other analytical and interpretative instruments than those known by previous theological tradition. Faced with the absence of an adequate established philosophy, the new theologians had to turn to *critical Latin American* social sciences. These were not just sciences that were "social" (such as sociology, economics, etc.), but also "critical" (because they tried to reveal and contextualize the reality of injustice) and "Latin American" (because our continent had so many of its *own* issues to resolve). The turn to these sciences was not, then, an *a priori*, dogmatic, or epistemological decision. Rather, on the basis of *Christian praxis and faith*, with essentially spiritual and pastoral criteria (stemming from Christians' commitment to fight politically against injustice, according to the social doctrine of the church), new categories for adequate analysis had to be found.

And so the nascent Latin American theology developed its use of Marxist categorical tools of analysis (proceeding historically from the French Marxist tradition, which used them with groups of students and workers). Juan Luis Segundo, José Comblin, Gustavo Gutiérrez, and I, were part of the generation that studied in France (or Belgium). These tools—we will see which ones and how they were used—permitted the new *theology*, which after 1968 began to be called *Liberation* (in Rubem Alves' Princeton thesis),[20] to achieve unexpected results in the analysis of historical, social and political realities (as well as in other areas such as sexism and racism, for, once discovered, the methodology was applicable to other areas of thought). All this produced, if you will, an "epistemological revolution" in the history of Christian theology. For the first time, the critical social sciences were used. Political economy and sociology, which had begun in the mid-nineteenth century, were now being used by Christian theology. As "modernism" gave rise to a crisis because of the use of *history* in theology (from Renán to Blondel), in the same way, liberation theology created a crisis when it adopted the *social sciences*, of which Marxism forms the critical nucleus. When we look at this crisis from the perspective of the twenty-first century, we will realize how important its missionary function was in the contemporary world—at the end of the twentieth century— that is, in the world of the poor of Latin America, Africa and Asia, and, especially in the real socialist nations, for whom liberation theology was the only intelligible and prophetic theology possible.

Which Marxism Does Liberation Theology Use?

As is commonly known, liberation theologians use a "certain kind" of Marxism—and implicitly or explicitly exclude another kind. We will come back to this point later when we explain the reasons for the *Instruction* against liberation theology of the Congregation for the Doctrine of the Faith in 1984.

First of all, in assessing the variety of Marxisms, liberation theologians universally reject "dialectical materialism." No liberation theologian accepts the materialism of Engels (in *The Dialectic of*

Nature) or of Lenin, Bujarín, and Stalin as philosophically conher-
ent.[21] Marx is accepted and used as a social critic. The contact with
Marx occurred in two ways: first, through secondary sources (as seen
in the works of Yves Calves in France or Bernhard Welte in Germany); or second, especially at the beginning of liberation theology,
through reading the "young" Marx directly, that is, up to the 1848
Manifesto. The influence of French thinkers was dominant in the
first generation of liberation theologians (Segundo, Comblin, Gutiérrez, Dussel, at the beginning of the 60s): after J. Maritain, there was
E. Mounier, and then Lebret. Teilhard de Chardin also provided
inspiration for this period. The Cuban Revolution (1959) drew attention to Marx: people began to read the young Marx together with
"Che" Guevara, Gramsci and Lukacs. Later we shall see how each of
these writers influenced theologians' use of a "humanist" Marx (in
the terminology of the time)—a Marx who is not dogmatic, nor
"economistic," nor naively materialistic. The French priests Cardonnel and Blanquart were also influential in the "reception" of Marxism by the future liberation theology. There was no systematic direct
contact with the "definitive" Marx (after 1857), nor is there much
use of this Marx today.

While such thinkers as Korsch, Goldmann, and even Trotsky have
not affected liberation theology (although Trotsky has had indirect
effect), other schools of thought have been influential since 1968.
Besides Antonio Gramsci, whose influence was present from the
beginning and grew even stronger, the first significant Marxist impact was that of the Frankfurt School through the works of the
"North American" Marcuse—who clearly influenced Rubem Alves'
work in 1968 and had a more diffuse effect on other liberation
thinkers (including J.B. Metz in Germany). Ernst Bloch also had a
widespread impact—especially in Moltmann's studies on utopian
vision and hope. Even more significantly, the work of Althusser,
translated for the classroom by Marta Harnecker,[22] would exercise a
strong influence not only on the theology of liberation (especially
on the second generation of theologians[23]) but also on the entirety of
Latin American Marxist thought.

Of the Latin American Marxists, not only "Che" Guevara, but also
Mariategui and Sánchez Vásquez have influenced the thought of
some liberation theologians. Of course, the ideas of Fidel Castro
since 1959 are required reading, especially his views on religion
(similar to those of Rosa Luxembourg, who influenced the Popular
Action movement in Brazil).

Along with the French thinkers already mentioned, Italian liberation theologian Giulio Girardi has also had a significant influence, mainly in the way his clearly Marxist position evolved from a decidedly "classist" posture at the beginning to a later view that incorporated the "people" as the historical subject of liberation praxis.

But the kind of Marxism that has most affected liberation theology has not been the "theoretical" kind we have been considering but rather the *Latin American* sociological and economical Marxism of "dependency theory," as elaborated by thinkers such as Orlando Fals Borda, Theotonio dos Santos, Faletto, Cardoso (many of whom, in reality, were not and are not Marxists). It is this sociology of "dependence," in its strong criticism of functionalism and of developmentalism, that brought about the epistemological rupture of liberation theology from the dominant theology. Therefore, the position of a Gunther Frank—despite all the criticism it has received—must be viewed as a determinative factor in liberation theology before 1972. In the same way, the views of F. Hinkelammert—as a Marxist and a theologian—represent perhaps the only presence of the "definitive" Marx, for at the end of the 60s in Santiago, a certain group at the Center for Studies of the National Reality did a serious study of *Das Capital* which made possible a unique opening to Marxism within one of the most creative currents of theology of liberation during the 80s.

To date, there has been no adequate study of this entire complex history; neither is there a history of contemporary Latin American Marxism, much less of its presence in Christian movements.[24] Our brief historical review shows, however, how simplistic it is for conservatives to accuse liberation theology of being ideologically "Marxist". *Long before its critics* mounted their charges, liberation theology accepted, with complete Christian responsibility, the difficult task of incorporating a "kind" of Marxism that was compatible with the Christian faith of the prophets and Jesus and with ancient and recent ecclesiastical (which means ecumenical) tradition. Stalinist dogmatism, or textbook economics, or "philosophical" Marxism, are not at all part of liberation theology's use of Marxism.

How Do the Liberation Theologians Incorporate Marxism?

An adequate answer to the above question would require a lengthy treatise. In these few pages, we offer only a preliminary sketch of how some theologians make use of Marxism; our intent is to provide a few examples rather than an exhaustive discussion.

The elaboration of the theory of development was pre-Marxist; so were the early works of Segundo or of Comblin.[25] The theology of revolution, however, did use Marxist tools for its analysis, but not in the same way as liberation theology did.[26] I believe that the historical difference between these theologies is to be found in dependence theory, in the way this theory "Latin Americanized" Marxism and gave it a sociohistorical dimension. Hugo Assmann was the first to explain adequately the "demarcation line" between such theologies as those of development, of revolution, of hope (Moltmann), and of politics (Metz).[27] We must not forget that the starting point of this entire development was a book that made history: *Marx and the Bible* by Porfirio Miranda, which presented the encounter of Marxism and Christianity in a direct and biblical manner.[28] But, paradoxically, it is a Christian who examines Marx and not a Marxist interpretation of the encounter.

Rubem Alves, in his Princeton thesis of 1968 ("Toward a Theology of Liberation"), analyzes the North American situation at that time from the perspective of H. Marcuse using, but, at the same time, transcending, the Protestant tradition of theology of revolution.[29] For Alves, the "political humanism" (of a Marcuse) surpasses mechanistic technologism and shows the importance of the political; on the other hand, "humanistic Messianism" (philosophical Marxism) does not grasp the element of transcendence present in all liberation movements (as does Christian "messianic humanism").[30] Alves' quotes from the young Marx, from Marcuse, from Alvaro Viera Pinto (*Conciencia e Realidade Nacional*), from Bloch, from Paulo Freire, reveal the kind of Marxism he is using.[31] It does not yet involve social analysis.

Hugo Assmann says:

> The language of "liberation" is language that articulates socio-political, revolutionary consequences to be drawn from the analytical language of "dependence." It is directly linked with an analytical focus on the phenomenon of underdevelopment.[32]

This is a criticism of "developmentalist" language used by certain Latin American social scientists—not necessarily Marxists—intent on explaining the poverty and oppression of the Latin American peoples. Although Assmann accepts the paradigm of super- and infrastructure, he is making a new use of Marxist categories by adopting the antieconomic theory of ideology proposed by Gramsci and Lukacs. From his broad background in Marxist thought, as well as in the German tradition, Assmann analyzes the "truth" of a statement on the basis of the praxis which grounds it. Nevertheless, again critical of traditional Marxism, he shows the revolutionary importance of the ideological struggle in which theology also takes part. For this reason, as we have said, he is the first to carry out the task of "marking" or distinguishing clearly between liberation theology and postconciliar European theologies (such as theology of hope, political theology, theology of Third World revolutions). His analysis of the symbolic structure as superstructure is very clear.[33] He also criticizes Stalinist dogmatism and even Althusserian thought for not treating adequately the question of fetishism and the relationship between theory and praxis.

Juan Luis Segundo, formed by the rather functionalist sociology of the 50s, also uses Marxist categories for analysis—in particular the concept of ideology.[34] He used social sciences in his early work (*Función de la iglesia en la realidad rioplatense*, 1962) and he is a master of the practice of "criticism." He lays bare the hidden and falsified parts of the European and North American—and even Roman—theologies (as in his critical work *Theology and the Church: A Response to Cardinal Ratzinger and a Warning to the Whole Church*.[35]

Gustavo Gutiérrez, who in 1964 had already begun his pioneering work, quotes Gramsci in the first note of his *A Theology of Liberation* (the first parts of which appeared in 1968 as a criticism of developmentalism); he thus makes clear which kind of Marxism interests him: not a dialectically materialist Marxism but one which is economically critical, decidedly political, and culturally analytical.[36] From this comes the fundamental idea that theology (like philosophy in a Gramscian sense) is a "critical reflection" on Christian praxis.[37] Like all liberation theologians in the 60s, Gutiérrez starts with the criticism of the "notion of development" and presents *liberation* as its antithesis.[38] He quotes authors such as Althusser, Kosik, Lukacs, Mariategui and Sánchez Vásquez, and, of course, Marx himself.[39] All of this shows how liberation theology uses a Marxism that is critical, Latin American, antieconomistic, to aid in political analysis. Gutiérrez also includes this quote from "Che" Guevara:

Let me say, with the risk of seeming ridiculous, that the true revolutionary is guided by strong feelings of love . . . They (revolutionaries) must
struggle every day so that their love of living humanity is transformed
into concrete deeds.[40]

Among the pertinent social sciences, Marxism is used, also indirectly, by Gutiérrez, as an instrument to discover and describe the
reality of the poverty of the Latin American people and the concrete
projects of liberation. Gutiérrez's work "Marxismo y Cristianismo,"
never published as a book, shows his thoughtful and profoundly
theological use of Marxist categories (such as class struggle, revolution, and utopia).

José Míguez Bonino's study *Cristianismo y marxistas*, subtitled
"El mutuo desafío para la revolución" ("The Mutual Challenge of
Revolution") is perhaps the only work dedicated explicitly to discussing the links between Marxism and Christianity among liberation theologians (although Miranda also took up this theme in *Marx
and the Bible*).[41] The Argentinian theologian's knowledge of Marx
was not new, for it could already be seen in his prologue to the work
of Rubem Alves, when he wrote in 1969:

Doesn't the renaissance of humanist Marxism grow out of the situation
of the developed countries . . . ? Isn't our situation very different, in
that the humanization we need requires a more elemental and "materialist" basis that effectively incorporates political, scientific and tech-
nological analysis, without which liberation becomes a mere dialectical
game?[42]

Here Bonino indicates the "sacramental" framing of the discussion which occurred during that period; I shall return to this point
below.

As a theologian of the movement Christians for Socialism in 1972,
Pablo Richard, together with Gónzalo Arroyo, its founder, made use
of Marxist categories.[43] For Richard, Gramsci is required reading,
especially his thesis on "Muerte de la cristianidad y nacimiento de
la Iglesia," which Richard used systematically to construct the
theoretical framework of his analysis.[44]

For Leonardo Boff, the rejection of capitalism "is oriented toward
a liberation within a different society."[45] Theology is constructed
from two sources: faith (biblical, according to the magisterium and
tradition) and social reality.[46] In order for the theologian to under-

stand that reality, "it is necessary to turn to the human social sciences, such as anthropology, sociology, psychology, political science, economics and social philosophy."[47] Marxism takes its place on this list, but Boff makes it clear that Latin American theology "does not make servile use of the analytic instrument developed by the Marxist tradition (that is, Marx and the different elaborations of socialism, of Gramsci, of French academic Marxism, and others); liberation theology separates the analytic instrument from its philosophical presuppositions (that is, dialectic materialism) and considers Marxism as a science, not as a philosophy."[48]

Clodovis Boff's *Teología do Político e suas mediaçoes (Theology and Praxis: Epistemological Foundations)* is perhaps the most systematic theological attempt to incorporate the theoretical structure of Althusser.[49] It is a rigorous theoretical study and use of the French Marxism of the 70s. It shows how a Marxist categorical framework can be used in a strictly Christian theology of the political. An analagous study in the 80s is needed, this time using Marx himself as referent. We will return to this topic later.

Jon Sobrino states that many of the European theologies respond to the objections of the "first Enlightenment," that of Kant, which questions the relationship between faith and reason, while the "second Enlightenment," that of Marx, questions the relationship between faith and historical change. What role does religion play in historical transformations? Faith is used as justification both for domination and liberation.[50] This is where liberation theology makes use of Marxism: theology must not only *interpret* reality but also justify its *transformation*—even a revolutionary one.

Otto Maduro has done some innovative studies on the question of religion in the young Marx and in the young Catholic Engels.[51] Juan Carlos Scannone, as well as Lucio Gera, formed part of the school of liberation theology that opposes Marxism—because of conditions specific to their national reality.[52]

We must not forget how Marxism has been used in the deeper currents of spirituality and mysticism, for example by Arthur Paoli, who studied Hegel and Marx in Italy, together with the future Paul VI then serving as advisor to the Italian Catholic Action. Also Ernesto Cardenal's *Santidad en la revolución*, which marked a historical clearing of the path to revolutionary processes, which in the case of the guerrillas of Teoponte reached a truly mystical level— disregarding its political or nonpolitical implications (Néstor Paz Zamora).[53]

We could name many others, such as Raúl Vidales, Luis del Valle, Jorge Pixtley, Elsa Tamez, Beatriz Melano Caouch, Julio Santana, Luis Alberto Gómes de Sousa, Gilbero Giménez, Alex Morelli.[54] We will leave for later my own position and that of F. Hinkelammert.

In summary, we have seen that liberation theology uses a *certain part* of Marxism in a *certain way*, never incompatible with the foundations of faith. Some liberation theologians have a more clearly "classist" position; others are more "populist"; some use only the instrument of ideological criticism, others social, and even economic. Some also oppose global Marxism—although it is difficult to define them as members of a theological movement. Some are inspired by a more French current of Marxism, others by the Italian or German currents; most move in different currents simultaneously. All of these theologians, however, use the thesis of dependency advanced by the Latin American current—defined with great care, conscious of the criticism it has received. Taking into account all of the indicated limitations, we can conclude that liberation theology is the first theological movement in the history of Christian thought worldwide to use Marxism (and in doing so it is ahead of other world religions).

III. The Accusation of Marxism

The Christian option for the poor and the oppressed, together with the use of social sciences as an epistemological tool, was interpreted by many—both in and outside the church—as a Marxist "manipulation" of or "infiltration" into theology. This accusation, unjust in what it intends, is not new; it is almost as old as liberation theology itself.

The 1984 Instruction

One of the earliest accusations that liberation theology is Marxist was made by Jaime Serna in October of 1972, on Bogotá television and in the newspapers.[55] *El Tiempo* of November 5 declared: "CE-LAM accused of Marxism." In the same year, the Conference of Latin American Bishops changed orientation. In the first issue of the magazine *Tierra Nueva,* the first article, by Bishop López Trujillo was entitled "La liberación y las liberaciones." The Vatican *Instruction* also included the issue of "liberation theologies," even though in reality there has never been more than *one* liberation theology.[56]

The Rockefeller Report in 1969 discussed Marxist infiltration in the church. And the Santa Fe Document of 1980, which read like an early political platform for Ronald Reagan, referred explicitly to the dangers of liberation theology.[57]

In 1975, R. Vekemans published his attack on liberation theology, *Teología de la Liberación y Cristianos para el socialismo;* in 1978, Bonaventura Kloppenburg also tried to link liberation theology and Christians for Socialism; Javier Lozano, in *La Iglesia del pueblo,* mounted an even more partisan criticism.[58] For Vekemans, the Christians for Socialism movement inspires liberation theology and results in the Marxist option for armed, violent struggle. According to Kloppenburg, for Marxists, both movements eventually combined to form a "popular church," a new sect. According to Lozano, although the starting point for the new movement is to be found in the "popular church" inspired by liberation theology, the origins of liberation theology are located in a Leninist Stalinist Marxism.

In the 1984 *Instruction,* part 7 begins a discussion of "Marxist analysis." (We are omitting any comment on the theology that underlies the *Instruction*).[59] With respect to our theme, the central idea is formulated in the following way:

> . . . the thought of Marx is such a global vision of reality that all data received from observation and analysis are brought together in a philo-sophical and ideological structure, which predetermines the signifi-cance and importance to be attached to them. . . . Thus no separation of the parts of this epistemologically unique complex is possible. If one tries to take only one part, say, the analysis, one ends up having to accept the entire ideology.[60]

The "thought of Marx" itself (leaving aside the interpretations of Engels, Lenin and Stalin) is philosophical-economic, and in his mature and definitive works—"scientific,"[61] from the perspective of the later tradition. We can find nothing of what the *Instruction* claims, when, for example, it states that "*atheism* and the denial of the *human person,* of his/her liberty and rights, are at the core of the Marxist theory."[62]

In a careful, line by line, reading of the volumes which compose section 2 of Marx's Collected Works, I have found nothing to substan-tiate such a description of his views.[63] On the contrary, Marx op-posed the militant atheism in the International—Bakunin attacked Marx for directing the International which "negated atheism."[64]

Marx wrote to Friedrich Bolte, on November 23, 1871, stating that, in 1868, he could not accept Bakunin's proposal to "dictate atheism as a dogma for the members," because "the International does not recognize theological sections (theologische Sektionen)."[65] On August 4, 1878, he wrote to George Howell, indicating that the proposed "Section on Socialist Atheists" that Bakunin tried to force through, was never accepted—and neither was that of the YMCA, because the International did not recognize "theological sections."[66] Marx was specifically opposed to militant atheism. The Instruction clearly ignores these facts, and ignores the difference between Marx, Engels, Lenin, Stalin, Gramsci, Lukacs, and Bloch.

With regard to the human person, we can state that for Mrax it is the "person" (Person in German) who is the starting point and constant referent for the establishment of his categories and his criticism. The "living work" (lebendige Arbeit) is the person who when "subsumed under" or "alienated" by capital (by "sin" for the Christian), becomes a "thing," an "instrument," merely a "commodity"[67]—as John Paul also teaches in Laborem Exercens.[68]

This means that, if we demonstrate that there are different traditions in Marxism, and even profound contradictions, the entire argument of the Instruction is wiped out at the roots.[69] Liberation theologians have been able to and have taken from Marxism those elements that are not incompatible with their faith (as we have shown above). For this reason, the Instruction's conclusion is false:

> This all-embracing conception thus imposes its logic and leads the "theologies of liberation" to accept a series of positions which are incompatible with the Christian vision of humanity.[70]

The Second Instruction of 1986

The 1984 Instruction evidently condemned liberation theology but in reality was unable to demonstrate its unorthodoxy. But the Instruction did achieve a practical intraecclesial effect: it provided justification for all those who wanted to exclude liberation theology from the centers of formation (whether for seminarians, nuns or lay people), universities, journals, etc. The practical effect was to prevent liberation theology from becoming the dominant theology of the Latin American church, as well as of the churches in Africa, Asia and the socialist countries—and in Europe and the United States. Consequently, the effect of the Instruction was "political".

As the title indicates, the *Instruction on Christian Liberty and Liberation*, dated March 22, 1986, deals principally with the problem of liberty, in particular, religious liberty; its significance for real socialist countries is indirect, and its bearing on the real issue of liberation is rather tenuous. The 1986 *Instruction* opens with biblical passages such as "the truth will make us free" and not with "I am the bread of life" or "Blessed are the poor." Liberation theology has as its starting point real, physical misery: that of hunger. The *Instruction*, on the other hand, concerns itself with truths, doctrines, with the struggle for liberty—assuming that the basic needs for food, drink, sleep, clothing, health have *already* been met (the "criteria" for the Final Judgment of Matt. 25). With such an attitude, the *Instruction* can announce:

> In its different forms [. . .] human misery is a manifest sign of the *congenital* weakness found in humanity after the fall.[71]

The response to this misery is "charitable works" or "aims."[72]

Still, one can say that the *Instruction* has not explicitly repeated the first *Instruction*'s accusations with respect to Marxism, although in its frequent reference to the 1984 document, it indirectly sustains those accusations. Theologically the position of this *Instruction* is very similar to that of the first one."[73]

IV. Paths Opening in the Present

In line with Thomas Aquinas' teaching that theology is a "science" insofar as it uses a definite *method* (for Aquinas, Artistotelian), liberation theology uses its scientific tools methodically and according to the tradition of the previous theologies, starting with the Apostolic Fathers and continuing through the Fathers of the church, the medieval Latin theologians, etc. Liberation theology is, however, *the first theology* to use Marxism as a valid mediation in a way not in contradiction with Christian faith. The church Fathers made use of Platonism, Saint Thomas of Aristotelianism, Rahner of Heideggerianism. In the nineteenth century, use of the "science" of history caused the crisis of modernism; today, however, this crisis has been resolved and all theology is "historical." The same process will occur with Marxism in the twenty-first century.

It is noteworthy that the marginalized nations of the world have been the first to adopt liberation theology, clearly because of their need for its practical and liberating option. Although liberation theology has suffered so much criticism, incomprehension, and even apparent condemnation, the paths have remained open, and future generations will be able to travel them safely, orthodoxly, and justly. In the remaining pages, we shall consider only some of the current challenges that lead the way to a promising future.

The Reception of Marxist Categories in the Magisterium

I offer only one, though highly indicative, example (from among many) of how the Magisterium has made use of Marxist categories. At present, the church, in millions of its members, lives in a non-capitalist world—that is, in the nations of real socialism. In this world, Marxism and its categories, are part of day-to-day life—of what Husserl or Habermas would call the Lebenswelt. John Paul II, in his 1981 encyclical Laborem Exercens, uses numerous Marxist categories, and paradoxically presents, on the one hand, an intelligent description of Marx, yet on the other, a portrayal of Marxism as ingenuous, economistic, and Stalinist.

The fundamental orientation of the encyclical is to explain the interrelatedness of work—bread—life.[74] Life stands at the origin of the relationship. Human persons are living beings; by living they consume their lives and thus have needs;[75] these needs demand the creative activity of work that produces bread (the "fruit" as defined in biblical thought); by being consumed bread satisfies needs and aids and increases life. This is the "vital cycle."[76] Marx offers a prototypical explanation of this cycle:

> In my production [read: my bread], I would have objectified my individuality, its specific character and therefore enjoyed no only an individual manifestation of my life during the activity, but also when looking at the object [the bread], I would have the individual pleasure of knowing my personality to be objective . . . and hence a power beyond all doubt. . . . My work would be a free manifestation of life, hence an enjoyment of life.[77]

Marx, speaking of the relationship between work or production and consumption or satisfaction, clearly indicates his "personalism":

> In the first [production] the person becomes objectified as a thing; in the second [consumption] the thing created by him/her is personified (personifiziert).[78]

And in this famous text he repeats:

> The commodity [read: bread] is . . . an external object, a thing which through its qualities *satisfies human needs*.[79]

Needs are *human* for Marx. According to the encyclical: "Work is one of the characteristics that distinguish man from the rest of creatures."[80]

In accordance with Catholic social doctrine, the encyclical explains that the *dignity of the human person* is the foundation of the dignity of work. On this point it coincides with Marx almost word for word:

> . . . different sorts of work that people do can have greater or lesser objective *value* . . . , nevertheless . . . each sort is judged above all by the measure of the *dignity of the subject* of work, that is to say, the person, the individual. . . .[81]

Marx says explicitly that:

> Labour as *absolute poverty (absolute Armut)* . . . existing without mediation, . . . can only be one [objectivity] not separated from the *person (Person)*; only one coincident with his/her immediate *corporality (Leiblichkeit)*.[82]
>
> . . . labour . . . is [the] not-objectified, therefore, non-objective; i.e., *subjective* existence of labour itself. Labour not as an object but as *activity*, . . . as the living source of value.[83]
>
> We mean by labour power or labour capacity the aggregate of those mental and physical capabilities existing in the *physical form*, the *living personality (lebendigen Persoenlichkeit)* of a human being.[84]

In some parts of the encyclical, the author seems to know Marx's work very well. He speaks of the *"capacity for labor (Arbeitsvermoegen),"* an expression that Marx uses in the *Grundrisse* (1857–1858), in the *Manuscripts of 1861–1863* and of *1863–1865*, but which he later replaces with *"labor power (Arbeitskraft)"* in *Das Kapital* of 1867. (For that reason later Marxism stopped using the term.)[85] For Marx, "labor" *in itself* has no (economic) value; only the "capacity for labor" does[86] because such capacity is the "creative *source* of value" and has dignity (as an *end*) and so is not a *means* (the *value* of the commodity).[87] And for Marx, as in the encyclical, the person, subjectivity, the dignity of work ("living work")[88] constitute the source of the value of all *things:* even the *thing* called *capital.*[89]

Marx and the encyclical coincide completely in that "*objective* labor"[90] (a Marxist category) receives its values from "*subjective* labor"[91] (also a Marxist category), for labor is described as subject and as subjectivity in the texts quoted from the *Grundrisse* and many of Marx's works.

The encyclical affirms "the primacy of humankind in the *production process,*[92] the primacy of humankind with respect to things" and thereby "the principle of the priority of work versus capital," because capital is only work objectivized, accumulated.[93]

Finally, the encyclical criticizes the isolation of people in capitalist societies, in contrast to the existence or "the sign of active persons within a community of persons,"[94] which reminds us of a text in *Grundrisse:*

> Free *individuality,* based on the universal development of the *individuals* and the subordination of their *communal,* social productivity which is their social possession . . . is the third stage . . . *social* production (*gemeinschaftliche*) is not subsumed under the *individuals* who *manage it as their common wealth* . . . [It is] the *free* exchange *of individuals* who are associated on the basis of *common* appropriation and *control* of the means of production.[95]

For Marx, as for the encyclical, human work ("living work" or the "subjectivity of work"), as individuality in community, is the starting point of ethical criticism: that is, the starting point is the human person of the worker. To talk about the "means of production," or about "objective" work as technology, or to state that "we cannot *separate* capital from labor, and in no way can we oppose labor to capital"—all these are, *strictly* speaking, categories or distinctions made by Marx himself; and the encyclical rightly uses these categories to criticize Stalinist Marxism as dogmatic and economistic. The encyclical, like liberation theology, uses Marxist categories in the same way that Saint Thomas used Aristotle.[96]

Theology and Economic Criticism

While liberation theology, from the beginning, has used sociological and political categories for its ideological analysis, a *theology of the economy,* consistent with the *sacramental nature* of bread (the product of work)[97] as a means of establishing social relationships and of building up or negating the Kingdom, is relatively recent. In this regard, the work of Franz Hinkelammert, *The Ideological Weapons of Death*, written to further a theology of life, has opened new perspectives.[98] Here Marxism is used adequately and on its own grounds (that is, economic and philosophical) and is incorporated from the perspective of a Christian faith that loses none of its own tradition. Hinkelammert points out that the criticisms leveled against fetishism by Marx are the same as those leveled against idolatry by Jesus and the prophets. Hinkelammert's reevaluation of "carnality" (*basar* in Hebrew and *sarx* in Greek, which is not merely the "body")[99] is consistent with Christian experience:

> However, the enormous value placed on real life in historical material-ism has a critical correlate in the Christian message. In the Christian message the resurrection means a resurrection of human beings in their real life. . . . Contrary to the way the forces of domination absolutize values, esteem for real life has always been the starting point for the ideologies of the oppressed. . . . The specific element in Marxism is praxis that leads to trancendence within real life. The specifically Christian element is hope in the potentialities of praxis, going beyond what can be calculated to be humanly achievable. The connecting link between them is real material life as the ultimate basis for all human life.[100]

No longer is it a question of separating a Marxist philosophy that has to be rejected from a Marxist analysis that can be accepted. Now it is a question of a complete and fitting *rereading* of Marx himself from a Christian, theological perspective. As Thomas of Aquinas *entered* into the field of "Aristotelianism" and "from within" began a *creative* process, the same thing has happened with this last, most recent and most promising, phase of liberation theology.

In my *Ethics and Community*, I have tried to create a theological Christian discourse that is essentially biblical, and, *at the same time*, strictly Marxist. The concept of "community" in *Acts* (2: 42–47) and in the *Grundrisse* (and in the later manuscripts up to *Das Kapital*) have served me as guides. Concepts (and categories) such as person, social relationship, work, value and "blood," product or "bread," are strictly Christian and traditional and are strictly in accord with the "categories" that Marx established in the definitive period of his life (1857–1880). A comparison of my two studies *La producción* teórica de Marx and Ethics and Community, will show that the epistemological hypothesis of the latter is the systematic and precise use of Marxist categories (as contained in the works published in MEGA by the West Berlin Marxist Institute), together with the use of the biblical categories in their Hebrew, Greek-Christian contexts. I have tried to overcome the dualism between the use of Marx's philosophy and analysis, without losing the clear difference between the two modes of discourses. In future years, liberation theology will make creative advances in both a missionary and prophetic sense, and will make itself comprehensible among ordinary people, especially among the exploited, as well as among real socialists.

Religion in Real Socialism

As just stated, one of the missionary virtues of liberation theology, is its ability to be understood in a world that until recently was considered atheist (actually, it was anti-superstitious) or materialistic (actually, it was concerned about the oppressed). The declaration of the Sandinista Government Sobre la religión in October of 1980 opened a new path for "real" worldwide socialism (see above). From now on, being a believer and a revolutionary are not two contradictory subjective (and objective) positions. The contradictions between faith and politics in the year 1968 have been overcome—and liberation theology has been a fundamental theoretical factor in bringing this about. In this context, Frei Betto's book Fidel and Religion is a historical work.[101] Providing more of a personal witness than a theoretical statement, the Cuban leader declared:

> I think that the enormous historical importance of Liberation Theology, or the Liberation Church—whatever you want to call it—lies precisely in its profound impact on the political views of its followers. It constitutes a point of contact between today's believers and those of the past—that distant past of the first few centuries after the emergence of Christianity, after Christ. [Fidel shows here his Luxemburgian position.] I could define . . . Liberation Theology . . . as Christianity's going back to its roots, its most beautiful, attractive, heroic and glorious history. It's so important that it forces all of the Latin American left to take notice of it as one of the most important events of our time.[102]

The critics of liberation theology, from within the church, totally forget the prophetic-missionary function of this theology.

If we add to these considerations the recent "opening" occurring in the Soviet Union because of the low level of productivity (which calls into question the previous naive economistic theory of Soviet Marxism), the significance of liberation theology, *because it has known how to use Marxism in a Christian fashion*, becomes universal. It is not only useful for Latin America, Africa or Asia, but also for real socialist countries. Doors are opening. Mikail Gorbachev, in his book *Perestroika*, harshly criticizes bureaucracy and dogmatism.[103] He has a positive view of religion, of "spiritual" values; he defends "humanism," democracy, demanding that "Lenin be read in a new way."[104]

It has been a long road: from the justification of a Christian praxis committed to the liberation of the poor and oppressed (by means of liberation theology), to the Nicaraguan Revolution, the improvement of church-state relations in Cuba, the discovery of religion not just as an "opiate of the people" but also as a "miraculous remedy"—to the elaboration of a theology fully conscious not just of using but of *rereading and discovering the internal creativity of Marxist thought itself.*[105]

Conclusions

Liberation theology originates and learns in an organized way from the praxis of the Latin American peoples, from the Christian base communities, from the poor and the oppressed. It first justified the political commitment of militant Christians, in order later, through praxis, to provide that same justification for the praxis of all the impoverished people of Latin America. It is therefore a critical theological discourse which analyzes traditional themes (sin, salvation, church, Christology, the sacraments, etc.) on a *concrete* relevant level. It does not reject *abstraction* (sin *in itself*, for example), but it situates such abstractions in a *concrete* historical reality (the sin of *the system of dependency*, for example).

The use of the human sciences, and particularly of Marxism, was made necessary by the need for a critical-concrete theological reflection based on the experience of the poor and the oppressed. It is the first theology in history to use this kind of analysis, and it does so based on the demands of faith, avoiding economism, naive dialectical materialism, and abstract dogmatism. It can then criticize capital or dependency as sin. Without recommending political positions— which is not the function of theology—it keeps from falling into a "third position" (not capitalism, nor socialism, but a Christian political solution). That does not keep it from being a theology that is orthodox (growing out of orthopraxis) or traditional (in the strongest sense of the word). It enters a missionary dialogue with Marxism—a dialogue which Latin American parties or political movements, and even persons in countries of real socialism can understand.

In a few decades, the prophetic calls of liberation theology will be passed on as the "common" and "long established" beliefs of Christianity. This is the message of liberation because of which prophets are criticized and persecuted. As Jeremiah, imprisoned in his own Jerusalem, recognized: "O Jerusalem, you kill the prophets and stone those who are sent to you!" (Luke 13: 34).

NOTES

1. Pope Pius IX indicated that there are some who accept "the criminal systems of communism and socialism". On socialism and Marxism in Latin America, see G.D. Cole, *Historia del pensamiento socialista*, vol. 3 (Mexico: Fondo de Cultura Económico, 1959; vol. 4: 1960, vol. 5: 1961). Also see Robert Alexander, *Communism in Latin America* (Rutgers University Press, 1959); Victor Alba, *Historia del comunismo en América Latina* (Mexico: Ed. Occidentales, 1954); Michael Loewy, *El marxismo en América Latina* (Mexico: Era, 1982); Sheldon B. Liss, *Marxist Thought in Latin America* (University of California Press, 1984); and my article "Encuentro de cristianos y marxistas en América Latina," *Cristianismo y Sociedad*, Mexico, 74 (1980), 19–36. See also Héctor J. Samour C., "Valoración del marxismo en la teología de la liberación" (Universidad Nacional Autónoma de México, Doctoral Thesis in Philosophy, 1988).

2. *Rerum Novarum*, Nos. 11–12. Also see my *Ethics and Community* (Maryknoll: Orbis Books, 1988), chapter 19, "The Gospel and the Social Teaching of the Church."

3. "Communism . . . teaches and desires two things: class struggle incarnated and the complete disappearance of private property," *Quadragesimo Anno*, No. 120. See also *Divini Redemptoris* (1937), Nos. 8–14, as well as *Humani Generis* (1950) of Pius XII.

4. See my article previously cited, "Encuentro de cristianos y marxistas en América Latina." The Latin American Communist parties, upon participating in some of the popular movements since 1936 (as directed by Moscow) lost their worker base (for the workers were at times absorbed by the popular movements); in 1941, the Communist parties were given a new order to join with the "Allies" against Nazism. In 1945 they were found allied with Anglo Saxon imperialism. These were irreparable mistakes.

5. See my *Los últimos 50 años (1930–1985) en la historia de la Iglesia en América Latina* (Bogota: Indo-America Press, 1986), pp. 13ff.

6. See E. Kadt, *Catholic Radicals in Brazil* (London: Oxford University Press, 1971); S. Silva Gotay, *El pensamiento revolucionario cristiano en América y el Cariba (Salamanca: Sígueme, 1981)*.

7. See *Camilo Torres por el Padre Camilo Torres Restrepo (1956–1965)* (Cuernavaca: CIDOC, 1967); *Obras escogidas* (Montevideo: Provincias Unidas, 1968); see also Rodolfo de Roux, *Historia general de la iglesia en América Latina* (Salamanca: Sígueme, VII, 1977), chapter 7.

See V. Bambierra et al, *Diez años de insurrección en América Latina* (Santiago de Chile, Prensa Latinoamericana, I–II, 1971); R. Goot, *Las guerillas en América Latina* (Santiago: Universitaria, 1971); INDAL, *Movimientos revolucionarios en América Latina* (Brussels, I–II, 1972).

8. Ives Vaillancourt, "La crisis del ILADES," *Víspera* (Montevideo), 22 (1971) 18–27; Pablo Richard, *Cristianos para el socialismo* (Salamanca: Sígueme, 1976); *Cristianismo, lucha ideológica y racionalidad socialista* (Salamanca: Sígueme, 1975); Roger Vekemans, *Teología de la liberación y cristianos para el socialismo* (Bogota: CEDIAL, 1976). Richard Shaull brings in elements from the experience of struggles for liberation in Africa and Asia and from the ecumenical movements; he must be considered one of the founders of liberation theology. See his "Consideraciones teológicas sobre la liberación del hombre," *IDOC* (Bogotá), vol. 43, 1968 and "A

Theological Perspective" in *Cultural Factors in Inter-American Relations*, Samuel Shapiro, ed. (University of Notre Dame Press, 1968).

9. See my *Religión* (Mexico: Edicol, 1977), pp. 212ff.

10. *Los cristianos y el socialismo. I Encuentro latinoamericano* (Buenos Aires: Siglo XXI, 1973), pp. 18–19. See Raúl Vidales' mimeographed anthology, *Praxis cristiana y militancia revolucionaria* (Mexico: CEE, 1978). For the context of the whole epoch, see my *De Medellín a Puebla* (Mexico: Edicol/CEE, 1979).

11. It is interesting to note that, beginning from approximately 1974, the "classist" position in liberation theology (in Chile, Perú and Brasil) accepted the category "pueblo" in political and sociological analysis. Finally, "pueblo" became a *historical subject*. See Giulio Giraldo, *Sandinismo, Marxismo y Cristianismo en la nueva Nicaragua* (Managua: CEE/CAV, 1986).

12. Raúl Vidales, op. cit., doc. I, IV.

13. *Comunicado oficial de la Dirección Nacional del FSLN sobre la religión* (1980), section 2.

14. *Compromiso cristiano para una Nicaragua nueva* (17 November 1979), p. 9.

15. Kenneth Aman, criticizes liberation theology for "using" Marxism as an "instrument" (like the medieval "ancilla theologiae"); see his "*Using* Marxism: A Philosophical Critique of Liberation Theology," *International Philosophical Quarterly*, 4 (1985) 393–401.

16. See my *El dualismo en la antropología de la cristiandad* (Buenos Aires: Guadalupe, 1974).

17. J.L. Segundo, *Theology and the Church: A Response to Cardinal Ratzinger and a Warning to the Whole Church* (New York: Seabury, 1985).

Paul Gathier, *Jésus, l'église et les pauvres* (Tournai: Ed. Universitaire, 1962).

18. See Roberto Oliveros, *Liberación y teología* (Mexico: CRT, 1977).

19. For the semantic evolution from "pobre" to "pueblo", see my article "El paradigma del éxodo en la teología de la liberación," *Concilium*, 209 (1987) 99–114.

20. *Theology of Human Hope* (Washington, Corpus Books, 1969).

21. See my *La producción teórica de Marx. Un comentario a los Grundisse* (Mexico: Siglo XXI, 1985), pp. 36–37.

22. *Conceptos elementales del materialismo dialéctico* (Mexico: Siglo XXI, 1974).

23. See Clodovis Boff, *Theology and Praxis: Epistemological Foundations* (Maryknoll: Orbis Books, 1987). Originally published in 1978.

24. See the works of S. Silva Gotay and R. Oliveros cited in notes 6 and 18.

25. F. Houtart-O. Vertrano, *Hacia una teología del desarrollo* (Buenos Aires, 1967); Vincent Cosmo, *Signification et théologie du développement* (Paris, 1967).

J.L. Segundo, *Función de la iglesia en la realidad rioplatense* (Montevideo, 1962); *¿La cristianidad, una utopia?* (Montevideo, 1964); *Teología abierta para el laico adulto* (Buenos Aires, 1968); José Comblin, *Théologie de la paix* (Paris, 1960–1963); *Théologie de la révolution* (Paris, 1970–1974).

26. See, for example, Helmut Gollwitzer, *Die reichen Christen und der arme Lazarus* (Munich: Kaiser, 1968) and Ernst Bloch, *Thomas Münzer* (1969) or Carlos Pinto de Oliveira, *Evangelho e revoluçao social,* (Sao Paulo: Duas Cidades, 1962); Jean Cardonnel, *L'évangile et la révolution* (Paris, 1968). See also R. Vekemans, *Teología de la liberación y cristianos para el socialismo*, pp. 100–112.

27. *Teología desde la praxis de la liberación* (Salamanca: Sígueme, 1973), chapter 2.

28. See its first edition in 1969 (Mexico), 1972 (Salamanca, Spain: Sígueme), 1974 (Maryknoll: Orbis Books).

29. See note 20.

30. Rubem Alves partially hides the meaning of these categories: "political humanism," "humanistic messianism," "humanist messianism," etc.

31. ISEB (Río de Janeiro, 1962).

32. ISEB, p. 122.

33. See, H. Assmann, "Teología de la liberación: Una evaluación prospectiva" (1971); also note 27.

The following article by Assmann is a classic: "El cristianismo, su plusvalía simbólica y el costo social de la revolución socialista" (in op. cit. pp. 171–202), in which the "symbolic" blindness of the left is criticized.

34. Up to his extensive analysis in a complete volume at the beginning of his Christology (Faith and Ideologies [Maryknoll: Orbis Books, 1984]). On our point, he wrote: "Evangelio, política y socialismo," in Actualidad Pastoral (1972), pp.303–306, 327–331, 356–357; "La iglesia chilena ante el socialismo (Talca, Chile: Fundación Larráin, 1971), p. 25, mimeographed.

35. See note 17.

36. Maryknoll: Orbis Books, 1973, p. 15.

37. ibid., p. 6.

38. ibid., p. 21ff.

39. Althusser, ibid., pp. 39, 97, 249, 277; Kosik, pp. 38, 40; Lukacs, p. 40; Mariategui, pp. 18, 97, 98; Sánchez Vargas, p. 18. He also uses Marcuse (pp. 31–32, 233) and Ernst Bloch (pp. 216–217, 220, 224, 243).

40. ibid., p. 98. He quotes F. Castro on pp. 98, 120, 123.

41. Published only in English (Grand Rapids: Eerdmans, 1976).

42. In the prologue to R. Alves, Religión: ¿opio o instrumento de liberación?, (Montevideo: Tierra Nueva, 1972), pp. x–xi.

43. "Racionalidad socialista y verificación histórica del cristianismo," Cuaderno de la Realidad Nacional, 12 (1972) 144–153. See Origen y desarrollo del movimiento Cristianos por el Socialismo: Chile, 1970–1973 (Paris: Centre Lebret, 1975).

44. E. Paulinos: Sao Paulo, 1984 (in Portuguese).

45. La fe en la periferia (Santander: Sal Terrae, 1981), p. 125.

46. ibid., p. 127.

47. ibid., p. 12.

48. ibid., pp. 75–76.

49. See note 23.

50. Liberación y cautiverio (Mexico, 1970), pp. 177–207.

51. See especially O. Maduro, Religión y conflicto social (Mexico: CRT, 1980).

52. Scannone, Teología de la liberación y praxis popular (Salamanca: Sígueme, 1976); Gera, "Aspectos eclesiológicos de la teología de la liberación" in CELAM, Liberación: diálogos en el CELAM, pp. 381–391; La iglesia debe comprometerse en lo político (Montevideo, 1970).

53. Paoli, Diálogo de la liberación (Buenos Aires: Lohlé, 1970; Meditazione sul Vangelo di Luca (Morcelliana: Brescia, 1972); Cardenal (Buenos Aires: Lohlé, 1971); Paz Zamora, edited by Hugo Assmann, Teoponte, una experiencia guerrillera (Oruro, Bolivia: CEPI, 1971).

54. Vidales, La iglesia latinoamericana y la política después de Medellín (Bogota:

Indo-America Press, 1972); id. Práctica religiosa y proyecto histórico (Lima: CEP, 1975).

Del Valle has numerous publications in the journal Christus (Mexico) since 1968 and is organizer of the Centro de Reflexión Teológica (Mexico).

Pixtley's On Exodus (Maryknoll: Orbis, 1987) and his work on God's Kingdom: A Guide for Biblical Study (Maryknoll: Orbis, 1984) open new paths in the exegesis of liberation.

Tamez is a pioneer of exegesis and Latin American feminist theology. Milano Caouch is an Argentinian feminist and theologian. Santana, "ISAL: un movimiento anti-imperialista y antioligárquico," in NADOC, 95 (1969); Teoría revolucionaria: Reflexión sobre la fe como praxis de liberación in "Pueblo oprimido, Señor de la historia," pp. 225–242; and many other works. Gomes de Sousa, "El futuro de las ideologías y las ideologías del futuro," in Víspera, 12 (1969), 23–31; "Condiciona-miento socio-político de la teología," in Christus, 479 (1975) 14–18. Giménez, "El golpe militar y la condenación de CPS en Chile," Contacto, 1–2 (1975) 12–116; and Cultura popular y religión de Anahuac (Mexico: CEE, 1978). Morelli, Libera a mi pueblo (Buenos Aires: Lohlé, 1971); "Fundamentación teológica de la acción por la justicia," Vida espiritual, 47–49 (1975) 36–63.

55. De Medellín a Puebla, pp. 282ff.

56. Instruction, 1984, IV, 3.

57. Department of State Bulletin, (Washington D.C., December 8, 1969), pp. 504ff. See Ana María Ezcurra, El Vaticano y la administración Reagan (Mexico: Nuevomar, 1984).

58. Vekemans, see note 8; Kloppenburg, "Informe sobre la iglesia popular" (Mexico: CEM, 1978); Lozano, Centro de Estudios y Promoción Social (Mexico, 1983).

59. See J.L. Segundo, Theology and the Church (see note 17), which shows the contradictions between the theology of the Instruction and that of the Second Vatican Council.

60. Instruction VII, 6. I leave aside the Instruction's ambiguities in formulation (because if it is a "hybrid amalgam" several conclusions can be drawn and not just one) and its contradictions (because in VII, 8, it says: "Marxist thought has diversified to create different currents that diverge notably one from the other").

61. "Science" for Marx has a precise meaning; see my work Hacia un Marx desconocido: Un comentario a los manuscritos del 61–63 (Mexico: Siglo XXi, 1988), chapter 14.

62. Instruction VII, 9.

63. The proposed complete edition of the works of Marx, in more than 100 volumes, is still incomplete. Section II will contain all the materials on Das Kapital, and they will comprise 17 volumes. Marx wrote Das Kapital in four drafts. We are finishing a commentary—in the style of Saint Thomas—on these "four drafts" (from 1857 to 1880) in three volumes, two of which we have quoted in notes 21 and 61.

64. Letter from Marx to Liebknecht on November 15, 1872 (MEW, 33, p. 402).

65. MEW 32, p. 328.

66. MEW 19, p. 144.

67. "Labour as absolute poverty . . . not separated from the person (Person)" (Grundisse; CP 28, p. 222; German edition, Berlin: Dietz, 1974, p. 203). See my work La producción teórica de Marx, chapter 7, pp. 139ff. "As such, according to his concept, the poor man (pauper) as person, is the bearer of the capacity for labour." (Manuscritos del 61–63; MEGA II, 3, pp. 34–35). See my Hacia un Marx desconocido,

chapter 3.2.b. "By capacity for labour . . . we understand *corporality*, the living *personality* of a human being." *El capital*, I, 4.3 (Mexico: Siglo XXI, 1980), I,1, p. 203; MEGA II, 5 (1983), 120. It would be easy to prove the "misinformation" and even superficiality of the *Instruction* on these issues.

68. Nos. 13–15. See my *Ethics and Community* (note 2), chapters 11–12 and 19.

69. See my work *La producción teórica de Marx*, pp. 34, 36–37, 177–179. Examples of two serious questions for theology: the negation of militant atheism by Marx and the solid affirmation of militant atheism by Stalin; the lack of dialectical materialism in the early Marx, and, on the contrary, his clear affirmation of it later.

70. *Instruction*, VIII, 1.

71. *Instruction*, 1986, No. 68.

72. No. 67.

73. Because of which it would be the object of a criticism similar to the analysis previously mentioned in note 60.

74. "With his *work*, man has to obtain his daily *bread*" (First line of the encyclical and Nos. 1, 9, etc.). For "maintenance of life," see: Prologue, nos. 1, 2, 3, 8, 10, 14, 18, etc.

75. " . . . in order to *satisfy* one's own *needs*" (No. 4); " . . . adapting it to his *needs*" (No. 5).

76. See my work *Filosofía de la producción*, on the "pragmatic circle" and the "poietic" or productive circle, the first need-consumption, the second, need-production-product-consumption.

77. CP 3, pp. 227–228; MEGA I, 3 (1932), 546–547. Italics in quotes from Marx mine.

78. *Grundisse*, I (Spanish edition, p. 11; German edition, p. 12).

79. *Capital*, I, 1 (trans. Ben Fowkes, New York: Random House, 1977, p. 127).

80. Prologue to *LE*. In *Manuscrito I* of 1844, Marx explains clearly the difference between human work that involves consciousness and freedom and that of mere animal action.

81. *LE* 6.

82. See note 67. See also *La producción teórica de Marx*, chapter 7, pp. 139ff.

83. ibid. The same text is found in the *Manuscritos del 61–63* (MEGA II, 3, p. 147); see also my *Hacia un Marx desconocido*, chapter 3.1.

84. *Capital*, p. 270. (1873, I, 4.3; Spanish edition, p. 203: MEGA II, 5, p. 120, from 1866). We will explore this issue in a work in progress which will discuss *Das capital* in the manner of a scientific commentary.

85. For example: "as capacity for work or aptitude for work" (*LE* 5); "The capacity for work" (*LE* 12).

86. "The only thing opposed to objectified work is the non-objectified work— living work. . . . The one has the value of use that is incorporated, the other exists as a human activity in process; the one is/has value, *the other is a creator of value*. It exchanges value for the *creative* activity *of value*" (*Manuscritos del 61–63*, Cuaderno I; MEGA II, 3, p. 30). See *Hacia un marx desconocido*, chap. 3.1.

87. For Marx, the "creation" of value is "from the nothingness" of capital: "How can one get out of production greater value than he put in it, unless he believes that *something can be created from nothing (aus Nichts)*" (*Das capital*, III, chap. 1, (edition in Spanish III, 6, p. 43; MEW 25, p. 48).

88. See my *Hacia un Marx desconocido*: chap. 14.2: "Crítica desde la exterioridad

del *trabajo vivo.*" Marx criticizes the reified objectivity of capital from the *personal subjectivity* of the worker.

89. The "fetishism" is only an inversion: the *person* of the worker becomes a thing; and the thing-capital is personified. See my article "El concepto de fetichismo en el pensamiento de Marx," in *Cristianismo y sociedad,* 85 (1985) 7–60.

90. Marx speaks of "objectified" labor or of the objective sense of labor.

91. Marx indicates that "living work" is work as an act, as activity, as subjectivity or subject: it is the individuality of the person of the worker, poor, naked, that is the constant reference of all of his critical thought. All of his work is an *ethic:* "If one wanted to choose to be an ox [*animal*], one could, of course, turn one's back *on the sufferings of humanity* and look after one's own hide. But I should really have thought myself unpractical *if I had begged out* without finally completing my book [*Das Kapital*], at least in manuscript" (CP 42, p. 366; MEW 30, p. 452; letter of April 30, 1867).

92. For Marx, "living work" subsumed under capital is used, consumed as "process of work" in the heart of capital itself (in the *Grundisse, Manuscritos del 61– 63* and *63–65.*

93. *LE* 11.

94. ibid., prologue.

95. *Grundisse,* I (CP 3, pp. 227–228; edition in Spanish, p. 86; German edition, pp. 75–77).

96. *LE* 5, 12, 13, 14, etc. At the beginning of *Cuaderno de París* (1844), Marx notes that it is "not possible to separate" work from capital as if they were two autonomous "things," because all capital is only objectified labor. They are not two *things:* there is *one* "subjectivity" (the labor) and capital is only that same subjectivity *objectified.* Thus he overcomes the "Trinity" (the three factors: labor, capital, land) which he criticized in *Das Kapital* (chap. 7 of the *Manuscrito del 65,* original folios 528ss., in the Amsterdam archives). For all of this, see my soon to be published work on the *Manuscritos del 63–65* (third version of *Das Kapital*).

97. See my article "El pan de la celebración eucarística," in *Concilium,* 172 (1982) 236–249.

98. Maryknoll: Orbis Books, 1986; originally published in 1977. See also his *Crítica a la razón utópica* (San José: DEI, 1984).

99. See my *El dualismo en la antropología de la cristianidad,* note 16.

100. *The Ideological Weapons of Death* (Maryknoll: Orbis Books, 1986), pp. 272– 273.

101. New York: Simon and Schuster, 1988. Originally published 1985.

102. ibid., p. 245.

103. Ed. Diana, Mexico, 1987, pp. 46, 49, 50, 52, 61, 102, 128, 138, 191, etc.

104. ibid., pp. 8, 30, 31, 33, 34, 36, 37, 39, 44, 59, 78, 84, 90, 150, 169, 171, 179, 191, 224, 347, etc.

On April 29, 1988, in the synod of the Orthodox Church, Gorbachev acknowledged that it was an error to have persecuted the church (*Los Angeles Times,* May 5, 1988, p. 9).

105. Op. cit. of F. Castro by Frei Betto, p. 276.

A LIBERATION PERSPECTIVE: PATRIARCHY, MONARCHY, AND ECONOMICS IN THE DEUTERONOMISTIC HISTORY

Alice L. Laffey

I. Introduction and Methodology

There are various perspectives from whicn one may approach biblical texts and depending on one's perspective, the texts may reveal very different—even conflicting—kinds of insights. For example, a liberation-critical perspective uses the results of historical criticism, literary criticism, and sociological criticism, but has as its goal an illumination of the several kinds of power relations which the biblical texts illustrate. Because this perspective recognizes that the texts themselves were produced in a patriarchal/hierarchical culture and have been consistently interpreted in one, it begins with a posture of suspicion. This suspicion extends not only to the texts' authors but also to the texts' past and present interpreters. Such an approach does not mean to deny the sacredness of the biblical texts, but rather seeks to acknowledge the *historical context* in which the texts were produced, the context in which the texts have usually been interpreted, and indeed, the context in which even present interpreters are situated and have been educated. It seeks to uncover

Alice L. Laffey holds a doctorate in Sacred Scripture from the Pontifical Biblical Institute in Rome, Italy, and is currently Chair of the Dept. of Religious Studies, College of the Holy Cross, Worcester, Massachusetts. Her publications include An Introduction to the Old Testament: A Feminist Perspective (Fortress, 1988), commentaries on 1 and 2 Kings and 1 and 2 Chronicles (The Liturgical Press, 1985) and articles in periodicals such as The Bible Translator and The Bible Today. She is presently preparing a manuscript which interprets biblical texts from a cosmic-ecological perspective.

the non-patriarchal/non-hierarchical threads which are interwoven throughout the biblical texts.

Historical Criticism

The period between one thousand BCE and two hundred BCE was patriarchal/hierarchical, and historical criticism which searches for a text's author(s), setting, genre, and purpose, has only confirmed that fact. Historical methodologies—tradition criticism, source criticism, form criticism, and redaction criticism—have uncovered that Old Testament history is men's history, that most if not all of the Old Testament was written *by men*, that it was written primarily *for men*, and that its contents are predominantly *about men*. Though occasional women emerge from the texts as leaders and heroines, such roles for women are *exceptional* and *not* the norm. Women are *normally* portrayed as male adjuncts. Their identity is located in their fathers until such time as they are transferred to husbands, and then later become mothers. Though historical criticism suggests that one period in Israel's history may have been more patriarchal than another, nevertheless, it recognizes that Israel's *pervading culture* was thoroughly *patriarchal*. In addition, the presumably male authors were literate, and we may conclude, since their texts were preserved, "significally connected"; similarly, the education of males who became interpreters of the biblical texts has frequently, though not always, implied a certain class status.

Further, historical criticsm has laid bare Israel's *hierarchical* social organization in which humans "rule over" and "subdue" other living things (e.g., Gen. 1:28–30) and some humans rule over other humans. It has explained the dissolution of judgeship and the creation of monarchy, for example, as the result of the unification of fearful Israelites who bonded together in order to defend themselves against their large and powerful Philistine foe; it has purported that the Israelites' desire to be "like the other nations" (1 Sam. 8:5.20) refers to their perceived need to have a king who could centralize their military efforts and thus provide a formidable opposition against the attackers. Historical criticism has concluded that the text which rejects a human monarch before one has yet been appointed (1 Sam. 8:7), as well as the verses of chapter 8 which describe the adversity to which the people will be subjected once a king has been appointed (vv. 11–18), are later additions, written to explain and justify the monarchy's demise.

Literary Criticism

Though the patriarchal/hierarchical history behind the biblical texts is not the concern of literary criticism, still, similar to historical criticism, literary criticism has functioned, for the most part, to highlight the patriarchal and hierarchical character of the texts. Because of its concentration on major characters (usually men!), central themes (e.g., patriarchal families, war and conquest, monarchical governance) and repeated motifs (the faithfulness or unfaithfulness of Israel and its male leadership), literary criticism has, for the most part, been almost as powerless as historical criticism to retrieve Israel's underclass (its women, children, slaves, outsiders, economically disadvantaged, etc.)

Sociological Criticism

Sociological criticism may shed light on the *function* of women and the underclass in ancient Israelite society and may even explain *how* and *why* they came to possess the stereotypical roles which they did, but nevertheless, it cannot change or justify those roles. When one understands, for example, the origins of the restriction of women, one may come to appreciate that "it was not always that way," that what developed as a temporary measure to respond to a particular historical necessity became in time an accepted and expected pattern of behavior, but even such knowledge cannot alter the texts and their portrayal of women.

Yet sociological criticism has served to uncover the enormous *differences* between the political, economic and social worlds of ancient Israel and our own, and to highlight the inadequacy of any simplistic biblical interpretation which would uncritically try to replicate ancient society in our own. In many nations, including most nations which are heirs to the biblical tradition, *monarchy* has been rejected in favor of democracy; democracy has been determined to be a more representative and, therefore, more just political system. Furthermore, what constituted equitable economic distribution in ancient Israel—a tribal society with explicit provisions for land distribution and re-distribution (e.g., Lev. 25; cf. Josh. 13–19; 1 Kgs. 21:3)—and what constitutes equitable economic policies in contemporary capitalist and socialist nation states, are *different* beyond compare. *Patriarchy*, though still alive and well, is no longer able to use the Bible to *endorse*, for example, polygamy, Levirate marriage, and rape. One might even conclude that historical-critical, literary-critical, and socio-critical studies of the Bible, if employed independently and not placed at the service of other biblical methods of interpretation, can shed very little light on appropriate political, economic, and social behavior for contemporary believers.

Liberation Biblical Criticism

A liberation-critical perspective is today calling into question the injustice which the biblical texts themselves, and traditional and modern interpretation, have done to women and other "minorities." The method self-consciously incorporates experience as a starting point of biblical interpretation. The reality experienced by the *economically* poor, by *racial* minorities, by the *politically* disenfranchised, by the *sexually* exploited—by all those socially marginalized for whatever "reasons"—is admitted as an interpretive tool in the search for meaning.

If one accepts Gerda Lerner's study, *The Creation of Patriarchy*, one understands patriarchy to be the source of other social inequities. Patriarchy has spawned the legitimation of hierarchies in general, including the political structure of monarchy, the economic structure of capitalism, the social preference of heterosexuality over homosexuality, and the legitimation of the exploitation of the world's natural resources. Can a community—or an individual—seeking *liberation* from patriarchy/hierarchy, from political, economic, and social domination benefit from reading the biblical texts? Can a community—or an individual—seeking to replace the paradigm of domination-subjugation with the paradigm of interdependence-mutual respect as those power relationships are played out in the political, economic, social, and ecological realms benefit from reading the biblical texts?

The answer to these two questions is affirmative for two reasons. As Mary Ann Tolbert so effectively admits, "the reader makes meaning." There is no "objective meaning" in a text apart from its reader/interpreter. Historical criticism (which sought the intention of the author and identified the intention of the author [once hypothesized] with the meaning of the text) was and is *historically conditioned*. The methods of historical criticism arose in response to the Enlightenment, which was the historical milieu of the historical critics. In a similar way the method I propose arises in response to the historical milieu of our own time—our cosmic crisis—nothing more, but nothing less. It disposes the reader to approach the texts from the perspective of the underclasses, of those for whom participation in the new decision-making that affects their lives has been either limited or denied, of women and other minorities.

Secondly, the reader so attuned will see the texts through new eyes. Despite the patriarchal/hierarchical culture which produced them and the patriarchal/hierarchical culture in which they have been interpreted, the biblical texts not only *contain* but *support* the paradigm of mutuality-interdependence. Because of the limitations of space this essay is able to explore only three examples of this paradigm.

II. A Liberation Analysis of Three Texts from the Deuteronomistic History

1 Samuel 8

The storyline of 1 Sam. 8, obliquely referred to above, is as follows. The narrator informs us that Samuel is now old, and consequently has appointed his two sons as judges to replace him. They, however, were corrupt. They turned aside after gain (*wayyiṭṭû 'aḥarê habbāṣaʻ*); they took bribes (*wayyiqḥû-shōḥad*) and perverted justice (*wayyaṭṭû mishpāṭ*). Because of this political and economic corruption (in Deut. 16:19 the judges are instructed not to pervert justice—*lō' taṭṭeh mishpāṭ*—and not to take bribes—*wølō' tiqqaḥ shōḥad*) the elders approached Samuel and requested from him that he appoint for them a king who would govern them, thus making them "like the other nations" (v. 5). The narrator tells us that Samuel prayed to the Lord. The Lord responded that Samuel should do what the people asked, that their request for a king was not a rejection of Samuel (of judges, *per se?*) but of the Lord as their king, and that this request was quite consistent with their repeated instances of infidelity and idolatry since the time they had left Egypt. They were merely treating Samuel now the way they had often treated God. Nevertheless, the Lord told Samuel to warn the people regarding how their life would be lived under a king. The warning is as follows:

(11) he will take *your* sons
        and appoint them to *his* chariots,
        and to be *his* horsemen
        and to run before *his* chariots;

(12) and he will appoint *for himself*
             commanders of thousands
             and commanders of fifties,
             and some to plow *his* ground
             and to reap *his* harvest,
             and to make *his* implements of war
             and the equipment of *his* chariots.

(13) He will take *your* daughters
             to be perfumers
             and cooks and bakers.

(14) He will take the best of *your* fields
             and vineyards
             and olive orchards
             and give them to *his* servants.

(15) He will take the tenth of *your* grain
             and of *your* vineyards
             and give it to *his* officers
             and to *his* servants.

(16) He will take *your* menservants
             and *your* maidservants
             and the best of *your* cattle
             and *your* asses
             and put them to *his* work.

(17) He will take the tenth of *your* flocks,
             and *you* shall be *his* slaves. (see Deut. 17:16–20)

Samuel is to warn the people that when this happens, the people will cry out because of their king, the one whom they have chosen to govern them, but the Lord will not hear. The chapter concludes with the narrator's report that the people were not persuaded by Samuel's warnings but continued to request from Samuel a king, one who would make them "like the other nations" (v 20), who would govern them and fight their battles. Samuel took the people's plea to the Lord who told Samuel to do as the people wished, to make a king.

Monarchy is here depicted as hierarchy, with the king sitting securely on the top of a cosmic pyramid. Human persons, including those very persons who ask for a king, *their* sons and *their* daughters, *their* menservants and *their* maidservants, will be the king's slaves and work *for him.* Moreover, the *animals* of the earth, including the best of *their cattle* and *their asses* will also be the *king's,* at *his* disposal; in addition, the *earth* and its *fruits,* including the best of *their fields,* and *vineyards,* and *olive orchards,* will also be at the *king's* disposal; the tithe normally offered to God—of *their grain* and *their vineyards* and *their flocks*—will be the *king's* also. The description of a human leader who takes out of the hands of the people what belongs to *them* and submits *their* property and *their* persons to *his own power and control*—this *patriarchy,* expressed here as *political* and *ecological* domination as well as *economic* hierarchy— is clearly condemned.

One can contrast the description given in 1 Sam. 8 with several other texts from the Deuteronomistic History which describe *God's blessings* on a *faithful Israel:* He "will bless you and multiply you; he will bless the fruit of *your body* and the fruit of *your ground, your grain* and *your wine* and *your oil,* the increase of *your cattle* and the young of *your flock,* in the *land* which he swore to *your* ancestors to give *you.*" (Deut. 7:13) "He will give the *rain* for *your land* in its season, the *early rain* and the *late rain,* that *you* may gather in *your wine* and *your oil.* And he will give *grass* in *your fields* for *your cattle,* and *you* shall eat and be full" (11:4–15).

While most historical critics focus on the probable exilic dating of 1 Sam. 8, written as an explanation of why Israel's monarchy was destroyed—because they wished to be "like the other nations," a phrase which literary critics also focus on because of its repetition in verses 5 and 20—a liberation-critical perspective is attentive to the contrast between monarchy (prosperity increasingly in the hands/power of the monarch) and the traditional assertions of the people's blessings from Yahweh in the form of the people's prosperity. The text of 1 Sam. 8 not only describes the paradigm of domination-subjugation; it condemns it. Further, 1 Sam. 8 can energize an attentive liberation-critical reader to work in his or her own situation toward a society in which there is a *more equitable distribution of resources,* toward a government in which there is a *greater distribution of power,* one which does not take bribes or act perversely, and one which does not steal from the people what rightly belongs to them.

2 Samuel 11—12:6

2 Sam. 11 is a famous text, whose *naming* is so obviously interpretation. Is it a text about the seduction of David or about the rape of

Bathsheba? That depends on *who* is reading the text and *how* the text is read.

In 2 Sam. 11:1 the narrator informs us that during the spring, when kings normally go out to war, David had sent out Joab, his servants, and all Israel, but David himself had remained behind in Jerusalem. The narrator continues with a report that on one afternoon David saw from the palace roof a beautiful woman bathing. Upon inquiry David learned that the woman was Bathsheba, the daughter of Eliam and the wife of Uriah, the Hittite. David sent and took the woman and lay with her. On discovering that she was pregnant, she sent to inform David.

What David did in response to this news was to send for Uriah from the battlefield. When Uriah returned to Jerusalem, David ordered him to go to his home "to wash his feet." (In Hebrew the word feet—*reqelîm*—is often used as a euphemism for the genitals and may refer in this context to sexual intercourse.) In any case, Uriah did not do as David directed. Instead, he spent the night outside the palace *with the king's servants.* When David discovered this, he asked Uriah why he had acted as he had, to which Uriah replied that it would not be fitting, when all Israel and Judah, including the ark, were on the battlefield, for him to go down and lie with his wife. (Men were to refrain from sexual intercourse both before and during battle, and Uriah—in contrast to David—had chosen to stand *in solidarity with* his fellow soldiers and *in company with* servants!) That night David attempted to get Uriah drunk, hoping that inebriation would weaken Uriah's resistance and that he would succumb to the opportunity to sleep with Bathsheba, his beautiful wife. Unfortunately for David, his efforts failed.

David then gave Uriah a letter to deliver to Joab on his return to the battle. The letter contained instructions for a battle plan that would surely result in Uriah's death. Joab executed the king's plan and Uriah was killed. Joab then sent David a message to that effect.

When Bathsheba learned of her husband's death, she made lamentation for him. Then, when the time of Bathsheba's mourning for her deceased husband was over, *David* made Bathsheba *his* wife, and she bore their son. Yet the last phrase of the chapter, like the first, is ominous: what David had done displeased the Lord (v. 27).

A liberation-critical interpretation of this text notes its patriarchal bias. Bathsheba is named, yet her identification is as father Eliam's daughter and husband Uriah's wife, and then as husband David's wife; the chapter also identifies her as fertile female and son's mother. What does a woman do, in the patriarchal culture of ancient Israel—or in any patriarchal culture—when a man, physically and socially more powerful than she, wishes to have sexual intercourse with her?

Bathsheba's passivity is herein highlighted. She submits to the king. What else can she do? David *should* have been out on the battlefield (vs. 1); he should *not* have taken another man's possession, in this case, Uriah's wife; and, certainly, he should *not* have covered up his adultery at the expense of Uriah's life. In contrast to a foreigner, the *Hittite* husband of Bathsheba, who would abstain from sexual pleasure in conformity to Israel's battle protocol, *Israel's* king David would seek sexual pleasure with an inappropriate partner at an inopportune time. The text clearly indicts David.

The interpretation of 2 Sam. 11, which relegates the woman to a mere *occasion*, a *literary instrument* in the story of David's sin, becomes, in the course of centuries, grossly distorted. The text as it reads does not laud patriarchy; it merely exhibits it. However, the text does leave open the possibility of even more patriarchal interpretation, for, centuries after its composition, when David's memory had become idealized in the minds and hearts of the Jews, the story came to condemn Bathsheba. How else could one account for the fact that David had been guilty of wrongdoing? Just as Eve had led Adam astray, so Bathsheba must have led David astray. *He* couldn't resist. It was *her* fault. She was too *tempting* to him; she *tempted* him. The beautiful Bathsheba had seduced David. By the time of the author of Chronicles, David could do no wrong; the entire episode is omitted from Chronicles.

A liberation-critical interpretation, making use of sociological criticism, wishes to emphasize the distance between the social situation which the text describes and our own. Women have a right to be identified by their own names; they should not belong to either fathers, or husbands, nor should they have to be so identified. Further, no woman should have sexual intercourse (and become pregnant) against her will—and certainly Bathsheba's situation is an ambiguous one! According to Deut. 22:22, had David been caught lying with Bathsheba, both of them would have died. But David was not caught; David was king. David could prevent his sin from becoming known—if not by recalling Uriah, then by commanding his placement in the front line of battle and thus securing his death. Nor should any woman become pregnant against her will. Furthermore, a woman who becomes pregnant with someone to whom she

is not at the time married should not have to marry the child's father
(see Deut. 22:28–29). In that patriarchal culture the widowed Bathsheba is likely to have considered marriage to the father of her child
(whether he was her rapist or not) the lesser of evils.

A liberation-critical interpretation would continue to name David
the culprit, but his sin would not only be, or even primarily be,
against Uriah. Rather, David's sins would be against Bathsheba,
whom he sexually violated, contrary to her unavailability, and
regardless of her willingness or unwillingness, whose husband he
killed, and whose child, because of his sins, would die (see 12:14).
Finally, a liberation-critical perspective sees the interconnectedness
of this instance with the political hierarchy of monarchy (the king
can do anything; he owns his subjects—as outlined in 1 Sam. 8) and
patriarchy.

2 Sam. 12 convicts David for his sin. The storyline runs as follows.
God sends the prophet Nathan to David. When he arrives, he tells
David a parable about two men in a city, one of whom was rich, the
other poor. The rich man had many flocks and herds; the poor man
had only one little ewe lamb, one which he had bought and of which
he had grown very fond. It was a pet; the poor man treated it like a
member of the household. One day a visitor came to the rich man;
the rich man provided for that visitor—not with meat from his own
herd, as one might expect; rather, he appropriated the poor man's
little ewe lamb and used *her* for *his* visitor.

When David heard the parable, he was outraged. What kind of a
person would do such a thing? How dare the rich man be so greedy?
How dare he abuse his power to dominate the (economically) vulnerable? Surely a generous restitution was in order! At that point
Nathan interrupted the self-righteous David with the assertion that
he was that man!

Two points in this part of the chapter are of particular interest
from a liberation-critical perspective. Monarchy and patriarchy are
here clearly linked with economics: the king can do what others
might not get away with—adultery and murder; he has *power over* a
married woman and his own general; the parable *equates* such power
with material wealth, though one may surely surmise that this
Israelite monarch also had material wealth. Just as the *power* of
monarchy had made possible David's *power over* Bathsheba and his
power over Joab in 2 Sam. 11, so now wealth, in this part of *the same
story*, makes possible *power over* the poor. And those who have—

power/riches, etc.—want more! 2 Sam. 12 clearly condemns such an economic system.

A liberation-critical perspective also looks carefully at the poor man's relationship to the little ewe lamb. In every way the little ewe lamb is vulnerable. She is "merely" an animal, and in the traditional western hierarchy animals are certainly inferior to humans—to be used and abused at humanity's will. Moreover, she is both young and female; these are, of course, other aspects of her vulnerability. But the poor man has no desire to dominate the lamb. Rather, he welcomes her into his home. The lamb grows up with him and his children, shares their food and drink and is treated like one of the family, "like a daughter" (kǿbat; v. 3).

The contrast between the rich man and the poor man is every bit as great as that between David and Uriah, and carries ecological as well as economic significance. Whereas greed leads to an insatiable urge to climb the ladder and ultimately, to the loss of life—Uriah's, the infant's and the ewe lamb's—the poor man is here presented as a model of one who approaches the world with cosmic interdependence and respect. *His* attitude, as here presented, is *not* to control, to have power over, but to be *in harmony with* and *to nourish*.

Finally, as has been noted, 2 Sam. 11 details David's patriarchal and monarchic behavior, and 2 Sam. 12:1–6 serve to condemn it. In fact, 2 Sam. 12 also condemns *any* hierarchical posture which would allow the rich to dominate and subjugate the poor, and to use *anything*, whether rightfully theirs or not, whether human or animal, for their own pleasure and enhancement. Above all, the two chapters illustrate as clearly as they condemn the interconnectedness of patriarchy, monarchic hierarchy, and economic and ecological domination.

1 Kings 5–7

1 Kings 5–7 detail the building of the Solominic temple. Chapter 5 explains that there had not been sufficient peace during David's reign to allow him to build Yahweh a temple but that greater "rest" came with Solomon's reign so he could do so (see 2 Sam. 7:13). Solomon arranged with King Hiram of Tyre to acquire building materials—cedar and pine logs—from Lebanon. These would be cut and later delivered to Jerusalem in exchange for large quantities of agricultural products. Both Hiram and Solomon would provide men to work on the project. Chapter 6 specifies the outer measurements

of the temple as well as its interior measurements, design, and elaborate decoration. Chapter 7 briefly describes the building of Solomon's own palace and then provides an inventory of additional furnishings which were made for the temple.

A superficial reading of the chapters leaves one with the impression of magnificence: Yahweh's temple is enormous in size and awesome in grandeur, a fitting dwelling place for Yahweh's Name. However, a closer reading of the text, one done from a liberation-critical perspective, notices that the chapters are replete with allusions to the king's power and wealth. For example, Solomon arranged to have King Hiram of Sidon's servants cut and then deliver to him cedars of Lebanon and cypresses for the construction of the temple, in exchange for an annual payment of twenty thousand cors of wheat and twenty (or twenty thousand) cors of beaten oil (5:6–12). More to the point, however, is the fact that the prosperity exhibited by Solomon was at the expense of the people. Having agreed to send some of his servants to help Hiram's servants with the wood, Solomon raised a levy of forced labor—thirty thousand men out of all Israel (v. 13). In addition, Solomon enlisted seventy thousand burden-bearers and eighty thousand hewers of stone in the hill country, besides an additional three thousand three hundred overseers of the others (v. 15).

The king's wealth is further evidenced by the generous quantity of pure gold with which parts of the temple were overlaid (6:20–22) as well as by the many pieces of gold and burnished bronze which he used to decorate the temple (7:15–51). A close reading of the text from a liberation-critical perspective suggests that Solomon had many things in common with the type of king about whom the prophet Samuel had warned (see 1 Sam. 8 above). He controled his people, even to the point of enslaving them. He created the hierarchy of some over others, with *himself* at the top. Moreover, he subjected not only persons, but also other living things which did not belong to him, to his use and abuse. The fruits of the *field*—the *wheat* and the *oil*—became objects of economic exchange. In addition, *living trees*—the *cedar*, the *cypress*, even the *olive* (6:23)—were, with seeming abandon, made to die; they too became mere objects at *his* disposal. And the *earth* itself was violated, with the hewing of stones (see 6:7).

Chapters 5–8 have been linked to 1 Kings 12—suggesting as they do that Solomon's treatment of his subjects was problematic. When his son Rehoboam made even heavier demands on the people, they rebelled, which led soon afterward to the division of the kingdom. A liberation-critical perspective is in sympathy with this explanation. A monarch who becomes a despot will be overthrown. His subjects will refuse to remain victims of his violence. In the name of religion—of Yahweh—Solomon acted like the kings of the "other nations" (see 1 Sam. 8:5.20) who built temples to their gods and thus enhanced *their* power.

And so one must ask, was the temple really built for Yahweh, since, by Solomon's own testimony in 1 Kings 8:27, not even heaven can contain God? or was the temple built for the sake of Solomon's own ego? How then should one interpret that verse in 2 Sam. 7 in which the word of the Lord declares to Nathan (the same prophet of 2 Sam. 12 above), that David is *not* to build a temple, that the Lord has never asked any of Israel's rulers whom the Lord commanded to shepherd the people Israel, "Why have you not built me a house of cedar?" (v. 7) Moreover, in this instance, does the end—the temple—justify the means? The temple was built by a king who took for granted *his power over* other persons, *his power over* other persons' possessions, over *animals* (e.g., 1 Kings 8:5) and *plants* (1 Kings 5:6), over material things in general. Finally, the building of the temple (as well as the building of Solomon's own palace and government buildings—1 Kings 7:1–12), is closely linked to the demise of the united monarchy. In other words, political domination that legitimates ecological and economic domination—including that which uses religion—may be, will be, perhaps *should be*, short-lived.

III. Methodological Conclusions and Suggestions for a Liberation-Critical Interpretation of Texts

What I have tried to do in this essay is to acknowledge, up front as it were, my own non-patriarchal/non-hierarchical bias toward interpretation. It is my conviction that patriarchy and hierarchy (often unacknowledged) have validated and continue to legitimate the paradigm of domination-subjugation in its many expressions. Once *power over* has been legitimated and becomes acceptable in any area of social organization—whether that be in relation to the environment, to politics, to economics, to gender relations including sexual preference (and these areas of social organization are always interconnected)—cosmic *harmony* and *balance*, the power relations paradigm of interdependence-mutual respect, can be lost sight of easily.

This has often occurred with respect to biblical interpretation. Yet, despite the patriarchal/hierarchical culture of ancient Israel, the paradigm of domination-subjugation is, within the biblical texts themselves, clearly *condemned*.

In addition, many of the biblical texts positively *support* a non-patriarchal/non-hierarchical perspective, the paradigm of interdependence-mutual respect. Those who approach the biblical texts as a believing community of the late twentieth century cannot afford other than this liberation-critical perspective. Such a perspective is able to facilitate new insights into the biblical texts; it also contains the potential to energize religious persons to the task, in collaboration with others, of liberating the cosmos from the many kinds of domination and subjugation which, if left unchecked, will ultimately lead to cosmic annihilation.

SELECTED BIBLIOGRAPHY

Albenda, Patricia. "Western Asiatic Women in the Iron Age: Their Image Revealed." *Biblical Archaeologist* 46 (1983) 82–88.

Batto, B. F. *Studies on Women at Mari.* Baltimore: John Hopkins University Press, 1974.

Bird, Phyllis. "The Images of Women in the Old Testament" in Rosemary Radford Ruether, ed. *Religion and Sexism.* New York: Simon and Schuster, 1974.

Gottwald, Norman, ed. *The Bible and Liberation,* Maryknoll: Orbis Books, 1983.

Lerner, Gerda. *The Creation of Patriarchy.* New York: Oxford University Press, 1986.

Lohfink, Norbert F., S.J. *Option for the Poor.* Berkeley: BIBAL Press, 1987.

Meyers, Carol. "The Roots of Restriction." *Biblical Archaeologist* 41 (1978) 91–103.

Trible, Phyllis. *God and the Rhetoric of Sexuality.* Philadelphia: Fortress Press, 1978.

———. *Texts of Terror.* Philadelphia: Fortress Press, 1984.

THE IDEAS OF GOD AND SUFFERING IN THE POLITICAL THEOLOGY OF DOROTHEE SOELLE

Mary Hembrow Snyder

I am a Catholic feminist theologian who is deeply concerned about those who suffer in our world. I have pursued the work of Dorothee Soelle within the hope that her concepts of God and suffering might better clarify for me, not only the whole question of suffering, but more specifically, the question of the connections that exist between personal and political suffering. In this essay I will briefly discuss the political theology of Dorothee Soelle as background to her ideas of God and suffering. Once these ideas are presented I will offer some closing reflections on both the strengths and weaknesses of Soelle's notions of deity and human affliction.

Let me begin with some biographical background about Soelle and myself, in the hope that such information will shed some light on both how and why the two of us struggle with questions about God and suffering in their personal and political dimensions.

Soelle states that initially Auschwitz and Vietnam politicized her. As a German raised in the 1930s, she anguished over how the Holocaust could have happened in her country. This monstrous tragedy provoked in her a deep reevaluation of the meaning of Christian faith. Gradually it impressed upon her an indelible conviction that theology done in a suprahistorical context is meaningless theology.

Mary Hembrow Snyder is Assistant Professor of Religious Studies at Mercyhurst College (Erie, PA.). She received her Ph.D. in Theology from the University of St. Michael's College, Toronto. Her recently published first book is The Christology of Rosemary Radford Ruether: A Critical Introduction (Mystic, CT.: Twenty-Third Publications, 1988).

Further, Vietnam was the locus that revealed the evils of capitalism to Soelle. The genocide of Vietnam became for her an expose of a military-industrial machine that warps technology and production to control the economy. In Vietnam she saw life from the victims' point of view, particularly the peasant women. This experience led her to identify with an alternative socialist vision of life, an alternative she witnessed in the struggles and hopes of the suffering poor in the Third World.

Personally, her divorce had a devastating effect on her. And while this agonizing experience moved her to pray for death, it also deepened her belief in God and her experience of the sufficiency of God's grace for life. Given this, (and more I am sure) Soelle has pursued the connections between personal and political suffering.

Like her, I, too, seek those connections. Like her, a particular event also politicized me, viz., the deaths of the four U.S. missionary women in El Salvador on December 2, 1980. More than anything previously, it made me realize that everything is linked: U.S. hegemony and Third World oppression, ideological blindness and "keeping the world safe for democracy," capitalism and imperialism, rampant social sin and a privatized faith, commitment to the poor and oppressed and martyrdom.

The December 2, 1980 tragedy in El Salvador led me to my first participation in a political demonstration. I marched on the Pentagon in May of 1981 with thousands of others protesting Reagan's policy in El Salvador. Indirectly, the death of those four women made me surer I had to simplify my lifestyle if I was to be freer to pursue my commitment to work for social justice.

Examples of personal suffering that I have been trying to integrate with the above have been several experiences of death over the years. My father died of cancer when I was thirteen. Between 1980 and 1983, my brother, mother, and grandmother also died. During this period I struggled very hard to keep my personal suffering in perspective. What comforted me the most was to begin to see my personal pain as part of the pain of all people who lose loved ones, especially the suffering poor of Latin and Central America with whom I identify most, having spent some time in Peru during the summer of 1983 where I witnessed incredible suffering and oppression.

While this perspective does not allay all my questions about God and suffering, it has provided me with a broader, more concrete framework in which to pursue the connections between personal and political suffering. Nonetheless, the fact remains that I cannot always make these connections. This essay is an attempt to do so.

I. The Political Theology of Dorothee Soelle

Because culture mediates a self-understanding, political theologians like Dorothee Soelle, in dialogue with the Frankfurt School, have taken the need to critique culture very seriously. One of the cultural corruptions resulting from the failure of the Enlightenment project has been the apotheosis of the private life. Consequently, ordinary people have looked upon political life as peripheral. Their perception has been legitimized by the church and a transcendent personalist theology. The latter, while signaling the value of the individual in his/her "I-Thou" relationship to God, has failed to take into consideration the socio-political implications of the Christian message. Such an existential interpretation privatized the Word of God and drained the eschatological promises of their socio-historical demands. Soelle and other political theologians[1] are primarily concerned with the concrete relationship between theory and praxis, faith and action. Using critical theory, they seek to dialectically transform those traditions (e.g., metaphysics, existentialism, positivism, neo-Thomism) which have failed historically to be fully liberating. By clarifying precisely the negative aspects of these traditions, they hope to retrieve and sublate their emancipatory thrust. Particularly, they seek to "deprivatize" the dominant theology which has failed to identify itself with the victims of unjust socio-economic and political orders throughout history.

Soelle's critique of Bultmann's existential theology led her to conclude ". . . that a political interpretation of the gospel is not antithetical to the essential intentions . . . of his theology.[2] Proceeding a step further, however, she maintains a theology must be created that will reflect in a systematic way upon the relationship between faith and politics. Thus, for Soelle,

> Political theology is rather a theological hermeneutic, which in distinction from a theology that interprets reality from an ontological or existentialist point of view, holds open a horizon of interpretation in which politics is understood as the comprehensive and decisive sphere in which Christian truth should become praxis.[3]

Political theology's basic hermeneutical principle, according to Soelle, is how authentic life can be mediated to *all* human beings,

vis-a-vis that of existential theology, which is concerned with authentic life for the individual. A presupposition of political theology
includes the question of individual existence, but only insofar as
the individual is seen in relation to society. Political theology affirms
the possibility that society can be transformed and that there is a
dialectical relationship between the transformation of unjust social
structures and the ongoing conversion of individuals. Both inform
and necessitate the other. As Soelle explains,

> A theology that understands itself apolitically will attempt to portray
> the gospel independently of this horizon of social transformations—
> which for us is indispensable. It makes as a preliminary demand the
> surrender of social, political reason, which regards the world as trans-
> formable. A theology like Bultmann's will view history as having come
> to an end and will always interpret redemption as an escape from the
> world.[4]

Essential to Soelle's methodology is the use of ideological criticism to counteract the tendency in some approaches to theology to
omit any consideration of their socio-political implications. Soelle
believes ideological criticism can unmask the biases inherent in the
gospel and the way that gospel has been traditionally interpreted.
The presupposition of this methodological tool is the belief germane
to any contemporary political theology that the fundamental message of the gospel is the call of all to human liberation. Primarily
this message is directed to the poor, oppressed, and marginated
victims of society. For political theologians such as Soelle, individual liberation has no merit outside the struggle for the liberation of
all peoples.

"Political theology as reflection on faith must give attention to the
social situation of those who are brutalized and uncover the social
roots of their brutalization."[5] It must expose forms of exploitation
that have been disguised under the aura of a greater freedom (e.g.,
consumerism); it must bring to light a new consciousness about
suffering and oppression concealed by an uncritical appropriation
of the religious tradition and the "progress" of society.[6] Political
theology as a critical dialectical theology, "prods men [sic] to combat
their own apathy, creating new anguish and inspiring new projects.
It entices them to seek transformation."[7]

II. The Idea of God in Soelle's Political Theology

Throughout Soelle's theology, I have found her discussion of who
God is, or is not, integral to her simultaneous discussion of the

search for Christian identity as a response to God. For her there is a dialectical relationship between the identity of God and that of the committed Christian making both an ongoing historical process ever subject to change and growth.

The False God and the False Christian

· In a response to the "death of God" movement some years ago, Soelle insisted that "God was not dead." Given the dissolution of the Enlightenment dream, and with it, the ascendancy of instrumental reason over practical reason, what died in a world dehumanized by an uncritical acceptance of science and technology, as far as Soelle was concerned, was ". . . in fact only the death of God's immediacy . . . the dissolving of a particular conception of God in the consciousness."[8] A supernatural *Deus ex machina* had lost any credibility in a world besieged by injustice, oppression, and alienation.

What had died was belief in an omnipotent, almighty ruler who demanded unquestioning obedience. Such an authoritarian image of God revealed a power-hungry deity whose impulse to dominate became embodied in the socio-political situation. Thus Soelle remarks, "God has been linked to the establishment, the political party, the law, patriotism . . . demanding unquestioning obedience from women and men. How does one distinguish who or what demands obedience?"[9] According to this concept, God is isolated from the world, is ahistorical and apolitical. Absolutely transcendent and "wholly other," God is independent from and unrelated to creation. Critiquing this idea of God, Soelle states:

> The theological presumption of God's absolute otherness has consequences in three dimensions: for God, for the earth, and for the human being. If God is absolutely transcendent, then God is rendered invisible as the Creator for whom there can be no human analogies. There is no interaction between such a creator and us. He creates the world out of his free will; he does not need to create it. His creation is an act of absolute freedom. Absolute transcendence literally means unrelatedness. Classical theology viewed the opposite of unrelatedness—relationality—as the weakness of a being bound through passion and suffering to other beings. Hence, the transcendent God in his absolute freedom is a projection of the patriarchal world view and its ideal of the independent king, warrior, or hero.[10]

This false God is the all-powerful, heavenly deity who desires that his followers suffer; this is a God who justifies misery and, in Soelle's perspective, is the product of sadistic and masochistic theologies of suffering:

> He fulfills the ideal of one who is physically beyond the reach of external influences and psychologically anesthetized—like things that are dead . . . his apathy signifies his spirit's freedom from internal needs and external injuries.[11]

Such an apathetic God is also "mute" in the face of suffering humanity and expects people to resign themselves to their circumstances. He thrives on the passivity, submissiveness, and unquestioning obedience of his subjects, whom he treats as objects.[12] This is the image of God the author finds in the Book of Job—a God whose ". . . essence is 'power' and not 'justice'."[13] In addition, Soelle criticizes this false God from a feminist perspective: "As a woman, I'd simply like to ask why people honor a God whose most important quality is power, whose interest is subjection, whose fear is equality."[14] She calls for the creation of a new language with which to talk about God—one more mystical than patriarchal. The latter enhances human passivity by speaking about the God who "directs," "controls," "judges," "destroys," and "rules over."[15] Soelle points to other God-symbols found in the mystics that would not embody authority and power, nature symbols such as light, water, and air. These reveal a deity who wishes harmony and union over obedience, wholeness, and intimacy rather than renunciation and distance.[16]

From a socialist perspective, she rejects a supernatural God who remains aloof from the struggles and hopes of people in history and who caters to individuals seeking personal fulfillment.[17] Such a God is unconcerned about the human body and the structures of society and, hence, human suffering.[18] His major preoccupation is the protection of his power and how to keep human beings from self-consciousness and self-determination.

The false Christian who believes in this false God is one who believes that Christian identity is an ontological or metaphysical given, that one's human effort and labor are unnecessary to the development of this identity, and that there is no process of God's ongoing creation and redemption of the world. All has been achieved in Christ for the false Christian and she is relieved, therefore, of any personal responsibility for history and the future. She is an obedient subject, unquestioning in her loyalty to an almighty, omnipotent Father. She perceives no tension between biological, cultural, and social determinism, on the one hand, and personal freedom on the other. She submits to the proposition that a just God nontheless expects people to suffer and that personal suffering is a means of purification, atonement for sins, and is necessary for individual salvation. The false Christian ultimately believes her *real* life will begin in heaven; consequently, her faith is privatized, ahistorical, and depoliticized.

Authentic Divinity and the Authentic Christian

Soelle claims that her repudiation of the false God enunciated above led her to embrace a "non-theistic theology" whose center is the suffering love of Christ.[19]

> The son was closer to me than the father, he revealed what the father could not communicate to me: love without privileges; love which empties itself and takes on the shape of a slave, a proletarian love which prefers to go to hell as long as others are condemned to stay there.[20]

The roots of this shift lay in her book, *Christ the Representative*, wherein she responded to the "death of God" movement. Rejecting any idea of God that conceives the divine as a heavenly, ahistorical, apolitical patriarch, Soelle insists in this book that Christ is our "temporary" representative before God; he does not replace us for we are unique and irreplaceable. Neither does he replace a dead God—for our God is the God of the living and Christ is God's "forerunner."[21] According to Soelle, our experience of God is Jesus Christ, and only by entering into the suffering love of Christ can we know and realize our Christian identity. Thus, as Christ provisionally represented us before God by temporarily assuming responsibility for human history, we provisionally represent God for each other until God comes again. The "death of God" is therefore negated by Christ the Representative, resulting in a Christian identity that continues to express itself in persons who represent others before God in history as Christ did. Thus, redemption is understood as an ongoing process which demands the participation of any who would claim to be disciples of Christ.

In *Beyond Mere Obedience*, the author says that God can only be experienced *as* and *in* Christ's powerlessness whose only "weapon" is love.[22] In a turn to the mystics, Soelle finds a theological language devoid of domination. God is, here, neither omnipotent nor authoritarian; rather, God is love and the "ground" of human existence. One's relationship to God is thus marked by union and solidarity rather than obedience and self-sacrifice.

Soelle acknowledges that we cannot know with any surety who God is or what God wills in any specific circumstance; however, she insists that if we are able to speak with any seriousness about God, we must do so immersed in history.[23]

In her *Political Theology*, Soelle understands that "God is love" only when human beings themselves become the incarnation of God through a "world-transforming praxis."[24]

Soelle's understanding of Jesus is thoroughly political, for she insists that his very words and actions challenged the social structures in which he lived.[25] His very manner of being negated relationships built on class divisions, familial ties, and sexual hierarchy. No one was to be called rabbi; those marginated by society—the sick, sinners, women, and the poor—were his companions and friends. Soelle claims it is not necessary to determine whether or not Jesus analyzed the social structures of his day as a basis for a contemporary call to discipleship. She maintains that the intention or tendency of Jesus' behavior was liberation of the oppressed; we are not called to imitate his actions but to be faithful to this intention and act creatively as our post-Enlightenment world demands. In Jesus' world, questions about the transformation of social conditions were not raised in the broad sense that they are today. This does not, however, release contemporary Christians from asking questions of a socio-economic and political nature when they directly impinge on how the gospel is to be interpreted in a manner faithful to the spirit of Jesus.

For Soelle then, God in Jesus becomes ". . . the symbol of our unending capacity to love. . . . Here the theme is love toward God, toward one who certainly is not over us like a perfect being but one who is in the process of becoming, as is everything we love."[26] God does not reside antiseptically in a heavenly realm, but suffers and dies daily on the cross wherever human beings are oppressed, tortured, and tormented. Thus, redemption is not achieved once and for all. The God of Dorothee Soelle expects human beings to identify with those who suffer in order to continue, in partnership, the work of creation, in order to build a truly just and human world.

Soelle has also developed the use of mystical language as a way to encounter a loving God. Such language would use different verbs to describe God's activity than does patriarchal language. The God of the mystics, "evokes," "empowers," "liberates," and "nourishes," human beings, making room for a human response issuing from love and a desire for union, rather than from fear and a sterile obedience.[27]

Soelle suggests that one way ". . . to become one with the movement of God in the world," is to be rid of the false God who yearns to dominate us; to do this is, with Meister Eckhart, to learn "the great surrender."[28] German mystics have enunciated three necessary steps for this surrender to take place. One of special interest to this essay is the third step: leaving God behind. Soelle explains that understood contemporarily, this means to abandon God only to find God in one's sisters and brothers. It is to thirst after solidarity instead of slavish obedience; it is to leave behind every relationship of domination, including that of a God who is an authoritarian ruler.[29]

Adopting a dynamic world view which understands nature as subject to change, the God of Soelle is ". . . the horizon of our life, wandering with us . . ."[30] Such a God is concerned with the body and society, legitimizing issues of economic justice, political freedom, and social equality as theological concerns demanding a unity of both theory and praxis. Thus, "no longer can incarnation be understood as an event that happened once and was completed, but rather as a process of God's self-realization in history."[31]

In Soelle's view, the authentic Christian lives in tension, and that tension is the creative arena where cultural determinism and personal freedom interact, provoking a fundamental dialectic between the identity of God and Christian identity. For her the most concrete identity she can ascribe to God is love, "the love that fashions human society in history."[32] Christ best embodied this love and by virtue of his suffering love, commissioned all would-be disciples to know him by suffering likewise in their own day and historical context. For Soelle, therefore, Christian identity, like the identity of Christ, is most fundamentally political—i.e., its substance lies in commitment to the liberation of the poor and oppressed. God as love is revealed every time a human being suffers with another, and the faces of God are as numerous as are the ways God's children suffer. The authentic Christian then, in relationship to God, prefers solidarity to obedience, harmony and union rather than domination, and cooperation instead of commandments. The authentic Christian eschews an almighty patriarchal being who desires human suffering. She understands, quite concretely, that to work against soci-economic and political oppressoin is to interpret the gospel's central message as one of redemption, particularly for the most dehumanized in this world. The authentic Christian believes social transformation is possible when faith and action, theory and praxis, are accountable to the wretched of the earth whom Jesus dearly loved. The authentic Christian, in the final analysis, is always critical and suspicious of those personal journeys (existential, psychological, religious) that result in a privatized faith. He desires an ever-deepening conversion that will plunge him continually into the struggles of his suffering sisters and brothers, so that community may replace excessive individualism and the eschatological promises may be experienced to some degree on this earth.

III. The Idea of Suffering in Soelle's Political Theology

The Pathology of "Christian" Suffering

1. Masochistic and Sadistic Theologies: The identity of the false God and the inauthentic Christian described above have been nurtured in what Soelle calls "masochistic and sadistic theologies." What this pathological tradition has done, primarily, is to keep suffering on a personal, individualistic plane. Thus, suffering was taught as something necessary for salvation, to pacify an angry, omnipotent God. Consequently, its possible social causes were hidden and questions of economic justice, political freedom, and social equality were not raised with any sense of their relationship to the suffering they caused for particular people. As a result, Christians were prevented from seeing any connection between personal and political suffering.

Christian masochism, as Soelle describes it, is an interpretation of suffering as something essential for one's growth as a true child of God. Suffering within this perspective came to be understood as 1) a way God tested one's fidelity, 2) punishment for sin, and 3) a means of purification.[33] Unquestioning submission was the premise of this Christian masochism. Meanwhile, the sadistic God who sent this suffering remained the omnipotent and omniscient ruler responsible for requiring people to pay for their sins. Unfortunately, this sadistic image has led many people to perceive God as having "contempt for humanity."[34]

2. Apathetic Christians: Soelle's definition of apathy as "the inability to suffer" is applied primarily to people in the industrial world.[35] She cites three sociological causes for this growing affection among people there: 1) in the industrial nations, a sufficient supply of basic commodities is available to most; as a result, "private property obscures public poverty" when the majority of people's basic human needs are satisfied; 2) much suffering has been eliminated by widespread education; 3) the situation of increased social mobility and common separation from what the author calls "primary relationships" has made the rupture caused by brokenness or geography in relationships easier to adapt to.[36] For example, she sees a link between this phenomenon and the direct inability of people from industrial nations to be sensitive to the suffering masses in the Third World. For Soelle the horror of this sociological situation is that on both a personal and political level apathy becomes

> . . . the no longer perceived numbness to suffering. Then the person and his circumstances are accepted as natural, which even on the technological level signifies nothing but blind worship of the status quo: no disruptions, no involvement, no sweat.[37]

Her solution to apathy would be to "serve the pain of God by [your] own pain.[38] It is an image of discipleship that connects personal and political pain with the pain of God. For Soelle this presupposes a theological understanding of God's pain as something that issues from the evil God sees in the world. The historical reality of pain then becomes the locus of divine revelation. Through unemployment, hunger, homelessness, sexism, racism, and militarism, etc. the pain of God is made manifest. Our response to realities such as these becomes a means by which we can serve God's pain. As Soelle explains,

> Our own pain, which we have accepted, will then be related to the pains of the people among whom we live. We stop hoping for a solution from without . . . To 'serve the pain of God by your own pain' is to lead suffering out of its private little corner and to achieve human solidarity.[39]

Suffering as "Death by Bread Alone"

"Death by bread alone" is an unnatural death which results from the imposition of violent social structures upon humankind.[40] Existentially speaking, it is a life filled with ennui and angst; biblically speaking, it is a life lived without meaningful relationships, where one's goal is survival and all *joie de vivre* is absent. It is a way of life characterized by estrangement and alienation. Describing this further Soelle argues:

> . . . our greatest enemy is a kind of creeping death, that living, breahting, lifelessness we see written on the faces of so many in our day. It is this kind of death and dying by bread alone that calls for our most resolute and passionate resistance and battle.[41]

Struggling with the suffering caused by a painful divorce, the author discovered that if often takes a death experience of some kind to make one realize that God's grace is sufficient. If her divorce taught Soelle that death is followed by new life, it is because the suffering it caused helped her to begin to see the link between the capitalistic values of her culture and the limited and distorted self-identities they create interrelationally.[42] But how was she to connect this personal suffering to that of people suffering in society? She looked to the suffering love of Jesus.

The Cross and Class Struggle

Soelle admits that Jesus' struggle may not be able to be called "class struggle," but insists nevertheless that he was on the side of the poor and oppressed.[43] She maintains that his struggle was the same as all historical struggles: to reconstruct a society marred by class divisions into one where sisterhood and brotherhood are possible. For Soelle, the cross and class struggle intersect wherever God and human beings struggle for liberation.[44] To take up one's cross is to actively engage in a struggle that is more than personal and devoid of any hint of passive acceptance.

Class struggle has two faces for Soelle: one "from above" and one "from below." The former is fought by people of wealth and power in order to maintain their privileges. Some methods they use to do this are cut-backs, plant closings or relocations where labor is cheaper. More covertly, they mask the struggle by propagating the myth that all are in the same boat.[45] While class struggle "from below" is often handicapped by fatalism and political apathy, its presence is felt by a consciousness awakened to oppression and the "weapon" of the non-violent strike.[46]

In relation to class struggle, Soelle has defined the cross as ". . . the place for Christians to stand when they become aware of the alienating culture of injustice in which they are living."[47] For her it has three dimensions: 1) to break neutrality—to view the world from the perspective of the victims and thus to join the struggle by naming and denouncing the enemy; 2) to make visible the invisible—to expose the victims and the economic, social, political, and religious structures which hide them. It is a call to participate in the revelations of God's love as it concretizes itself in the struggle; and, 3) to share a vision—to anticipate the kingdom of God by embodying the eschatological promises of peace, justice, and reconciliation. It is a challenge to keep alive the memory of the dead and the suffering they endured by an active commitment to building the kingdom of God on earth.[48]

Mysticism's Contribution to Soelle's Idea of Suffering

For Soelle, the search for self-identity and the search for God's identity are dialectically interrelated in the tension between personal and political suffering—i.e., the cross. This search demands the rejection of what she calls "bourgeois theology," of "individualism as the deepest and ultimate category."[49] Here every cross is a personal struggle devoid of any political dimension. "A new interpretation, which thinks of the cross and political struggle together, begins with the active conscious decision of a life for the poor and oppressed."[50] Mysticism has helped Soelle better understand the dialectics that encompass her theological and faith commitments. The relationships between the identity of God and Christian identity, between personal and political suffering, have been nuanced for her by the mystics' view of God, self, suffering, and the world.

The mystics saw suffering as a way of loving God *practically*—a way of becoming more authentically one's self. They rejected a God who punishes sinners in favor of a God who desires union with the victims. They expected suffering to change them—that somehow it would strengthen them in their weakness.

> It is the mystic sufferer who open his [sic] hands for everything coming his way. He has given up faith and hope for a God who reached into the world from the outside, but not hope for changing suffering and learning from suffering.[51]

Such suffering enables one to be there for others, common sojourners offering each other a compassionate embrace.

Because mysticism is based on experience, because it speaks of a non-authoritarian God and enables one to learn "the great surrender," Soelle believes that for women, particuarly, the latter can be a vehicle for liberation from a patriarchal theology and church.[52] "The greatest surrender," the leaving of world, self and God, is an inward journey where the false identity created by capitalistic values and a bourgeois theology are shed. It is a search for meaning where one discovers that "God is love," concretely, in the struggles for liberation. "The return journey" thus becomes a way to deepen one's commitment to the poor and oppressed through solidarity and justice-making. While this "return journey" is not clearly articulated by Soelle, she understands it as a kind of Exodus event. As such it seeks to make further connections between public and private spheres of life, between the personal and the political, between an authentic Christian identity and the identity of a God who is love.

IV. Reflections

The major strength of Soelle's idea of God is that it is unsystematic and in process. While some may criticize this as a weakness, its strength, to my mind, lies in the fact that it makes her notion of God dependent upon an interpretation of reality that is historical, political, biblical, and contemporary. It is a heuristic concept in dialectical relationship with the meaning of Christian identity. It defies rigid, dogmatic categorization, for it seeks to communicate to all people the possibility of authentic life in a world victimized by a capitalistic economic system, the threat of nuclear annihilation, the growing presence of national security states, and the widening gap between rich and poor. It seeks to articulate a radically relational understanding of the divine as that which is profoundly connected to all that has been created, thereby challenging human beings to live in harmony with self, others, God, and the environment.

According to Soelle, if God is to speak meaningfully to us human beings amid these ealities, we must in some way embody " . . . the as yet unrealized totality of our world and the truth of our life which is yet to appear."[53] The transcendence of such a God is not characterized by alienation as dualism, but rather by praxis, i.e., ". . . not a state but an act, the capacity of creatively overcoming the given act of conditions in a historical situation."[54] God cannot be known apart from the creative efforts of human beings to build a more just and human world.

Implicit in the above major strength is a second strength—i.e., the presupposition that Christians are adults who prefer a God who is partner and friend rather than patriarch. Given this, they are willing to assume their responsibility as co-creators, to make the incarnation of God a "real presence" in the world.

A weakness I perceive in Soelle's idea of God is that it is too "Christian"—i.e., her idea of God is limited by her failure to include the insights of neo-pagan feminists such as Carol Christ, who has written passionately on the value and significance of Goddess spirituality, or the work of theologians such as Paul Knitter who has called our attention to the urgent need for dialogue between theologians of liberation and those engaged in interreligious dialogue.[55] Soelle's idea of God could only enrich and be enriched by such conversations.

With regard to her critique of suffering, its first strength lay in its exposure of how pathological theologies have kept Christians low in self-esteem, fearful, isolated and preoccupied with personal sin. Secondly, her critique provides an invaluable insight into the connection between personal and political suffering by calling our attention to the following prerequisites essential to making that connection:

1) the abandonment of belief in a supernatural DEUS EX MACHINA who is ahistorical and apolitical;

2) a commitment to the poor and oppressed;

3) a belief that history is where God is revealed and that theory and praxis, faith and politics dialectically illuminate that revelation;

4) the self-discipline of a socio-economic and political consciousness;

5) the perception that most suffering is socially caused;

6) a willingness to live with the ambiguity of a powerless God whose only "weapon" is love;

7) the capacity to see one's suffering as a privileged way to enter into solidarity with one/s victimized sisters and brothers;

8) ongoing conversion—openness to learn and be changed by suffering so as to engage in a commitment to social transformation.

A weakness I see in the author's concept of suffering is in her stereotype of people living in industrialized nations as apathetic.

While I do not deny its obvious presence, at least since Soelle's initial observations, fewer and fewer people in these nations can be categorized as "satiated." Among other things, rising unemployment, homelessness, and poverty, along with a more broadly-based suspicion of the ideology behind the arms race and U.S. presence in Central America, have contributed, I think, to a growing identity of First World people with suffering Third World people, as well as to a reduction of apathy among more and more middle class people in the western world.

"Political theology is not simply a call to activism. It is a search for an integrating wisdom capable of being practiced cooperatively in reversing dehumanizing injustices."[56] Through her ideas of God and suffering Dorothee Solee has challenged us to participate in the search for such wisdom. Meanwhile, "We know that the whole creation has been groaning in travail together until now . . . " (Rom. 8:22).

NOTES

1. I am referring here specifically to Johannes B. Metz and Matthew L. Lamb. See particularly Metz's groundbreaking article, "The Church and the World in the Light of a 'Political Theology'," in his *Theology of the World* (New York: Herder & Herder, 1969), pp. 107–124, and also Matthew L. Lamb, *Solidarity With Victims: Toward a Theology of Social Transformation* (New York: Crossroad, 1982).

2. Dorothee Solee, *Political Theology*, John Shelley, tr. (Philadelphia: Fortress Press, 1974), p. 55.

3. Ibid., p. 59.

4. Ibid., 62.

5. Ibid., p. 67.

6. Ibid., p. 69.

7. Ibid.

8. Dorothee Soelle, *Christ the Representative* (London: SCM Press, Ltd., 1967), p. 133.

9. Dorothee Solle, *Beyond Mere Obedience*, Lawrence W. Denef, tr. (New York: The Pilgrim Press, 1982), p. 12.

10. Dorothee Soelle and Shirley Cloyes, *To Work and to Love: A Theology of Creation*, (Philadelphia: Fortress Press, 1984), p. 14.

11. Dorothee Soelle, *Suffering*, Everett R. Kalin, tr. (Philadelphia: Fortress Press, 1978), p. 42.

12. Ibid., p. 77.

13. Ibid., p. 114.

14. Dorothee Soelle, "Mysticism, Liberation and the Names of God," *Christianity and Crisis*, June 22, 1981, p. 182.

15. Ibid.

16. Ibid., p. 183.

17. Dorothee Soelle, *Beyond Mere Dialogue: On Being Christian and Socialist* (Detroit: Christians for Socialism, 1978), p. 18.

18. Ibid.

19. Ibid., p. 38.

20. Ibid.

21. *Christ the Representative*, p. 134.

22. *Beyond Mere Obedience*, p. xix.

23. Ibid., p. 10.

24. *Political Theology*, p. 107.

25. Ibid., pp. 64–67.

26. *Suffering*, p. 92.

27. Soelle, "Mysticism, Liberation, and the Names of God," p. 184.

28. Ibid.

29. Ibid., p. 185.

30. *Beyond Mere Dialogue*, p. 12.

31. Ibid., p. 18.

32. Ibid., 35. Here Soelle is quoting Juan Luis Segundo.

33. *Suffering*, p. 19.

34. Ibid., p. 26.

35. Ibid., p. 36.

36. Ibid., p. 40.

37. Ibid., p. 39.

38. Ibid., p. 44. Here she is using the idea of Japanese theologian Kazoh Kitamori.

39. Ibid., p. 45.

40. Dorothee Soelle, *Death by Bread Alone*, David L. Scheidt, tr. (Philadelphia: Fortress Press, 1978), p. 6.

41. Ibid., p. 12.

42. With regard to this Soelle has also stated that capitalistic values " . . . rule not only our economy and politics but our whole way of thinking." Ibid., p. 77.

43. *Beyond Mere Dialogue*, p. 24.

44. Ibid.

45. Ibid., p. 21.

46. Ibid., p. 22.

47. Ibid., p. 16.

48. Ibid., pp. 25–30.

49. Dorothee Soelle, *Choosing Life*, Margaret Kohl, tr. (Philadelphia: Fortress Press, 1981), p. 54.

50. Ibid.

51. *Suffering*, p. 145.

52. For the German mystics, "the great surrender" consists of three steps: abandoning the world, the ego, and God. See Soelle's interpretation of this in "Mysticism, Liberation, and the Names of God," pp. 184–185.

53. *Death by Bread Alone*, p. 132.

54. *Beyond Mere Dialogue*, p. 17.

55. See Carol P. Christ, *Laughter of Aphrodite: Reflections on a Journey to the Goddess* (San Francisco: Harper & Row, 1987), and Paul F. Knitter, "Toward a Liberation Theology of Religions," in *The Myth of Christian Uniqueness: Toward a Pluralistic Theology of Religions*, John Hick and Paul F. Kittner, eds. (Maryknoll, New York: Orbis Books, 1987), pp. 178–200.

56. Matthew L. Lamb, "Political Theology," 1987. Department of Theology, Boston College, Boston, Massachusetts. Unpublished manuscript. This article has since been published by Michael Glazer, Inc., in *A New Catholic Dictionary*, 1987.

MYSTICISM AND POLITICS AND INTEGRAL SALVATION: TWO APPROACHES TO THEOLOGY IN A SUFFERING WORLD

William L. Portier

It remains true that one of the major phenomena of our time, of continental proportions, is the awakening of the consciousness of people who, bent beneath the weight of age-old poverty, aspire to a life of dignity and justice and are prepared to fight for their freedom.[1]

These are not the words of Gustavo Gutierrez or John Luis Segundo or even Johann Metz or Edward Schillebeeckx, but of Joseph Ratzinger. The names of Schillebeeckx and Ratzinger are rarely associated except in an adversarial context. We tend to assume, and with some reason, that they represent polar positions on the spectrum of contemporary Catholic theology. While not wishing to minimize real differences of theological method and conclusions, I will emphasize in this essay certain convergences in their thought. These center on how our awareness of human suffering in the world, as expressed in the opening quotation, ought to shape our sense of the way scholars and teachers in the western academy should do theology.

William L. Portier is Associate Professor of Theology at Mount Saint Mary's College in Emmitsburg, Md., where he has taught since 1979. He received his Ph.D. in Theology from the University of St. Michael's College, Toronto, in 1980. From 1986 through 1988, he served as Vice President of the College Theology Society. His publications in the areas of historical and systematic theology include Isaac Hecker and the First Vatican Council *(1985) and* The Inculturation of American Catholicism, 1820–1900: Selected Historical Essays *(1988), which he edited. Work in progress includes an introductory theology text, a biography of John R. Slattery, and continuing work on the thought of Edward Schillebeeckx.*

This comparison will be based primarily, though not exclusively, on two texts. The first is a series of lectures given by Schillebeeckx at the Free University of Amsterdam May 27 through May 30, 1986. They were translated into English as *On Christian Faith. The Spiritual, Ethical, and Political Dimensions* (Crossroad, 1987). In the last lecture, entitled "Jesus as the Question of Men and Women to God: Mysticism, Ethics and Politics," Schillebeeckx develops the categories of *mysticism* and *politics,* as he reflects on the experiences of middle class Christians in the West who try to live in solidarity with those who suffer. This lecture will be the focus of our attention in this essay.

The second text is the Congregation for the Doctrine of the Faith's "Instruction on Christian Freedom and Liberation," dated March 22, 1986, released April 5, 1986, and signed by Joseph Ratzinger. While Ratzinger is doubtless the principal author of this document, its fifth chapter is so close to the thought of Pope John Paul II that, if he did not write or at least significantly edit it, he certainly could have. In the fourth chapter, entitled "The Liberating Mission of the Church," Ratzinger draws from the documents of the Latin American bishops the concept of "integral salvation" or "integral liberation" (LC 62, 63).[2]

Schillebeeckx and Ratzinger affirm with one accord that the voices of those who suffer, both within and beyond the confines of the western, industrial states, must be included in western theology. This mutual concern testifies to the impact which Latin American liberation theology has had on western theology. In the texts considered below, both Schillebeeckx and Ratzinger respond as citizens of the industrial West to the challenges posed by liberation theology on behalf of those who suffer needlessly.

Schillebeeckx and Ratzinger diverge in their estimates of the impact suffering voices ought to have on western theology. Their respective approaches to the experience of salvation in a suffering world represent two divergent views of the theological task. One might see in them as well reflections of two trends in contemporary Catholic theology. I will call them the "anthropological" and the "contextual." My contention here is that, while these two orientations represent sometimes widely diverging theological perspectives on contemporary experience, they are, like the texts to be considered below, not incompatible in principle. In order to make this clear, it is also necessary to consider a third orientation, that of liberation theology.

I. Three Orientations in Contemporary Catholic Theology

Since Vatican II, the "turn to the subject" or the anthropological turn has become a commonplace for interpreting the recent history of Catholic theology. In this interpretation, a generation of theologians, represented in Europe by Karl Rahner and Henri de Lubac, helped to move Catholic thought from a classical cosmological worldview to a modern or anthropological one which thematized questioning human subjects as well as the objects of their questioning. The young Metz even argued that the anthropological turn had begun with Aquinas. It is important to emphasize, however, that *anthropological* does not here refer to the kind of purely formal and abstract account of individual human subjectivity typical of eighteenth-century thought.

Key to the twentieth-century anthropological approach is an orientation toward history, a sense of the historicity or situatedness of human subjects. Both Rahner and Bernard Lonergan, the latter in the North American context, urged theologians to attend to their situatedness in the particularities of a time and place. In the closing paragraph of *Spirit in the World*, first publichsed in 1939, the year Germany invaded Poland, Karl Rahner directed our search for God to "the here and now of his [man's (sic)] finite world." We should expect to encounter God, Rahner thought, "where we already and always are, in an earthly place, at an earthly hour."[3] This emphasis on human historicity led at Vatican II to the kind of concern for dialogue with modernity that we find in the *Pastoral Constitution on the Church in the Modern World*.

In the intervening years, voices from at least three different concrete standpoints have criticized this early form of the anthropological orientation. Each of these lines of criticism expresses serious reservations about the modern European project of rational emancipation. These three critical voices or perspectives can be named: 1) political, or better, contextual theology, 2) liberation theology, 3) concrete anthropological theology. I intend this latter term as a reference to the thought of Pope John Paul II and, in his better moments, that of Joseph Ratzinger. The adjective *concrete* is intended to distinguish this perspective from the earlier anthropological approaches mentioned above, namely those of the eighteenth and early twentieth centuries.

1. Contextual theology: Some western Europeans, in dialogue with critical social theory, have argued that the earlier generation's

sense of the historicity of theologians and their theologies tended to remain too abstract, too bound to the framework of early modern European thought with its separation of the religious and the political, the spiritual and the temporal. The later Metz and, in his own turn, Schillebeeckx represent this line of criticism. Since the term *political theology* is closely associated with the thought of J.B. Metz, and since it is foreign to the North American setting, I prefer to call this critical perspective *contextual* theology.

Contextual theologians in Europe and North America give critical attention to the relationship of theological ideas to the particular situatedness of theologians as embodied persons in social and economic settings in particular cultures and places at particular times. The voices and experiences of those who suffer unjustly in and from such concrete settings provide theologians with an epistemological corrective for their own points of view as creatures of the modern West. Such a critical perspective or view from below helps western theologians to bring their own acting and reflecting into closer relationship, helping to heal the modern schism between theology and spirituality, between dogmatic theology and moral theology. Contextual theologians who seek to take as their own the critical perspective of those who suffer have also been called *"liberationists."*[4]

2. Liberation Theology: In the years since Gustavo Gutierrez published *A Theology of Liberation* in 1971, Latin American theologians have challenged the dominance of the early anthropological approach as failing to do justice to the experiences of suffering people in their countries. Schillebeeckx, for example, credits Gutierrez with inaugurating "a theological practice which mobilized an entire continent and opened the eyes of European and North American theologians to their unhistorical and often idealistic way of thinking."[5]

In his comments on Ratzinger's August, 1984 "Instruction on Certain Aspects of the 'Theology of Liberation',", Leonardo Boff contrasts the method of liberation theology, with its starting point in the experience of needless suffering in Latin America, and what he calls the "Central European perspective" in which liberation is one theological topic among many. He summarizes it as follows:

> Liberation is a fundamental concept in blibical theology and in the tradition of emancipation found in modern culture. When dealing with it theologically, the theologian researches scripture, tradition, the teachings of the church and the recent opinions of theologians. The

idea is to systematically reconstruct the idea of liberation and to establish a critical grounding for the topic; once this is done, its consequences for the everyday life of the faithful are deduced and advice and instruction for future action are drawn up.[6]

Many contemporary North American theologians should be able to recognize ourselves in what Boff calls the "Central European perspective." He is not talking about some form of manualist neo-scholasticism but a species of the basic theological approach that led to Vaticin II and in which most of the present generation of theologians, including those from Latin America, were trained. Boff's characterization is a fair description of the 1984 Instruction he was commenting upon, but an incomplete description of Ratzinger's usual anthropological approach to theological questions.[7]

3. Concrete Anthropological Theology: While Ratzinger's perspective is an avowedly anthropological one, it would be a mistake to interpret him as uncritically repeating earlier forms of the anthropological approach in a purely formal or abstract way detached from concrete history. He has tried to develop the turn to the subject in a way that would purely the modern project of some of its reductionist tendencies. Commenting on *Gaudium et Spes* in 1975, he wrote:

Let is be said once and for all: the progress of the Church cannot consist in a belated embrace of the modern world—the theology of Latin America has made that all too clear for us and has demonstrated thereby the rightness of its cry for liberation.[8]

As his able discussion of the anthropological foundations of tradition shows, he shares the emphasis on human historicity characteristic of the earlier anthropological approach.[9] At the same time, he denies that his anthropology is purely formal. Such a treatment is "just as little possible as the pure self-reflection of praxis, new context slips in unnoticed."[10]

Ratzinger's development of the anthropological approach, therefore, is not incompatible in principle with the contextual approach. Though their emphases are different, both have developed from the earlier anthropological approach with its stress on human historicity. Ratzinger himself has spoken of "the inseparate connection between humanity and history." "Tradition, as the *constitutivum* of history, is constitutive of a humanity that is truly human, of the *humanitas hominis*."[11] What Ratzinger refuses to do is discuss the relationship between humanity and history in Marxist terms. This makes it difficult for him to handle questions about what happens when tradition distorts the human through the maintenance of unjust social and economic structures.[12] As we shall see below, the pope's greater facility in dealing with such questions illustrates that the concrete anthropological perspective is not closed to them.

II. Ratzinger and Schillebeeckx Diverge on Marxism

More than the differences between anthropological and contextual theologies, therefore, what separates Ratzinger and Schillebeeckx is that, for whatever reasons of personal make-up, history and choice, they occupy sharply divergent ground in what might be called the "political culture" of Europe.[13] They diverge most sharply in their attitudes toward the epistemological insights of Marxist thought and the possible application of those insights to the present interpretation, in action and reflection, of the Christian theological tradition. This leads to differing attitudes toward Christian experience, and particularly the experience of suffering, as a source of theology.

Ratzinger's distrust of neo-Marxism or critical theory is deep and long standing. He knows well that a Marxist thinker would likely dismiss his formal anthropology as reflective of bourgeois interests. But he regards such criticism as based on a false view of the human which refutes itself by its own repressive performance. With such a basis, any genuine concern for suffering humanity is bound to go out of control and inflict more needless suffering. In a *New York Times* interview, he explained the origin of his attitude toward neo-Marxism:

> For so many years, the 1968 revolution and the terror created—in the name of Marxist ideas—a radical attack on human freedom and dignity, a deep threat to all that is human. At the time, I was dean of the faculty of theology at Tübingen, and in all the university assemblies in which I participated, I could notice all kinds of terror, from subtle psycho-terror up to violence. This was accomplished in the name of freedom, with theories that were so hypocritical, if one only compared them with the praxis. Up to then, I had known Marxism and neo-Marxism only from books and thought it was good to discuss; I even thought at the beginning that this could be a corrective of Bultmann's existentialism that was dominating Tübingen . . . However, I learned that it is impossible to discuss with terror and on terror, as there are no premises for a discussion—and such a discussion becomes collaboration with

terror. I think that in those years, I learned where discussion must stop because it is turning into a lie and resistance must begin in order to maintain freedom.[14]

Schillebeeckx and others who have drawn from critical theory believe that the epistemological priority it gives to the interests of those who suffer unjustly can work in the context of a Christian-oriented vision of the human.[15] For his part, Ratzinger fears that orthopraxis in its most radical sense presumes that no truth about the human can exist prior to praxis. Truth, he insists, can never be a "product of fact."[16] Here one can only wonder which theologians the Cardinal has in mind. On the other hand, Ratzinger also insists that the move from theory to practice can never be mere application. He emphasizes this in concluding his discussion of the impact of the Marxist notion of "base" on the theology of the local church.

> But it is equally impermissible to reduce 'praxis'—to reduce life in the concrete units that form the Church—to simple application. Rather the 'local church' is to be regarded as a place of learning by experience, of the real testing of faith, as a place of suffering but, at the same time, as a place of knowledge that derives from suffering.[17]

Given this, as well as his nuanced view of tradition as the "base" and "precondition" for humanness, Ratzinger could doubtless agree in principle with Schillebeeckx that the dichotomy between a beginning with Christian tradition and a beginning with Christian experience is a false one. Nevertheless Ratzinger seems less inclined than Schillebeeckx to acknowledge and reflect upon the relationship between his situatedness or context and his interpretation of tradition. He is less inclined than Schillebeeckx to extend criticism of tradition in the name of those who suffer to the Church's own traditions.[18]

The difference between Ratzinger's concrete anthropological approach and Schillebeeckx' more contextual one is captured at the connotative level by the two terms in the title of the 1986 CDF Instruction, *freedom* and *liberation*. Significantly, both Ratzinger and Schillebeeckx are aware of the deep ambiguities of modernity and its concept of freedom. In the name of freedom from needless external domination, western history has produced a surplus of further domination. This "dialectic of enlightenment," as some critical social theorists have named it, raises perspectival questions about whose freedom is under discussion, as well as more praxis-oriented questions about humane ways to achieve a more inclusive freedom. The texts of Schillebeeckx and Ratzinger both begin with the ambiguities involved in the dialectic of enlightenment.

III. Mysticism and Politics

The term *mysticism* and *politics* represent the direction in which Schillebeeckx has taken his theology during the past decade. He has made his own critical theory's concern for the history of needless human suffering.[19] The terms *mysticism* and *politics* also represent Schillebeeckx' attempt to overcome the dualism (between the private or spiritual and the public or political) which afflicts western discussions of religious freedom. The May 1986 Abraham Kuyper Lectures at the Free University of Amsterdam provide straightforward working definitions of these terms. Mysticism is "an intensive form of experience of God or love of God"; politics is an "intensive form of social commitment," open to all and not limited to the professional activity of politicians.[20]

The liturgical and political involvements of the "critical communities" with whom he has associated since the early 1970s provide the experiential basis for these conceptions. No dobut the presence of medium range U.S. nuclear missiles on Dutch soil has also had an effect. Within the life experience of middle class Christians, members of the relatively privileged classes in the dominant culture, citizens of nation states which possess and threaten to use nuclear weapons, Schillebeeckx searches as theologian for the call and salvation of God. In his remarks on the occasion, September 17, 1982, of receiving the Dutch Government's Erasmus Prize for his contribution to European culture, Schillebeeckx dwelt upon the theologian's responsibility amid the ambiguities of modernity. Noting theology's past complicity, he wrote:

> But whatever one thinks of contemporary theologians, one thing should be granted them: by means of a historical praxis of commitment to mysticism and politics, they are trying to discover the human face of God and, starting from there, to revive hope in a society, a humanity with a more human face.

He went on to describe the main task of theology: "to preserve the transcendence of the God who loves men [sic], hidden and yet so near, in the face of the idols which human beings set up." This means opposing any claims of human science to "provide the only effective solution to vital human problems" and implies "a truly interdisciplinary approach."[21]

If it is the business of theologians to "preserve the transcendence of the God who loves men," and they do this by means of a "historical praxis of commitment to mysticism and politics," the phrase "experience of God" in the working definition of mysticism above takes on special significance. Through all the stages of the development of his thought, Schillebeeckx has consistently maintained that our experience of God is always mediated in some way. Even in personal prayer, the immediacy of God is mediated by "the historical human and natural world of creation, the constitutive symbol of the real presence of God for us."[22]

Because of our finitude, we do not experience the absolute presence of God "pure and undiluted, available on its own . . ." How God's cause comes, within the historical horizon of our lives, to be one with humanity's cause and vice versa is what "the theologian aspires to unravel."[23] There is not initially ordinary human experience which we, by a process of reflection, subsequently identify as religious experience. "Experience is always interpreted experience."[24] Christians are people who experience life in terms of the story of Jesus Christ. If there is to be an attempt at reflection on why or how one can do this, it cannot be separated from Christian ethical and liturgical life. We simply do not have access to a purely theoretical why or how.

Because of our present historical and cultural situation in the West, the absolute presence of God can, and even needs to be, mediated through the domain of politics as defined above. Our times cry out for what Schillebeeckx calls "political love." In the May 1986 lecture on "Jesus as the Question of Men and Women to God: Mysticism, Ethics and Politics," he explains this in a particularly clear way. He treats it as a development of the New Testament teaching on the unity—full of tension—between love of God and love of neighbor (Luke 10). Ratzinger too will treat "integral salvation" within the context of the two great commandments. For Schillebeeckx in this text, the bond which units mysticism and politics into a fitting contemporary possibility for Christian experience is this clear ethical dimension of the Christian faith expressed in the two great commandments.

In our time love of God and love of neighbor can and need to be experienced in a new form, a political form. Mysticism was formerly thought to be a form of contemplative prayer; love of neighbor took on the form of compassion in interpersonal exchanges, embodied best in the traditional corporal and spiritual works of mercy. With the realization that the conditions which produce poor and hungry neighbors throughout the world are often of human rather than natural origin, and therefore changeable, love of neighbor acquires a new political dimension or form in the struggle for social justice. Participation in this struggle for justice on the side of the needy is what Schillebeeckx means by "political love." It does not replace Christian kindness or compassion, works of charity at the individual level, but rather becomes still another form of love of neighbor. Present within each is the same implicit love of God. Mysticism and politics then have the same relationship of unity in tension as love of God and love of neighbor.

This new form of love of neighbor and love of God opens up a new field of holiness which Schillebeeckx, following Jon Sobrino, calls "political holiness."[25] World travel and mass media communication heighten our awareness in middle class society of the suffering of the needy throughout the world and even in our own cities and rural communities. In this context, the call to political holiness opens the possibility for a new two-fold experience of transcendence.

First, those who are excluded, the poor as well as those who have tried to make the cause of the oppressed their own, experience what Schillebeeckx calls, following Theodor Adorno's conception of critical negativity, "a negative contrast experience." This is an experience of God's absence or of the distance between our present society and God's Kingdom. In his reflections on nuclear deterrence cited above, he describes this experience as an "extra-scientific cognitive certainty," the source of the "force obliging us to engage in social action."[26]

The absolute character of the negative experience of contrast, however, doesn't mandate the particular projects, policies, or actions with which we respond. This leads to the second aspect of his new experience of transcendence. Through the shared resistance against injustice and the struggle to bring about liberating political change, believers know the revelatory attraction of the burning bush. They can experience "an intense contact with God, the presence of the liberating God of Jesus."[27] Such glimpses of transcendence are often as cloudy, if not so dramatic, as the moving example, developed earlier in the lecture, of the soldier who suffers execution himself rather than carry out a command to murder the innocent. In such "liberation praxis," the reality of God is made known to us as "the deepest secret, the heart and soul of each truly human liberation." This realization summons us even in the unfulfilled present to the praise and thanksgiving of liturgical prayer and celebration.

Although something new and different appears in this added political dimension of Christian love of God and neighbor, Schillebeeckx still finds in this new struggle or *ascesis* a dynamic similar to more traditional conceptions of the mystical life with its dark nights (he prefers Ruysbroeck's "dark light"), its cleansing *agon*, its faith and hope in God unseen, the strange mutuality of mystical union. No less formidably ambiguous than the multifaceted depths of the interior castle are the inherent dangers and temptations waiting in the murky depths of politics. As with traditional mystical experience, Schillebeeckx insists, the limited emancipations achieved by genuine political love, in spite of this mystery and ambiguity, are experienced and not merely interpreted as God's own saving work. "Without prayer or mysticism," he concludes, "politics soon becomes cruel and barbaric; without political love, prayer or mysticism soon becomes sentimental or uncommitted interiority."[28] Such an understanding of Christian experience challenges the theologians who reflect on it to join the "ecumene of suffering humanity." "One can no longer theologize and make church pronouncements in the same old way."[29] This is more than a new way of theologizing, however, it is also a new spirituality, "the spirituality of solidarity with the poor."[30]

IV. Integral Salvation or Liberation

Others have commented at length on the CDF "Instruction on Christian Freedom and Liberation." My purpose here is limited to an exposition of Ratzinger's use of the concept of "integral salvation." As Gustavo Gutierrez has explained, the term originated as a polemical qualification placed on the liberation called for by liberation theology. In fact, as he goes on to point out, the term expresses one of liberation theology's "most classic themes." He warns, however, that those who use this term have often blinded themselves to "the historical implications of Christ's salvation."[31]

In his discussion of the recent emergence of what he calls the "liberationist" orientation in the church since Vatican II, Gregory Baum distinguishes a "liberal, reformist" or "soft" liberation from "hard" liberation, which "names the concrete conditions of oppression and implies a certain rupture or discontinuity with the prevailing order."[32] In view of Gutierrez' warning about the term "integral salvation" or liberation, we can ask whether Ratzinger's use of the term is an example, in Baum's terms, of "hard" or "soft" liberation. A good place to begin looking for an answer might be the biblical theme which Juan Luis Segundo has described as "one of those closest to the heart of liberation theology," Israel's Exodus from Egypt.[33]

In the August 6, 1984, "Instruction on Certain Aspects of the 'Theology of Liberation,'" Ratzinger acknowledges that the Exodus "represents freedom from foreign domination and from slavery." But it is "ordered to the foundation of the people of God and the covenant cult celebrated on Mount Sinai (Ex 24)." While it is less than clear that any liberation theologians have presented the Exodus this way, Ratzinger denies, on the basis of its religious purpose, that the Exodus can be "reduced to a liberation which is principally or exclusively political in nature."[33a]

In his book-length reply to the 1984 Instruction, Segundo criticized this interpretation of the Exodus. He charged Ratzinger with distorting exegetical evidence in the interest of a particular theological agenda which would impose on the text a form of the modern dualism between the secular or political and the religious or spiritual. Like Schillebeeckx' above, Segundo's point is that God is experienced precisely in the liberation from domination of a people "who are already his." The Hebrews who were delivered from Egypt were not modern westerners who had a political experience to which they subsequently gave a religious interpretation. What we would call the *secular* and the *religious* are not clearly distinguished here. In arguing that Ratzinger has imposed on the text a particular theology in which "the religious and the secular are opposed," Segundo has in effect charged him with spiritualizing the sense of scripture to fit a modern western "religion of the heart" characterized by "individual worship and piety."[34]

Whether or not it is intended as an implicit reply to Segundo's criticism, Ratzinger's incorporation of the theme of integral salvation is clearly a response to objections of this kind which come from contextual or liberationist perspectives. The Exodus, therefore, is a prominent feature of the 1986 Instruction and its treatment is more positive in tone and more nuanced in content.

In the Old Testament the liberating action of Yahweh which serves as
model and reference for all others is the Exodus from Egypt, the 'house
of bondage.' When God rescues his people from hard economic, political and cultural slavery, he does so in order to make them, through the
covenant on Sinai, "a kingdom of priests and a holy nation" (Ex 19:6).
God wishes to be adored by a people who are free. All the subsequent
liberations of the people of Israel help to lead them to this full liberty
that they can only find in communion with their God.

The major and fundamental event of the Exodus therefore has a
meaning which is both religious and political. God sets his people free
and gives them descendants, a land and a law, but within a covenant
and for a covenant. One cannot therefore isolate the political aspect for
its own sake; it has to be considered in the light of a plan of a religious
nature within which it is integrated. (LC, #44).

The Exodus liberates people to be free for communion with God
through God's own law. At the heart of this law are the two great
commandments and "the justice which must govern the relations
between people." In this context, Ratzinger describes the poor, the
needy, the widow and the orphan as having "a right to justice
according to the juridical ordinances of the people of God." (LC,
#45) Of the "poor of Yahweh" he claims that "their fight against
injustice finds its deepest meaning and its effectiveness in their
desire to be freed from the slavery of sin" (LC, #47). This is in
keeping with his perfervid insistence that human liberation is primarily liberation from sin (LC, #37–42, 53).

Ratzinger further develops this interpretation of the Exodus as the
model of integral salvation which is both religious and political in
his July 19, 1986 address at Lima, Peru. He finds in a certain
unidentified type of liberation theology a "reversal of symbols"
whereby the relation between Old and New Testaments is inverted.
Where Christians had previously interpreted the Exodus as a type of
baptism, some contemporary theologians find in such interpretations "a retreat from the political-real into the mystical-unreal and
the merely individual."[35]

In seeking to clarify the question about the goal of the Exodus
raised by Segundo and others, Ratzinger argues that the goal of
Israel's own land and political autonomy must be set in the wider
context of Sinai, the covenant and Torah.

Thus one can definitely say that the goal of the Exodus was freedom.
But one must add that the figure of freedom is the covenant and that

the form in which freedom is realized is the right relation of men to one another described in the Law of the Covenant, and this relation is derived from the right relation to God.[36]

Were Israel to lose the covenant but retain the land, the people would have "returned to its pre-Exodus condition." Through Christ the liberating forces of Exodus/Sinai are universalized with the consequence that "in the future the religious and civil communities, Church and state, are no longer identical, but clearly distinguished from each other."[37]

In the Instruction of 1986, chapter 4 introduces the theme that the church's mission is "for the integral salvation of the world." According to the model of Ratzinger's interpretation of the Exodus, the political is "integrated" into "a plan of a religious nature" (LC, #44). The church's essential mission is described as one of "evangelization and salvation" (LC, #63). In a phrase which partially echoes the 1971 Synod of Bishops teaching that action on behalf of justice is a constitutive element in the preaching of the gospel, Ratzinger insists that teaching about "the justice which must regulate human relations" is "part of the preaching of the Gospel."

In the subsequent emphasis on "integral liberation" (#63), Ratzinger is clearly trying to prevent those who wish to keep the church "out of politics" from using against the poor his words about the primacy of the religious. The same love which moves the church to want to share the gospel and the sacraments with the world moves Christians "to pursue people's true temporal good, help them in their needs, provide for their education and promote an integral liberation from everything that hinders the development of individuals" (#63). The church's teaching on social justice, therefore, does not go "beyond her mission." The integral liberation which it is the church's mission to foster is both spiritual and temporal. Like Schillebeeckx' unity in tension between love of God and love of neighbor, Ratzinger proposes a unity and distinction between evangelization and human promotion. (#64).

As the difference between the phrases *the unity and the distinction* and *unity in tension* suggests, there is still considerable disparity between the more harmonious theme of "integral salvation" and Schillebeeckx' more conflictual theme of "mysticism and politics." Segundo, for example, might find it difficult to see how integral salvation provides anything more than a juxtaposition which retains the basic individualism of modern western piety.

Integral salvation, however, does go beyond traditional appeals for voluntary charity on an interpersonal basis. Ratzinger clearly wants the church, through its social teaching and through the activities of Christians in the world, to respond to "the awakening of the consciousness of people . . . bent beneath the weight of age-old poverty" (LC, #17). Work for justice is an inner demand of the church's own mission. Although Ratzinger claims that one can call structures "sinful" only in "a derived and secondary sense," he shows a clear understanding of the relation of "structures marked by sin" to the suffering of the poor. While "social sin," according to Ratzinger, is not sin strictly speaking, Christians are nevertheless taught by him that it is "necessary to work simultaneously for the conversion of hearts and for the improvement of structures" (LC, #75).

One of Ratzinger's chief concerns, perhaps even his central one, is that the church's teaching on social justice and the political activities of Christians not be coopted by revolutionary movements which have sub-Christian, materialistic understandings of what a human person is. He therefore insists that Christian action on behalf of justice must be based on a Christian anthropology, a vision of the human which respects the spiritual dignity of each person, a vision that advocates a liberation based on a sense of true freedom. That Ratzinger thought he was laying this anthropological foundation in the first three chapters of the Instruction is clear from his remarks in the Lima speech cited above:

> A vision without praxis is insufficient; but conversely, a praxis that did not rest on a coherent view of man [sic] and his [sic] history would be groundless—an external system of rules that cannot do justice to the magnitude of the question.[38]

V. Ratzinger and Schillebeeckx Converge on Solidarity

Must we in conclusion acknowledge an irreconcilable opposition between Ratzinger's anthropological approach and Schillebeeckx' more contextual one, between integral salvation and mysticism and politics, between the church's social teaching as a branch of moral theology and a more praxis-oriented understanding of theology as theoretical activity? Many western theologians are looking for ways to make their work responsive to the cries of those who suffer. I do not think they are faced with an either/or choice between the anthropological and contextual approaches. Without wishing to deny real conflicts in church and society by imposing an alien harmony on these two approaches, I want to argue that they are broadly compatible. The theme around which they can converge, one that is common to all three contemporary theological orientations and which has received increasing attention in recent Catholic social teaching, is solidarity. This argument unfolds in five steps. The first two are preliminary. The final three are more substantive and based in the text of Ratzinger's 1986 Instruction. Strong text-based reasons lead to the conclusion that the Instruction's concrete anthropological vision is open to, and in part based on, a contextual approach of its own which transcends theology as a disengaged form of pure theory.

1. Theology cannot be reduced to political activism. Some would argue that western theologians can only respond to the aspirations of the poor by becoming political activists, or by going to work in clinics or other helping institutions in the Third World, for example. Theology in this view is not an authentic Christian calling but an escape from the real world. While I am not in a position to analyze such attitudes, I do not think that their truth is self-evident. Since I am firmly convinced that I live in the real world, I will continue under the assumption that theology need not be inherently ideological and self-alienating. It can indeed respond in its limited way to the cry of the poor, not as some guilty afterthought, but as a structural part of the activity itself.[39]

2. Radical disjunctions such as the apparent opposition between anthropological and contextual approaches in theology are often ideological. Sometimes they serve to exclude significant sectors of contemporary experience, the experiences of those represented by either Ratzinger or Schillebeeckx, for example, from the theological task, and perhaps even from the church itself. Sometimes they serve to turn theologians and other Christians into observers who feel they cannot choose between them. Disjunctive thinking often works to the advantage of those who have power understood as some form of external coercion over others.

3. The Church's social teaching, and its concrete application by Christians in particular contexts, cannot be dismissed as meddling in politics. Only on an understanding of theology which uncritically reflects the western political arrangement of separation of church and state, can salvation be understood as purely spiritual and based on a purely interior experience of God. Ratzinger clearly rejects such a view.

The inner bond between the two great commandments, emphasized by both Ratzinger and Schillebeeckx, excludes such a privatized view of Christian experience as purely interior. Neither Schillebeeckx nor Ratzinger simply repeats the two great commandments in an ahistorical manner. Rather both insist that, if Christians are really to hear the gospel, with its link between love of God and love of neighbor, in the modern western context, they must listen to its appeal for justice on behalf of those who suffer unjustly.

Ratzinger's Instruction emphatically and not just in passing recognizes the aspirations of the suffering poor as a sign of the times in which the church is bound to respond. The Instruction's opening paragraph declares that the church "makes these aspirations her own." It goes on to call for concrete applications of liberation and freedom themes to different local situations. Local churches, "in communion with one another and with the see of Peter," are left to "make direct provision for" such applications (LC, #2).

Whether he takes sufficient measures to prevent it, Ratzinger clearly doesn't want his words about "integral salvation" to be used against the poor. He wants to present the gospel message in such a way that modern Christians will be challenged by its call for justice for the poor and suffering. In spite of these intentions, however, he tends to pass over the extent of the conflict that may result from trying to put the church's social teaching into practice, and in general fails to subject the church's own language and behavior to a rigorous ideology critique. The extent of the qualifications placed on the church's solidarity with contemporary aspirations for liberation, and the rhetorical emphasis given to the primacy of liberation from sin, seem to provide an excess of aid and comfort to people such as Third World dictators and privileged westerners who profit in worldly terms from interpreting their religion as a purely spiritual affair. This is often a rhetorical matter where Ratzinger's embattled and pessimistic tone, his *Weltschmerz*, as one commentator has called it, tends to work against the content of the Instruction.

4. Theological reflection, grounded in particular contexts, contributes to the development and application of the church's social teaching. What the Instruction refers to as "the new basic communities" of the Latin American church have become the paradigm for the contextual approach in theology. With the qualification that they take care to remain united within the faith and order of the universal church, the Instruction describes them as "a source of great hope." Given this communion with the universal church, the experience of

basic communities "rooted in a commitment to the complete liberation of man [sic], becomes a treasure for the whole church" (#69).

> Similarly, a theological reflection developed from a particular experi-
> ence can constitute a very positive contribution, inasmuch as it makes
> possible a highlighting of aspects of the word of God, the richness of
> which has not yet been fully grasped. (#70)

Further, the Instruction's understanding of the nature of the
church's social teaching, to which it is contributing, is remarkably
historically sensitive and contextual. At the beginning of chapter V,
the church's social teaching is described as:

> born of the encounter of the gospel message and of its demands
> summarized in the supreme command of love of God and love of
> neighbor in justice with the problems emanating from the life of society
> (#72).

The church's social teaching is further described with such terms
as "essentially oriented toward action," and as developing "in
accordance with the changing circumstances of history." It is not a
closed system, but "remains constantly open to the new questions
which continually arise." Finally, it requires "the contribution of all
charisms, experiences and skills" (#72).

5. Solidarity can be the common theme which transcends the
differences between anthropological and contextual theologies. In
its fifth and most potent chapter, Ratzinger's Instruction presents a
vision which local Christians can use in their work for "integral
salvation" and "political love." In his insightful commentary on the
Instruction, Alfred Hennelly locates its most significant contribution
as "the integration of Pope John Paul's groundbreaking encyclical
Laborem Exercens into a liberation context." Hennelly views the
Instruction as a kind of threshold where liberation themes meet the
mainstream of Catholic social thought and are integrated in a preliminary way by the Pope's insistence on the priority of human labor
over capital.[40]

If "integral salvation" is to be more than a handy formula for
defusing Latin American liberation theology, it must, in Baum's
terms, be intended as "hard" liberation. Near the end of chapter V,
having acknowledged in paragraph 74 that the church's social teaching provides criteria for identifying and opposing unjust social

structures, the Instruction appeals, in the face of international injustice, for new forms of solidarity. This theme of solidarity, properly interpreted, can turn a potentially abstract concern for "integral salvation" into "political love."

Pope Paul VI used the term *solidarity* in his 1967 encyclical *Populorum Progressio*. The Latin America bishops used it at Medellin in 1968. It is Pope John Paul II, however, who has made *solidarity* an important theme in Catholic social teaching. He speaks of it in philosophical terms as an aspect of human intersubjectivity, an "attitude of community," or "a constant readiness to accept and to realize one's share in the community because of one's membership within that community."[41] In his 1981 encyclical, *Laborem Exercens*, published a few short months before the suppression of the Polish labor union, Solidarity, he applied the anthropological notion of solidarity to the question of human work. To achieve social justice in and among the various countries he recognized "a need for ever new movements of solidarity of the workers and with the workers." The pope firmly committed the church to this cause as the "Church of the poor."[42]

These sentiments echoed his speeches in Mexico on the occasion of the 1979 conference of Latin American bishops at Puebla. Some had hoped that Puebla would repudiate liberation theology in Latin America. But the key theme of solidarity was conspicious in the Final Document's ringing reaffirmation of the preferential option for the poor. As Christ established solidarity with us through the incarnation, so chapter I of Puebla's Final Document urged the Latin American Church to a gospel poverty "understood as solidarity with the poor and as a rejection of the situation in which most people on this continent live.[43]

In his 1987 encyclical, *Sollicitudo rei socialis*, the pope explained solidarity at length. He called it a "virtue," "a moral and social attitude." we begin to practice it when we recognize the moral dimension of the world community's interdependence. In a powerful paragraph, the Pope fleshes out solidarity's meaning:

> This [solidarity] then is not a feeling of vague compassion or shallow distress at the misfortunes of so many people, both near and far. On the contrary, it is a firm and persevering determination to commit oneself to the common good; that is to say, to the good of all and of each individual because we are all really responsible for all. This determination is based on the solid conviction that what is hindering

full development is that desire for profit and that thirst for power already mentioned. These attitudes and 'structures of sin' are only conquered—presupposing the help of divine grace—by a diametrically opposed attitude: a commitment to the good of one's neighbor with the readiness, in the Gospel sense, to 'lose oneself' for the sake of the other instead of exploiting him and to 'serve him' instead of oppressing him for one's own advantage (cf. Matt 10:40–42; 20:25; Mark 10:42–45; Luke 22:25–27).[44]

If the western press' generally apprehensive response to this encyclical is any indication, those who wish to spiritualize the gospel will find little aid and comfort in the pope's understanding of solidarity. Having placed the theme of solidarity within the context of recent Catholic social teaching, we can return to the Instruction (paragraph 89) and read it as an echo of Puebla and *Laborem Exercens* and as an anticipation of *Sollicitudo Rei Socialis*. Against this background, Ratzinger's call for new forms of solidarity signals a notion of integral salvation with teeth, an example of what Baum has called "hard" liberation.

Solidarity is a direct requirement of human and supernatural brother-hood. The serious socio-economic problems which occur today cannot be solved unless new forms of solidarity are created: solidarity of the poor among themselves, solidarity with the poor to which the rich are called, solidarity among the workers and with the workers. Institutions and social organizations at different levels, as well as the state, must share in a general movement of solidarity. When the Church appeals for such solidarity, she is aware that she herself is concerned in a quite special way. (LC, 89).

VI. Conclusion

There remains a certain potential tension between the nuanced and open-ended anthropological approach represented by the 1986 Instruction, *Laborem Exercens* and *Sollicitudo Rei Solicalis* and the more contextual approach represented by Schillebeeckx. Nevertheless, the theme of solidarity as an attitude and a practical virtue, as well as an epistemological posture, provides a means for giving flesh to such notions as political love and the promotion of integral salvation. It also provides a name for the common commitment shared by contextual and anthropological theologians from various parts of the world.

Theologians in North America and Europe are left to determine the concrete forms this solidarity will take. Schillebeeckx provided one example when in 1982 he publicly opposed his country's possession of nuclear weapons. He accepted the consequence that peace would have to include "a liberating renewal of economic and socio-political structures, as well as an inner conversion." "Love of God," he concluded, "and the loving solidarity of human brotherhood and sisterhood are one single inviolable 'divine virtue.' "[45]

In our own country, theologians buy books by Jon Sobrino of El Salvador and Miguel D'Escoto and Ernesto Cardenal of Nicaragua. We write papers and attend conferences and teach courses on liberation theology while money from our government continues to pay for widespread destruction of life and resources in Central America. Each of us must decide how we will express the solidarity with our Central American brothers and sisters to which the gospel calls us at this time. But there are two things we ought to avoid.

First, the urgent moral imperative for solidarity with those who suffer needlessly ought to preclude any comfortable embrace of an abstract anthropological approach in teaching and studying theology. Second, we ought not permit our secular culture to divide the church according to its political categories, thereby separating from one another, on the basis of non-religious criteria, those I have called contextual, liberation, and concrete anthropological theologians, and those upon whose experience they reflect. Solidarity, as understood in recent church teaching, ought to be a commitment which helps us bridge the divides of our political culture.

NOTES

1. The Congregation for the Doctrine of the Faith, "Instruction on Christian Freedom and Liberation" (*Libertatis Conscientia,* LC) in *Origins,* 15 (April 17, 1986), 713–28. Hereafter this document will be cited by paragraph number in the text. The opening citation is from LC #17.

2. On "integral salvation" or liberation, see the 1968 Medellin document on "Justice," #4 in L.M. Colonnese, ed., Second General Conference of Latin American Bishops, *The Church in the Present-Day Transformation of Latin America in the Light of the Council* (Bogota, Columbia: Ediciones Paulinas, 1970), II, p. 59. See also I, p. 121 and II, p. 141. On the history of the concept, see Gustavo Gutierrez, *The Power of the Poor in History,* Robert R. Barr, tr. (Maryknoll: Orbis Books, 1983), pp. 144–48.

3. Karl Rahner, *Spirit in the World,* William Dych, tr. (New York: Herder & Herder, 1968), p. 408.

4. On the liberationist organization, see Gregory Baum, *Theology and Society* (New York/Mahwah: Paulist Press, 1987), chs. 1 & 10.

5. This is part of a long quotation from Schillebeeckx which appears on the dustjacket of Gutierrez' *The Power of the Poor in History.*

6. Boff's remarks appear in LADOC, 15 (Jan/Feb, 1985) 8–12. The above appears on p. 8.

7. For an early example of Ratzinger's method, see the "completely general analysis of the basic attitude of 'belief' " which precedes discussion of the specifically Christian mode of belief at the beginning of Ratzinger's 1968 *Introduction to Christianity,* J.R. Foster, tr. (New York: Herder & Herder, 1970), pp. 43, 50. For a later example, see Ratzinger's illuminating discussion of the "anthropological foundation of the concept of tradition" (1974) and the discussion of "faith and experience" (1980), part of a longer section entitled "The Anthropological Element in Theology." The latter two examples appear in *Principles of Catholic Theology,* Sister Mary Frances McCarthy, S.N.D., tr. (San Francisco: Ignatius Press, 1987), 85–101; pp.343–55.

8. Ratzinger, *Principles,* p. 390.

9. See the section on the "anthropological foundation of the concept of tradition" in ibid., p. 85–101.

10. Ibid., p. 319.

11. Ibid., p. 87.

12. Ibid., pp. 89–94.

13. On European "political culture," see H. Stuart Hughes, *Sophisticated Rebels, The Political Culture of European Dissent, 1968–1987* (Cambridge/London: Harvard University Press, 1988). Schillebeeckx and Ratzinger appear in chapter 5.

14. E.J. Dionne, Jr., "The Pope's Guardian of Orthodoxy," *New York Times,* Nov. 24, 1985, p. 58. Cf. the discussion of "local ecumenism" in Ratzinger, *Principles,* pp. 302–23.

15. See Schillebeeckx' discussion of the seven "anthropological constants" in *Christ, The Experience of Jesus as Lord,* John Bowden, tr. (New York: Seabury Press, 1980), pp. 731–43. See also Schillebeeckx, *Jesus, An Experiment in Christology,* Hubert Hoskins, tr. (New York: Seabury, 1979), p. 591.

16. Ratzinger, *Principles,,* p. 310.

17. Ibid.

18. "Tradition is the precondition of man's [sic] humanness, but it is also its peril. Whoever destroys tradition destroys man [sic]—he is like a traveler in space who himself destroys the possibility of ground control, of contact with earth. But even he who would preserve tradition falls likewise into the danger of destroying it.

"We must, consequently, analyze tradition from two different perspectives. From the thological point of view, it is necessary first of all to guard tradition against traditions . . . But there is, above and beyond all this, a deeper question that is not so readily applicable to the Church but that is all the more surely to be found in the content of human history: Is the basic tradition itself really intact, or is it perhaps itself marked by the forces of alienation? . . .

"To the concept of tradition as the basis of man's [sic] humanity there is opposed the concept of an emancipated rationality that is hostile to tradition; the present crisis in the Church is due not least of all to the fact that, within her, advocates of both concepts are now engaged in a lively conflict with regard to her own traditions." Ibid., pp. 90–91.

19. On Schillebeeckx and critical theory, see William L. Portier, "Interpretation and Method" in The Praxis of Christian Experience, Robert Schreiter and Mary Catherine Hilkert eds., (New York: Harper & Row, 1989) forthcoming.

20. Edward Schillebeeckx, On Christian Faith, The Spiritual, Ethical, and Political Dimensions, John Bowden, tr. (New York: Crossroad, 1987), pp. 71–72; cf. pp. 65–70.

21. Edward Schillebeeckx, God Among Us, The Gospel Proclaimed, John Bowden, tr. (New York: Crossroad, 1983), p. 253.

22. Schillebeeckx, Christ, p. 809.

23. Edward Schillebeeckx, "Christian Conscience and Nuclear Deterrent," Doctrine and Life, 32 (1982) 98.

24. Schillebeeckx. Christ, p. 81.

25. Joh Sobrino, Spirituality of Liberation, Toward Political Holiness, Robert R. Barr, tr. (Maryknoll: Orbis Books, 1988), pp. 80–86.

26. Schillebeeckx, "Christian Conscience and Nuclear Deterrent," p. 107.

27. Schillebeeckx, On Christian Faith, p. 73.

28. Ibid., p. 75.

29. Ibid., p. 84. See also Schillebeeckx' sermon on Luke 6.17, 20–26, entitled "The Gospel of the Poor for Prosperous People" in God Among Us, pp. 175–79. Compare the treatment of the beatitudes in chapter IV of "Instruction on Christian Freedom and Liberation," where Ratzinger uses the beatitudes to introduce the theme of integral salvation.

30. From the same dustjacket quote cited in note 5 above.

31. Gutierrez, Power of the Poor in History, pp. 144–45.

32. Baum, Theology and Society, pp. 8–9.

33. Juan Luis Segundo, Theology and the Church, A Response to Cardinal Ratzinger and a Warning to the Whole Church, J.W. Dierksmeir, tr. (Minneapolis: Winston Press, 1985), p. 44.

33a. Congregation for the Doctrine of the Faith, "Instruction on Certain Aspects of the 'Theology of Liberation'," The Tablet, Sept. 8, 1984, p. 869.

34. Segundo, Theology and the Church, pp. 44–47, 51.

35. Joseph Cardinal Ratzinger, "Freedom and Liberation: The Anthropological Vision of the Instruction 'Libertatis conscientia'," Communio, 14 (1987) 64.

36. Ibid., p. 66.

37. Ibid., p. 67.

38. Ibid., p. 58.

39. See Gregory Baum's comments in *Theology and Society*, pp. 26–30.

40. Alfred T. Hennelly, "The Red-Hot Issue: Liberation Theology," *America*, May 24, 1986, pp. 427–28.

41. Karol Wojtyla (Pope John Paul II), *The Acting Person*, Andrzej Potocki, tr. [*Analecta Husserliana*, Vol. X] (Dordrecht/Boston/London: D. Reidel Publishing Co., 1979), pp. 284–85.

42. Pope John Paul II, *Laborem Exercens #8*, in Gregory Gaum, *The Priority of Labor, A Commentary on Laborem Exercens* (New York/Ramsey: Paulist Press, 1982), pp. 110–111.

43. Final Document, Chapter I in *Puebla and Beyond*, John Eagleson and Philip Scharper, eds., (Maryknoll: Orbis Books, 1979), p. 266.

44. Pope John Paul II, *Sollicitudo Rei Socialis, #38* in *Origins*, 17 (March 3, 1988) 654.

45. Schillebeeckx, "Christian Conscience and Nuclear Deterrent," pp. 111–112.